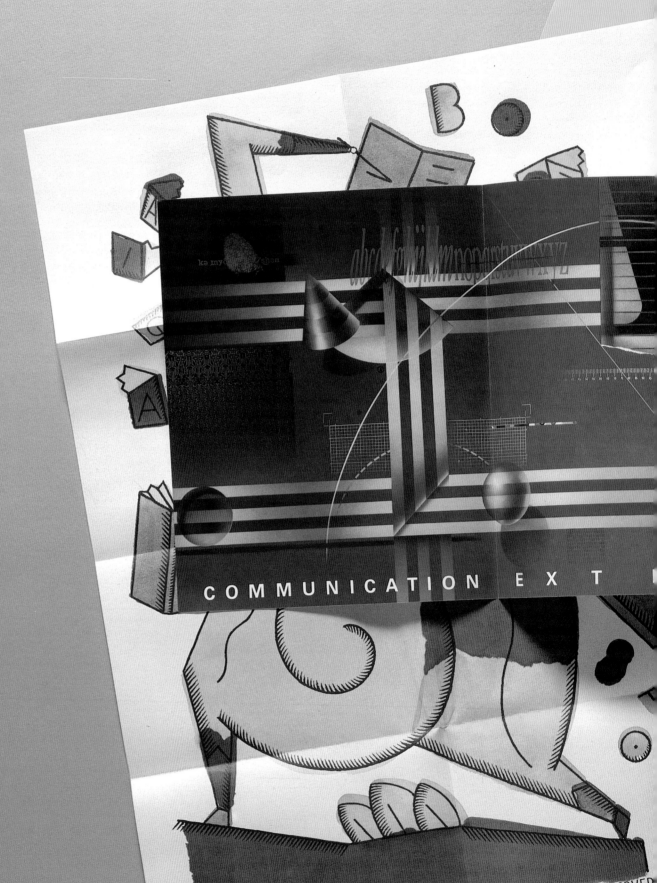

COMMUNICATION EX T

CALL FOR ENTRIES · AIGA BOOK SHOW 1987 & BOOK JACKET & PAPERBACK COVER

Graphic Design USA: 9

The Annual of the American
Institute of Graphic Arts

Written by Steven Heller,
Andy Grundberg, and
Ellen Lupton

Designed by Massimo Vignelli

Contents

Watson-Guptill Publications
New York

The American Institute of Graphic Arts

The American Institute of Graphic
Arts is the national non-profit organization which promotes excellence
in graphic design. Founded in 1914,
the AIGA advances the graphic
design profession through competitions, exhibitions, publications,
professional seminars, educational
activities, and projects in the public
interest.

Members of the Institute are involved
in the design and production of
books, magazines, and periodicals
as well as corporate, environmental, and promotional graphics. Their
contributions of specialized skills
and expertise provide the foundation for the Institute's program.
Through the Institute, members form
an effective, informal network of
professional assistance that is a
resource to the profession and to
the public.

The most important development
within the AIGA in recent years has
been the growth of chapters throughout the country. Separately incorporated, twenty-three AIGA chapters
enable designers to represent their
profession collectively on a local
level. Drawing upon the resources
of the national organization, chapters sponsor a wide variety of
programs dealing with all areas of
graphic design.

By being part of a national network,
bringing in speakers and exhibitions
from other parts of the country and
abroad, focusing on new ideas and
technical advances, and discussing business practice issues, the
chapters place the profession of
graphic design in an integrated and
national context.

The competitive exhibition sched-
ule at the Institute's gallery includes
the annual Book Show and Communication Graphics. Other exhibitions
may include Illustration, Photography, Covers, (book jackets, record
albums, magazines, and periodicals), Posters, Signage, and Packaging. The exhibitions travel nation-
ally and are reproduced in *Graphic
Design USA*. Acquisitions have been
made from AIGA exhibitions by the
Popular and Applied Arts Division
of the Library of Congress. Each
year the Book Show is donated to
the Rare Book and Manuscript Library of Columbia University, which
houses the AIGA collection of
award-winning books dating back
to the 1920's. For the past five
years, the Book Show has also been
exhibited at the Frankfurt Book Fair.

The AIGA sponsors a biennial national conference covering topics
including professional practice, education, technology, the creative
process, and design history. The
1989 conference will be held in
San Antonio, Texas.

AIGA also sponsors an active and
extensive publications program.
Publications include *Graphic Design
USA*, the annual of the Institute; the
Journal of Graphic Design, published quarterly; the AIGA Salary
Survey 1987; Graphic Design Education Statement; a voluntary *Code
of Ethics and Professional Conduct*
for AIGA members; *Symbol Signs
Repro Art*, a portfolio containing 50
passenger/pedestrian symbols
originally designed for the U.S.
Department of Transportation and
guidelines for their use; and a *Membership Directory*.

Past Presidents of the AIGA

This volume and the exhibitions it represents make an important statement about the Institute's mission to promote excellence in graphic design.

During our program year, in particular with the momentum of chapter growth and programming, it is sometimes possible to lose sight of the fact that the essential energy of this enterprise is the power of design. To walk through the AIGA exhibitions, as to turn the pages of this book, is to be reminded once again of the impact, variety, and personal vision of American design. It makes a more profound statement on the contribution of the profession than any impassioned treatise on the value of design.

The work presented here represents a growing constituency. This year we had a significant increase in the number of individuals who entered AIGA competitions for the first time, as well as the number of individuals whose work was accepted for the first time. Though the perception that we are a New York organization persists, the chapter movement is effectively dissolving geographic boundaries. Entries to our competitions came from 43 states and Canada. The preponderance of entries this year came from the Northeast, and the majority of acceptances came from the West and Southwest. Also, despite difficult odds (i.e., 5,670 entries to Communication Graphics, 207 acceptances), five individuals entered one piece each and got in.

The AIGA is growing and changing, and the profession we represent is alive and well. We have had a rewarding program year: over 20 chapters and provisional chapters held more than 200 events this past year, ranging from exhibitions and seminars to auctions to fund chapter scholarship programs.

The Conference in San Francisco reminded us that we represent a large community of individuals with common cause; AIGA exhibitions traveled to 42 locations as diverse as Taipei, Taiwan to Bozeman, Montana; we are collaborating with the Walker Art Center on the first major exhibition of the history of graphic design in America. This book is the culmination of our publishing program for the year. The *Journal* continues to receive high praise for the vitality of its ongoing critical, historical, and professional comment on issues related to graphic design; a formal statement on a Graphic Design Education and a succinct statement on *What is Graphic Design?* were published, and we have begun to survey educational institutions in preparation for the second edition of our Education Directory; and we have published the AIGA standard contract and our first salary survey.

To Massimo Vignelli, our thanks for graphic design at its best in the service of graphic design at its best, and to Rudy de Harak, whose jacket design speaks to the inherent complexity of making a statement about graphic design on many levels. Andy Grundberg, Steven Heller, and Ellen Lupton wrote the prose that brings those individuals and institutions which received our highest awards into the context of an important contribution informed by talent, will, and wisdom.

On behalf of the AIGA, I would like to thank Bruce Blackburn, our outgoing president, whose calm intelligence and philosophical take on the role of institutions proved invaluable through two years of consolidation and growth.

Caroline Hightower, *Director*

The AIGA Medal

For 66 years, the Medal of the American Institute of Graphic Arts has been awarded to individuals in recognition of their distinguished achievements and contributions to the graphic arts. Medalists are chosen by an awards committee, subject to approval by the Board of Directors. This year the committee chose to recognize two individuals, Alexey Brodovitch (posthumously) and Gene Federico.

1987 Awards Committee

Chairman
Cheryl Heller
Chief Executive Officer and
    Creative Director
Heller Breene

Committee

Alvin Eisenman
Director of Studies in
    Graphic Design
Yale School of Art

Douglass Scott
Senior Designer
WGBH

Deborah Sussman
President
Sussman/Prejza & Co., Inc.

Past Recipients

Norman T.A. Munder, 1920
Daniel Berkeley Updike, 1922
John C. Agar, 1924
Stephen H. Horgan, 1924
Bruce Rogers, 1925
Burton Emmett, 1926
Timothy Cole, 1927
Frederic W. Goudy, 1927
William A. Dwiggins, 1929
Henry Watson Kent, 1930
Dard Hunter, 1931
Porter Garnett, 1932
Henry Lewis Bullen, 1934
J. Thomson Willing, 1935
Rudolph Ruzicka, 1936
William A. Kittredge, 1939
Thomas M. Cleland, 1940
Carl Purington Rollins, 1941
Edwin and Robert Grabhorn, 1942
Edward Epstean, 1944
Frederic G. Melcher, 1945
Stanley Morison, 1946
Elmer Adler, 1947
Lawrence C. Wroth, 1948
Earnest Elmo Calkins, 1950
Alfred A. Knopf, 1950
Harry L. Gage, 1951
Joseph Blumenthal, 1952
George Macy, 1953
Will Bradley, 1954
Jan Tschichold, 1954
P.J. Conkwright, 1955
Ray Nash, 1956
Dr. M.F. Agha, 1957
Ben Shahn, 1958
May Massee, 1959
Walter Paepcke, 1960
Paul A. Bennett, 1961
Willem Sandberg, 1962
Saul Steinberg, 1963
Josef Albers, 1964
Leonard Baskin, 1965
Paul Rand, 1966
Romana Javitz, 1967
Dr. Giovanni Mardersteig, 1968
Dr. Robert L. Leslie, 1969
Herbert Bayer, 1970
Will Burtin, 1971
Milton Glaser, 1972
Richard Avedon, 1973
Allen Hurlburt, 1973
Philip Johnson, 1973
Robert Rauschenberg, 1974
Bradbury Thompson, 1975
Henry Wolf, 1976
Jerome Snyder, 1976
Charles and Ray Eames, 1977
Lou Dorfsman, 1978
Ivan Chermayeff and
Thomas Geismar, 1979
Herb Lubalin, 1980
Saul Bass, 1981
Massimo and Lella Vignelli, 1982
Herbert Matter, 1983
Leo Lionni, 1984
Seymour Chwast, 1985
Walter Herdeg, 1986

ALEXEY BRODOVITCH

1898-1971

Alexey Brodovitch, Modern Man

Alexey Brodovitch is remembered today as the art director of *Harper's Bazaar* for nearly a quarter of a century. But the volatile Russian emigré's influence was much broader and more complex than his long tenure at a fashion magazine might suggest. He played a crucial role in introducing into the United States a radically simplified, "modern" graphic design style forged in Europe in the 1920's from an amalgam of vanguard movements in art and design. Through his teaching, he created a generation of designers sympathetic to his belief in the primacy of visual freshness and immediacy. Fascinated with photography, he made it the backbone of modern magazine design, and he fostered the development of an expressionistic, almost primal style of picture-taking that became the dominant style of photographic practice in the 1950's.

In addition, Brodovitch is virtually the model for the modern magazine art director. He did not simply arrange photographs, illustrations, and type on the page; he took an active role in conceiving and commissioning all forms of graphic art, and he specialized in discovering and showcasing young and unknown talent. His first assistant in New York was a very young Irving Penn. Leslie Gill, Richard Avedon, and Hiro are among the other photographers whose work Brodovitch nurtured during his long career. So great was his impact on the editorial image of *Harper's Bazaar* that he achieved celebrity status; the film *Funny Face*, for example, which starred Fred Astaire as a photographer much like Avedon, named its art-director character "Dovitch."

Brodovitch and his father

Before leaving Russia

Despite his professional achievements and public success, however, Brodovitch was never a happy man. Born in Russia in 1898 of moderately well-to-do parents, he deferred his goal of attending the Imperial Art Academy to fight in the Czarist army, first against the Austro-Hungarian Empire and then against the Bolsheviks. In defeat, he fled Russia with his family and future wife and, in 1920, settled in Paris. There, despite the burden of exile, he prospered; in 1924 his poster design for an artists' ball won first prize, and in 1925 he won medals for fabric, jewelry, and display design at the International Exhibition of Decorative Arts (the landmark "Art Deco" exposition). Soon he was in great demand, designing restaurant decor, posters, and department store advertisements.

He came to the United States in 1930 to start a department of advertising design at the school of the Philadelphia Museum (later known as the Philadelphia College of Art). There he trained students in the fundamentals of European design, while embarking on numerous freelance illustration assignments in Philadelphia and New York. In 1934 Carmel Snow, the new editor of *Harper's Bazaar*, saw his design work and immediately hired him to be its art director. It was the beginning of a collaboration that was to revolutionize both fashion and magazine design, and that catapulted *Bazaar* past its arch-rival, *Vogue*.

At *Harper's Bazaar*, where he was art director from 1934 to 1958, Brodovitch used the work of such European artists as

Man Ray, Salvador Dali, and A. M. Cassandre, as well as photographers Bill Brandt, Brassai, and Henri Cartier-Bresson. He was the first to give assignments to emigré photographers Lisette Model and Robert Frank. Starting with a splashy, sometimes overly self-conscious style largely borrowed from his early counterpart at *Vogue*, Dr. M. F. Agha (AIGA medalist, 1957), he gradually refined his page layouts to the point of utter simplicity. By the 1950's, white space was the hallmark of the Brodovitch style. Models in Parisian gowns and American sports clothes "floated" on the page, surrounded by white backgrounds, while headlines and type took on an ethereal presence. At his best, Brodovitch was able to create an illusion of elegance from the merest hint of materiality. Clothes were presented not as pieces of fabric cut in singular ways, but as signs of a fashionable life.

Besides his achievements at *Bazaar*, Brodovitch's legacy as a publications designer includes the short-lived but influential magazine *Portfolio*, three issues of which were published in 1949 and 1950. A flashy, innovative quarterly aimed at the design profession, *Portfolio* contained profusely illustrated features on Alexander Calder, Charles Eames, Paul Rand, Saul Steinberg, and others, as well as articles surveying the graphic variations of cattle brands and shopping bags. As art editor, Brodovitch helped conceive the magazine's contents, as well as creating its distinct design with the help of die-cuts, transparent pages, multi-page fold outs, and other elaborate (and expensive) graphic devices.

Throughout his career, he continued to teach. His "Design Laboratory," which focused variously on illustration, graphic design, and photography and on occasion were offered under the auspices of the AIGA, provided a system of rigorous critiques for those who aspired to magazine work. As a teacher, Brodovitch was inspiring, though sometimes harsh and unrelenting. A student's worst offense was to present something Brodovitch found boring; at best, the hawk-faced Russian would pronounce a work "interesting." Despite his unbending manner and lack of explicit critical standards —Brodovitch did not formulate a theory of design—many students under his tutelage discovered untapped creative reserves.

Even at the height of his powers, however, Brodovitch's personal life remained linked to loss and disappointment. His family life was evidently unhappy. In addition, a series of house fires in the 1950's destroyed not only his country retreat but also his paintings, archives, and library. In the 1960's, after he left *Harper's Bazaar*, he continued to teach but did little design work. He died in 1971 in a small village in southern France where he had spent the last three years of his life.

Today Brodovitch's legacy is remarkably rich. His layouts remain models of graphic intelligence and inspiration, even if seldom imitated, and the artists, photographers, and designers whose careers he influenced continue to shape graphic design in the image of his uncompromising ideals.

—Andy Grundberg

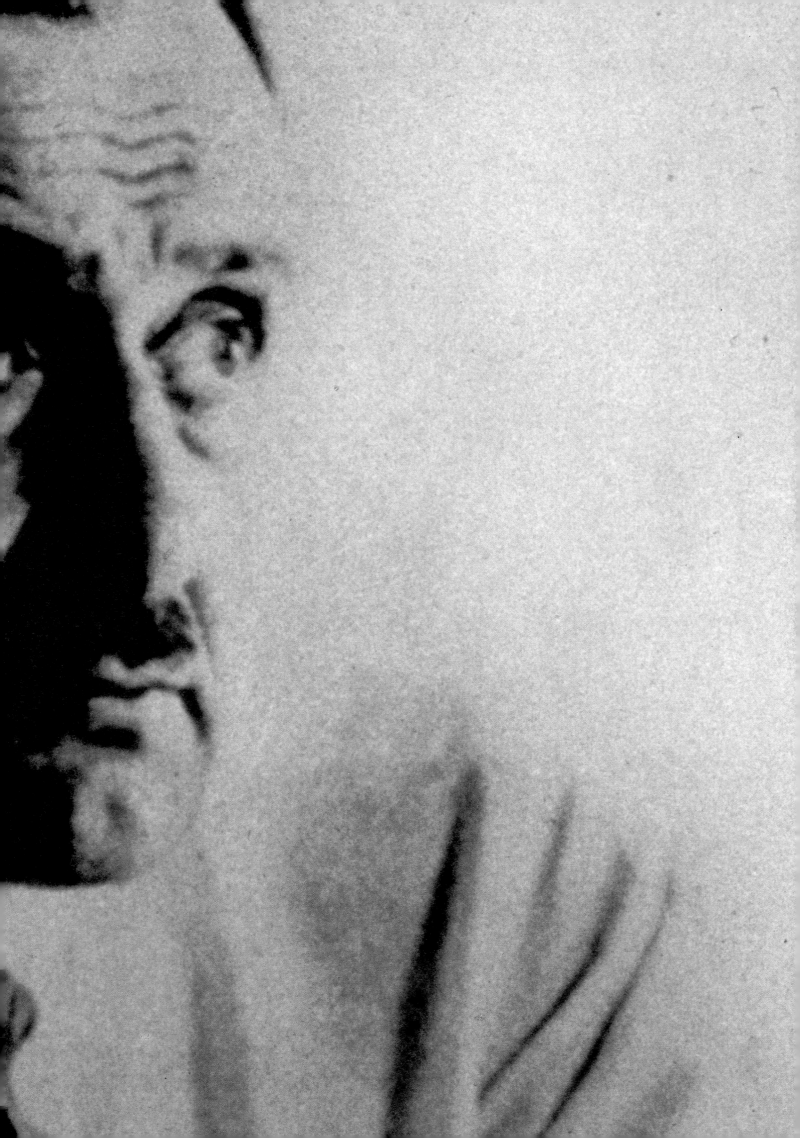

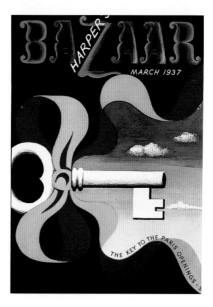

March 1937. Copyright © 1937.
The Hearst Corporation.

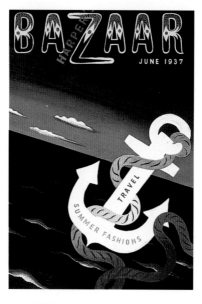

June 1937. Copyright © 1937.
The Hearst Corporation.

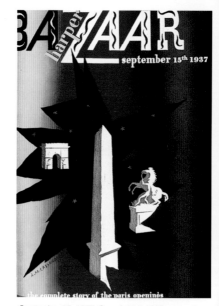

September 15, 1937. Copyright © 1937.
The Hearst Corporation.

February 1939. Copyright © 1939.
The Hearst Corporation.

September 1, 1939. Copyright © 1939.
The Hearst Corporation.

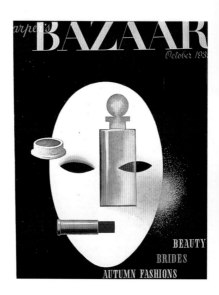

October 1939. Copyright © 1939.
The Hearst Corporation.

December 1946. Copyright © 1946.
The Hearst Corporation.

May 1947. Copyright © 1947.
The Hearst Corporation.

November 1952. Copyright © 1952.
The Hearst Corporation.

March 1, 1938. Copyright © 1938.
The Hearst Corporation.

May 1938. Copyright © 1938.
The Hearst Corporation.

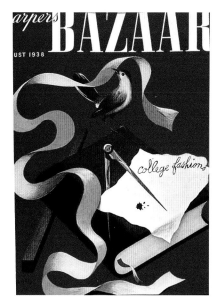

August 1938. Copyright © 1938.
The Hearst Corporation.

February 1940. Copyright © 1940.
The Hearst Corporation.

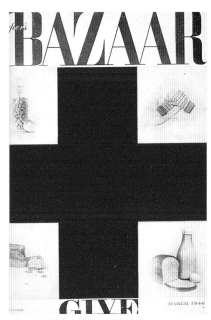

March 1946. Copyright © 1946.
The Hearst Corporation.

November 1946. Copyright © 1946
The Hearst Corporation.

July 1956. Copyright © 1956.
The Hearst Corporation.

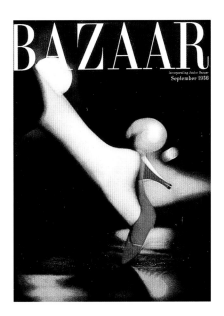

September 1956. Copyright © 1956.
The Hearst Corporation.

October 1957. Copyright © 1957.
The Hearst Corporation.

Courtesy of *Harper's Bazaar*.

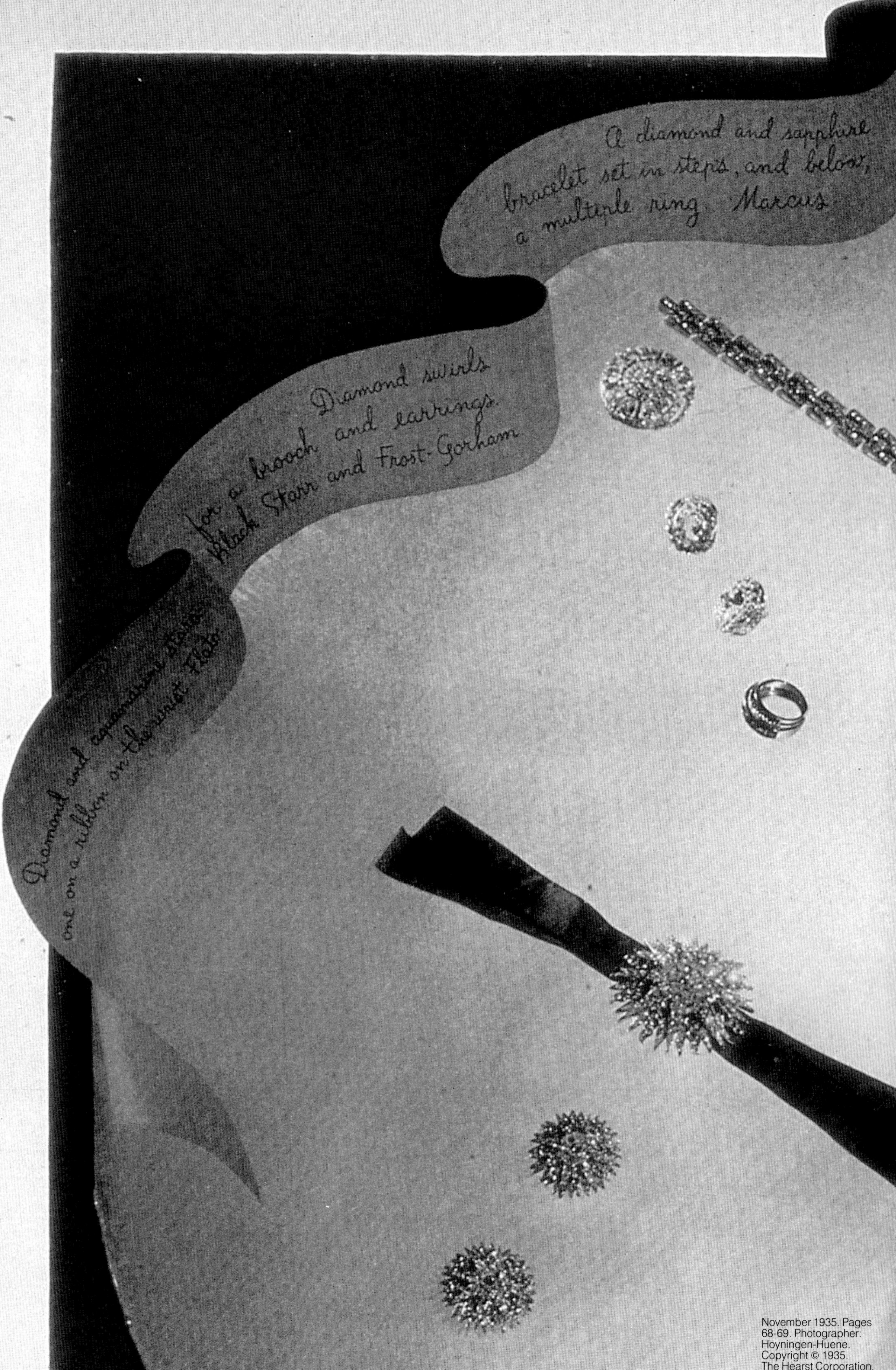

A diamond and sapphire bracelet set in steps, and below, a multiple ring. Marcus.

Diamond swirls for a brooch and earrings. Black Starr and Frost-Gorham

Diamond and aquamarine stones on a ribbon on the wrist. Flato.

November 1935. Pages 68-69. Photographer: Hoyningen-Huene. Copyright © 1935. The Hearst Corporation.

Courtesy of *Harper's Bazaar*

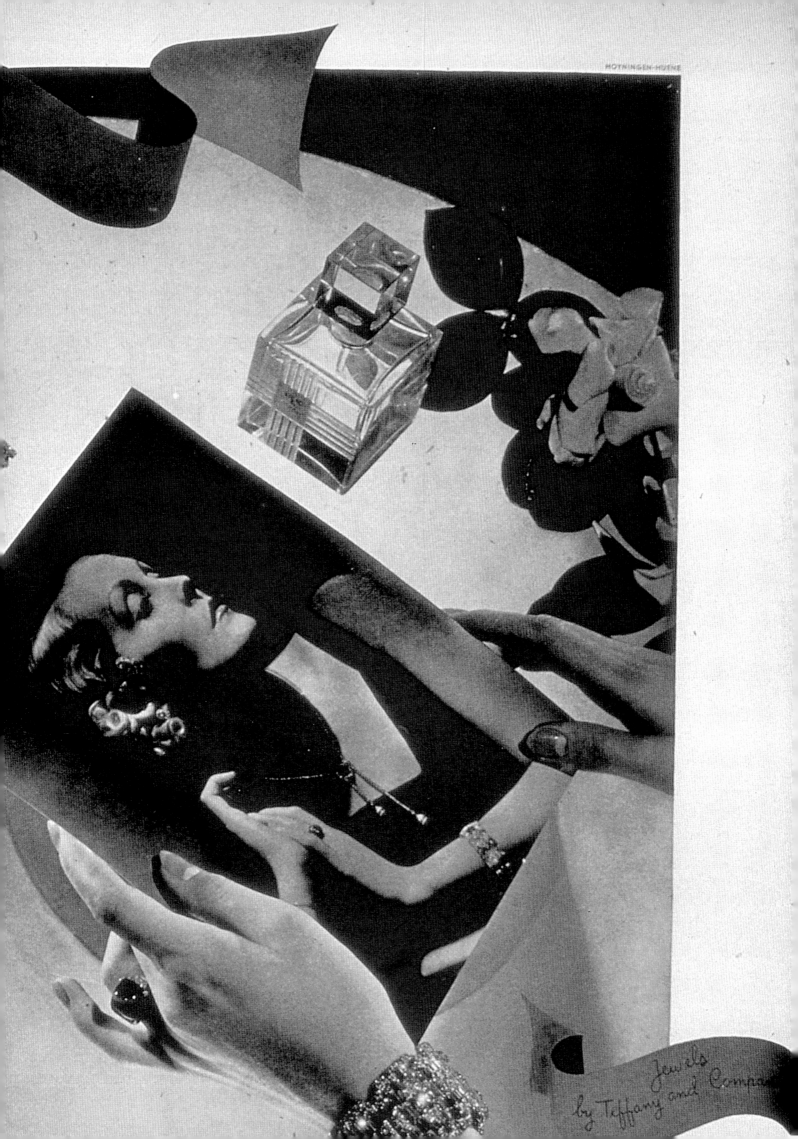

Jewels
by Tiffany and Company

October 1938. Pages 64-65. Photographer: Hoyningen-Huene.
Copyright © 1938.
The Hearst Corporation.

October 1940. Pages 58-59. Photographer: Ma
Copyright © 1940.
The Hearst Corporation.

June 1938. Pages 92-93. Photographer: Hoyningen-Huene.
Copyright © 1938.
The Hearst Corporation.

April 1948. Pages 158-159. Matisse's *Jazz*.
Copyright © 1948.
The Hearst Corporation.

February 1946. Pages 122-123. Photographer: Lisette Model.
Copyright © 1946.
The Hearst Corporation.

Courtesy of *Harper's Bazaar*.

September 1955. Pages 214-215.
Photographer: Richard Avedon. Copyright ©
The Hearst Corporation.

BEAUTY IN ULTRA VIOLET

• You live and grow and are beautiful by grace of a large, impervious ball 92,900,000 miles away. Without the beneficent heat of the sun, you would freeze and die. Without the glowing light of the sun, you would walk in perpetual darkness. And without the magic of its ultra-violet rays, you could hope for neither vitality nor beauty.

Zone beauty, beauty of teeth, wholesome blood, and loveliness of skin—all these are impossible without your proper measure of ultra-violet bounty.

Ultra violet is at once more and less mysterious than it sounds. Specifically, it is that group of the sun's rays from which you can get a sunburn. It is also the source of the all-important sunshine vitamin, Vitamin D.

During the winter months, however, the sun has a way of letting you down. There's less sunshine, and what there is loses much of its ultra-violet content before it reaches you, because of the angle at which the rays hit the earth. As some wit once remarked, the sun is the greatest physician of all; the only difficulty is in getting an appointment with him. Well, that's no problem in dealing with science's new substitute for the sun. You can always make a date with a machine!

Ultra-violet lamps were invented quite recently, but they've already found an important place in your daily life. They are used industrially for such diverse purposes as the irradiation of milk and the purification of air in pullman cars. Your doctor and your dermatologist use them for their excellent results upon the body in general, as well as their specific value in the treatment of acne and the clearing up of minor skin blemishes.

Some of the best beauty experts, who know that beauty is health, health beauty, and are never slow to take a good hint from a doctor, have now brought this lamp to their salons. They've discovered how effectively it brings your skin to life—like an exhilarating massage, but far less strenuous. This, of course, is extra velvet, for at the same time you are storing up precious Vitamin D from your ultra-violet treatment.

These new ultra-violet machines are no ordinary sun lamps. Five minutes under one is the equivalent of twenty-five minutes under a scorching sun, at the season and hour when only mad dogs and you-know-who are reputed to go out in it. You react to the machine much as you would to the sun; that is, you get a reddish burn first, and later this turns to tan. There's one difference for you to remember, though. The lamp does not bring you the hot infra-red rays of outdoor sunshine, so you mustn't depend on perspiring discomfort to warn you when to stop. Which means, of course, that you have to time yourself very carefully. Start out with a more smidgen of this super-concentrated sunshine. You can increase the doses gradually, but never take more than five minutes of it on any one day.

Just like frequent sun baths, frequent sessions with an ultra-violet machine will tend to dry your skin. This may be a fine problem-solver for you if you have an excessively oily skin. But if yours is a bit on the dry side, be sure you use plenty of lubricating oil or cream after your treatment. Anything on your face during your session with the lamp will interfere with its efficiency.

Your doctor will approve ultra violet for you because of the general boon to your health. But you'll have to go to your mirror to learn what exciting things a clear, rosy color can do for your complexion, how shining white your eyes and teeth will look against an all-year tan.

by Elmer Guthrie Neff

Chiffon set to music

February 1935. Pages 56-57. Photographer: Munkacsi.
Copyright © 1935.
The Hearst Corporation.

Silk jersey is the most important material of the season. Here Alix flings it into motion with a sensuous restraint. Jay Thorpe.

October 1936. Pages 82-83. Photographer: Hoyningen-Huene.
Copyright © 1936.
The Hearst Corporation.

The Little Black Dress Grows Up

• Opposite: The "little" black dress
is out to get attention, this spring,
and here the news runs to the hemline—
just eleven-odd inches off the floor, to give
the skirt of this black silk dress a look
of almost infinite extension. Also in its favor:
the loose-front pleats at the waist, and a pair
of ultra-pointed inserts to add inches to the pretty legs
beneath. The bodice, bloused above the waist,
has a shallow V-neck and brief sleeves,
swathed in a nearly floor-length style.
In Chardon Marche silk. About $25.
Saks Fifth Avenue; Julius Garfinckel; Nicholas Ungar's,
Portland. Dress, stole, and the hats on both pages
by Christian Dior-New York, now celebrating
M. Dior's tenth anniversary in the couture.
• Right: Black rayon crepe is coming back
into its own with the new loosed-out lines
of fashion, and a little back-dipped
capelet buttons still more fashion over
the shoulders of this slender, short-sleeved
dress. By Larry Aldrich, in Onondaga crepe
of acetate and Avisco rayon. About $90.
Saks Fifth Avenue; Julius Garfinckel;
Sakowitz. Both paper gloves
by Kislav; Herbert Levine mules.
• A final fashion note: Mr. Bolger, squiring
both young ladies shown here, wears black, too.

RICHARD AVEDON

February 1957. Pages 92-93. Photographer: Richard Avedon.
Copyright © 1957.
The Hearst Corporation.

Courtesy of *Harper's Bazaar*

$40

Blue-Flowered
Shirtwaist I

By Suzy Perette, in Onondaga
About $40. Russeks,
Joseph Magnin, Wanamaker
Philadelphia. Pink-flowered
by Mr. Arnold, about $45

February 1955. Pages 92-93.
Photographer: Richard Avedon.
Copyright © 1955.
The Hearst Corporation.

Courtesy of *Harper's Bazaar*.

$25

ted Tangerine
Shirtwaist Dress

By Jerry Gilden, in silk
coin-dotted with white. About $25.
Lord and Taylor; A. Harris; Joseph
Magnin; May Company, Los Angeles
Straw soufflé hat by Emme,

Paris Report (Continued)

• The current silhouette owes everything to the new words. Tweeds, for instance, look bulky and rough on the surface, as if they were hand-woven, but they're really very thin, light and soft. This new development in the weaves makes it possible to wear capes over jackets over dresses— to mold a woman up to her chin in layers of tweed so heavy, plus thistledown. Often, the tweeds are mixed, and often the mixer is black— black with red, with brown, with gray; or black and white, even Stephen. Other tweeds have a sort of basket-case that makes them look tweely too, and even rustic. All the new words have dull, rough surfaces, never slick or flat. Mohair sometimes gives a glossy depth to tweed; wool and mohair are mixed together in a gigantic herringbone; and Shetland and Angora are sometimes woven together, but occasionally subdued colors— charcoal crossed with light gray, for instance. Checks are gray and white, black and white, gray and black. Tweeds are Parma violet, lichen red, seaweeds and silver greens, and red. Black is very black, like the raven's wing, and for dinner dresses, there is black wool as soft and supple and sending as silk crepe. (Continued on page 192)

The Capes of Paris:

Short or full-length, theirs is the most influential new silhouette of the collections— the very model of the new day line, wrapping up suits and dresses alike in giant woolly cocoons. Dior's long form, opposite, is sparkly blue and white tweed (one of the new leatherweights, by Labbey), gathered into a huge drawstring "collar," with slots for sleeves. • Above: Dior's short-brim cape is dark blue Rodier wool with a magnified tab to button in its barrely fullness over a slender matching dress. Holt Renfrew of Canada; I. Magnin; Marshall Field; Neiman-Marcus; Frederick and Nelson.

September 1956. Pages 182-183. Photographer: Richard Avedon.
Copyright © 1956.
The Hearst Corporation.

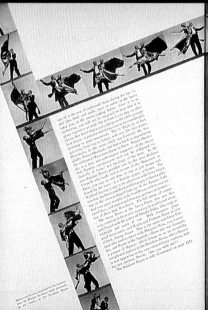

November 1935. Pages 52-53. Photographer: Munkacsi.
Copyright © 1935.
The Hearst Corporation.

February 1955. Pages 90-91. Photographer: Richard Avedon.
Copyright © 1955.
The Hearst Corporation.

*interestingly sustain than repetition). No, there was never
a mite of bun-hokum about Bogart; he was an actor without theories (well, one: that he should be highly paid),
without temper but not without temperament; and, because
he understood that discipline was the better part of artistic
survival, he lasted, he left his mark.*

November 1952. Pages 116-117. Photographer: Richard Avedon.
Copyright © 1952.
The Hearst Corporation.

September 1956. Pages 212-213. Photographer: Richard Avedon.
Copyright © 1956.
The Hearst Corporation.

Courtesy of *Harper's Bazaar*.

Observations
Photographs by Richard Avedon
Comments by Truman Capote
Designed by Alexey Brodovitch
Published by Simon & Schuster, Inc.
New York, 1959.
Copyright © 1959 by Richard Avedon Inc.

The publication of *Observations* in 1959 represents an
important collaboration between Alexey Brodovitch and
Richard Avedon, colleagues at *Harper's Bazaar*, and
established Avedon as one of the leading photographers
of the twentieth century.

Marilyn Monroe, actress
New York City, 1958

Escudero, dancer
New York City, 1955

Late in the last decade, Escudero, the Granadian grandee of flamenco, gave his farewell exhibition on a New York stage. He was **ninety** years old; though unable to perform in the fullest sense, he managed, by the program's end, to mass his audience into one steep tidal-wave of vein-swelling olés: this though he simply (but, as happens with most things that are done simply, very intricately, really) sat the whole evening in a chair snapping his fingers. His furious, tough-as-teak fingers: bony castanets hurling a rainfall of rhythm, a mosaic of sound as echoing, as honeycombed as the Alhambra's curved chambers. It was eerie, it was exciting; more than that, for reasons altogether unsentimental, will-power being the least sentimental of manly attainments, it was moving. Moving as only a triumph of will over old mortality can be.

101

The only important artists that have been exclusively developed by the movie medium are, till now, obviously, Garbo, Chaplin, a couple of cameramen, several directors, and the Italian screenwriter Cesare Zavattini.

In amiable hysteria with jutting chipmunk teeth, soft mustache and a would-be-bonvi, Zavattini is the single original literary figure for which films can assume credit: if the films had gone uninvented, it is not likely that his writing would have amounted to much—pictorial plays are his true modes of expression and, living in the hills beyond Rome far from the Via Veneto poseurs, he works on them with that isolated intensity one associates with the more dedicated poets; in result, he is in good measure responsible for the successes of De Sica, for whom he composed, among others, The Bicycle Thief, Shoe Shine, Miracle in Milan, Umberto D., and, lately, The Roof. It is interesting that De Sica has never made a first-rate film not derived from Zavattini's work; after reading a half dozen of his scripts, the reason would seem to be

Charles Chaplin, actor
New York City, 1952

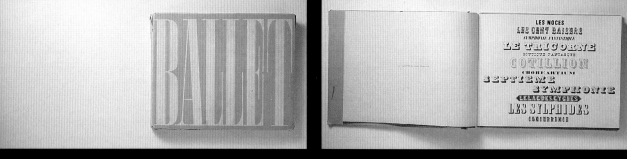

From the collection of Harvey Lloyd.

AIGA Medalist 1987

Gene Federico: The Art Director's Art Director

Good design has been an anomaly in American advertising ever since the turn of the century when copywriters were given total rein over imagemakers. Unlike European advertising of the same period when the foremost artist/designers were made culture heros, it was virtually inconceivable that an American art director could be more than just a layout person. This changed in the 1930's when the advertising pioneer Ernest Elmo Caulkins, realizing the strength of word and picture, devised the forerunner of the creative team. By 1939, when Gene Federico, a twenty-one-year-old Pratt Institute graduate with a special interest in typography, entered the profession, a few exceptional designers had already begun to change the look and content of some mainstream advertising, paving the way for a distinctly American modern style.

By the late 1940's, after an apprenticeship at an ad agency, a tour of duty in the Army, and an unexceptional stint as a magazine art associate, Federico realized that graphic design was his passion and advertising his métier. Soon he became one of America's premiere advertising art directors and designers, bridging the often wide gap between the two jobs. His selection as the 1987 AIGA Medalist is important for two reasons: It honors someone who, for over four decades, has responsibly stretched the boundaries of advertising design with typographic elegance and conceptual acuity, and, as a principal of Lord Geller Federico Einstein, continues to contribute to an American graphic design vocabulary.

Born on February 6, 1918 in New York's Greenwich Village, Federico was the middle child with two sisters. When the family moved to the Bronx, he attended P.S. 89 which, in keeping with a venerable New York City public school tradition, sponsored a number of poster competitions for city agencies and events. Federico's earliest advertisement was a poster painted in tempera for the ASPCA. When the family moved to Coney Island a few years later, he enrolled in Abraham Lincoln High School. This was the home of the legendary *Art Squad* led by Leon Friend, who taught intensive classes in commercial design and illustration for over fifty years. As an *Art Squad* member Federico

2.

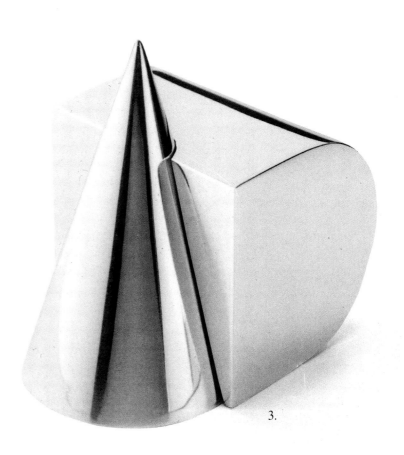

3.

was exposed to the work of the leading European advertising artists. One inspiration was an arresting, Cubist-inspired poster by A.M. Cassandre promoting the *S.S. Amsterdam*. Awed by its stark geometry and subtle hues, he modeled his own early poster style on Cassandre's use of bold lettering and dominant painted image. Though he designed pages for school publications, Federico explains that "it was the direct message of a poster that propelled me into advertising."

Brooklyn's Pratt Institute was the next stage in his education. In its voluminous library, Federico pored through the current European design magazines and American design annuals soaking up the influence of Cassandre, Lester Beall, and Paul Rand (the latter, only a few years older than Federico, was already making significant inroads into advertising design). At Pratt *form* became an enduring watchword, which Federico says is the basis of "a work so powerful that it is hard to find any weakness in it."

Tom Benrimo, a popular advertising designer and illustrator at the time, was a formidable teacher who recommended that Federico take a job with his client, the Abbott Kimball Company, a small advertising agency in New York. One of Federico's first professional assignments was a clever conceptual piece entitled "Brains and Luck," a brochure promoting the agency that was accepted into the 1939 New York Art Director's show. Concurrently, he took a few weeknight classes at the Art Students League in Manhattan under the tutelage of Howard Trafton. One lesson was on the effects of *dumb light* in which Federico recalls "you just hang a naked lit bulb to see its effects on a model." Another was Trafton's analysis of African sculpture, "his emphasis on distortion and negative space explained the root of all graphic experience." On those seemingly endless, noisy subway rides back to his home in Brooklyn he would often discuss the evening's lessons with Norman Geller, a younger classmate, who years later would become his business partner.

In 1941, seduced by a job offer in the ad department at Bamberger's Department Store, he decided to migrate to Newark, New Jersey. There he could do good work, double his salary, and most important, live away from home for the first time. Four months later, Uncle Sam of-

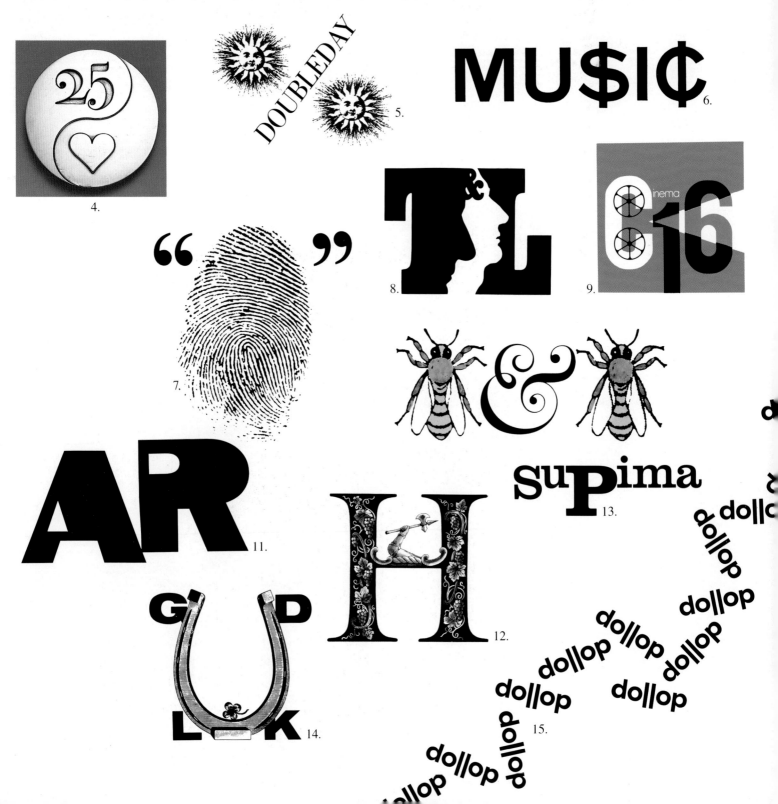

fered a less comfortable home away from home. From April 1941 to November 1945 Federico was a GI first stationed in the United States and then sent to North Africa and Europe, where he served in a camouflage unit. Field work allowed the occasional respite to design manuals, posters, paint a mural for an officer's club, and, in Oran, organize an enlisted man's art show. Federico returned from the war to the job at Abbott Kimball, where he stayed less than a year.

Federico's pre- and postwar design was exhibited in 1946 at the prestigious A-D Gallery in a show entitled "The Four Veterans." Will Burtin, then art director of *Fortune* magazine, impressed by what he saw, asked the young designer to become his art associate. "I thought that I should try editorial," he painfully recalls,

"but I hated it. I loved Will, but I couldn't follow the way he designed. So completely analytical, he could take the most complex subject and then build it into a dramatic structure. It was brilliant, but it wasn't my kind of design." Federico resigned after ten months, and took a temporary job supervising layouts at *Architectural Forum* where, admitting to his preference for the single image and a definite problem with achieving kinetic flow through pictures, he did merely a so-so job. At this point, he decided to freelance.

For a year and a half Federico struggled while his wife, Helen, worked as an assistant to Paul Rand. "With Helen's salary, we were able to manage," he says. Rand suggested that Federico take a job at Grey Advertising where he met Bill

Bernbach, Phyllis Robinson, Ned Doyle, and Bob Gage. They left shortly to open an agency with Mac Dane, called Doyle Dane Bernbach. Three years later, Gage invited Federico to join the new firm, and he was given the *Woman's Day* magazine account. This resulted in a series of ads that revealed Federico's deft pictographic sensibility.

Though some advertising designers, like Rand and Beall, signed their already distinctive work, Federico's signature was found in the construction of the typographical image. "Lester Beall opened my eyes to the idea that type could be used to emphasize the message," says Federico talking about his roots. "One of his ads had the great line, 'To hell with eventually. Let's concentrate on now.' The 'e' in 'eventually' was

very large and 'now' was the same size. The simple manipulation of these letter forms allowed the viewer to immediately comprehend the message." Federico's method is also based on the integration of text and image and so he has always worked intimately with a copywriter. He says, "I too look for those simple elements in copy." And warns that "when the designer doesn't read the copy to catch the sound of the words, he runs the risk of misusing the typography. If the rhythm of the words is disregarded, the copy is likely to be laid out incorrectly." Federico's best-known ad for *Woman's Day* typifies this rhythmic sensitivity. It has the catch-line "Going Out," and shows a photo of a woman riding a bicycle with wheels made from the two lowercase Futura 'o's in the headline. The aim

of this ad was to persuade potential advertisers that three million-plus devoted readers went out of their way to buy this check-out counter magazine. The ads apparently did well for the client, but more importantly proved the power of persuasive visual simplicity in a field that often errs on the side of overstatement.

Federico's advertising approach is more related to attitude than style. Despite Lou Dorfsman's assertion that Federico is the prince of Light Line Gothic (admittedly one of his favorite typefaces), few of his ads conform to a single formula or evoke stylistic *deja vu*. Nevertheless, one trait is dominant: his love of and skill with type. This talent matured during the mid-1950's. He fondly remembers, "It was then that Aaron Burns (who was working at the Composing

Room) introduced me to a range of new typefaces. He would get so excited about new developments, and we would have fun working together." This was more than the typical designer and supplier relationship; Burns also developed formative outlets for Federico and others to experiment with expressive typography. One was a series of four sixteen-page booklets (written by Percy Seitlin) that allowed designers total freedom to interpret a specific subject with type, photography, and illustration. Herb Lubalin did one on jazz, Lester Beall did cars, Brownjohn, Chermeyeff and Geismar did New York City, and Federico did *Love of Apples*. "I wanted to try something where I used metal type in extreme ways without having to cut it—without cutting up proofs or playing with stats," explains Fe-

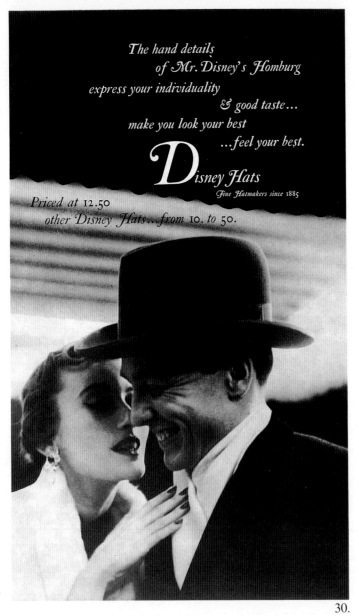

30.

you take the car... I'll take the Lambretta!

Push a button and off you glide—
to the club, to the 8:02, to Math class, to the supermarket.
You'll be the smartest thing on wheels when you
drive the Lambretta, Italy's darling, America's newest love!
For information or your nearest dealer, call or write
Lambretta Div., Innocenti Corp., 350 Fifth Avenue, N.Y., BR 9-8476

31

32.

Thanks giving

...over a million times as strong in

1950

★ ★ ★ ★ ★ ★ ★ ★ From less than 100 Pilgrims united in the
★ ★ ★ ★ ★ ★ ★ ★ first thanks giving...to more than 150 *million*
★ ★ ★ ★ ★ ★ ★ ★ Americans joining in national thanks giving
★ ★ ★ ★ ★ ★ ★ ★ this year...thus has our great American holiday
★ ★ ★ ★ ★ ★ ★ ★ grown. ★ Never has Thanksgiving been more
★ ★ ★ ★ ★ ★ ★ ★ widely observed than it will be in 1950. And
★ ★ ★ ★ ★ ★ ★ ★ never has it been more important! ★ This year,
we give thanks more than ever before, for the *idea* of America. For the idea of
freedom. And for our strength to protect our freedom. ★ During the past few months
America has seen that freedom seriously challenged. Thousands of men have died
in its defense. All of us have been affected, in one way or other, by the changes this
defense of freedom has brought in our way of living. All of us are united in the
conviction that, cost what it may, freedom *must* be defended. ★ We at Magee join
all other Americans in giving thanks that we live in a free land, and in
the determination to do all we can to preserve it!

magee
carpets and rugs

derico about this masterpiece of descriptive typography. "For some time, I had known that if you stacked Title Gothics they would have a different look than traditional types. So the whole book was based on that simple idea." But the aesthetics of type were not his only concern, as he says, "The message of the book was that nature's beauty is being radically altered. There's a line that reads 'When we, in business, industrial America, began to get smart about apples, we packaged them and packaged them and packaged them until the apple itself became a package.' I illustrated that point with a photograph of an apple with a string tied around it." In another designer's hands, this subtle environmental critique might have become a screaming polemic, yet Federico's elegant touch transformed these

34.

35.

a smart woman puts her money in a **jana** bag

33.

36.

37.

She's got to

go

38.

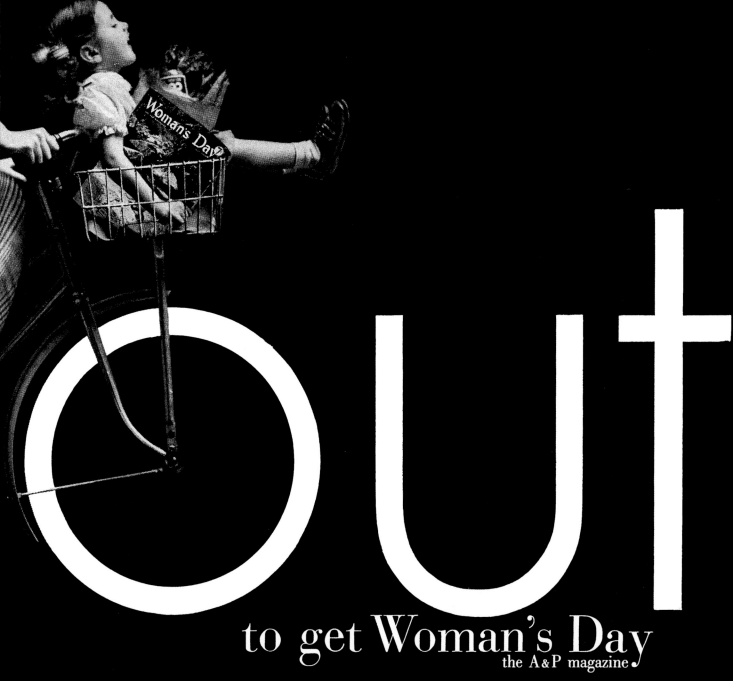

Out
to get Woman's Day
the A&P magazine

...and Woman's Day isn't all she buys.

ause Woman's Day's circulation is all single copy sales,

you can be sure of 3,811,000 readers out shopping where your products are sold.

few pages into memorable visual poetry. One could say the same for a great deal of his advertising.

After the stint with Doyle Dane Bernbach, he went to Douglas D. Simon and then spent seven and a half years at Benton and Bowles. There he says "practically nothing happened," though he actually created some memorable advertising for IBM's Office Products Division, including those for the introduction of the early electric and first Selectric typewriters. For the Selectric, the first office machine to use a type element, Federico wrote a slogan, "A new type of writer," which, like some other excellent ideas for IBM went unused. One of his favorites, and therefore the most frustrating rejection, is a 'knotted pencil,' a symbol to announce IBM's new 'Stretch'

Wonderful family resemblance

L'**A**iglon admirers are finding similar smartness, similar sparkle, similar high quality in junior sister · ...Jeanne d'**A**rc!

L'AIGLON APPAREL, INC., JEANNE D'ARC (DIVISION OF L'AIGLON APPAREL, INC.) 1350 BROADWAY, N. Y. 18.

39.
40.

41.

computer, which at the time could solve more problems than any other computer. With his creative-teammate copywriter Bob Larimer, Federico devised the archetype of one of today's favored visual cliches. Larimer has recently written about it, saying, "When longer ago than we care to admit we created an ad for IBM illustrated with a knotted pencil, we thought the symbol was totally original. Since that distant day, the knotted pencil has turned up repeatedly in art, advertising, and commercial illustration." Despite the reasons for IBM's rejection (and Federico never really found out why), it underscores the heart of the advertising dilemma: How effectively does good design contribute to selling an advertising concept? Federico says, "It depends on who is doing the selling. If I were a salesman like George Lois or Lou Dorfsman, I could sell almost anything. But you don't always have such good fortune. Your work is presented by account people who lack sufficient feeling for it."

The need for more control over the quality and destiny of his work motivated Federico to start his own agency. However, the process was not rapid or easy. In the early 1960's at Benton and Bowles, Federico ran an art group that included Emil Gargano, Roy Grace, and Dick Hess. There he met a copywriter named Dick Lord, who left to become creative director of Warwick & Legler and invited Federico to join him. Four years passed before taking up the offer to become art supervisor. Eight months later in early 1967, citing general malaise, both Lord and Federico decided to form a partnership called Lord Southard Federico. Southard, who was brought in to lure accounts, soon left making it Lord Federico. "That add_d a sort of regal sound to my name," muses Federico. One day on the street, he ran into Norman Geller, his former classmate and subway companion, who as a former art director turned business wiz had done quite well with his own agency. Wanting to take on a new challenge, he joined the fledgling firm. Soon the name of copywriter, Arthur Einstein, was added to the shingle. With two writers and two art people as principals, Lord Geller Federico Einstein was built on a solid creative foundation. At first business was slow, but in time the firm acquired some fashion, beauty, and "nuts and bolts" accounts. One of Federi-

42.

43.

44.

Adele Simpson recreates the magic of old Baghdad in Breeze, a Hope Skillman fabric woven of Supima... dramatizing the debut of this champagne of cottons. Born and bred in America, Supima reveals unprecedented lustre, unheard of strength, undreamed of grace. At Bonwit Teller, all stores · Neiman-Marcus, Dallas · Harzfeld's, Kansas City, Supima Association of America, 40 Worth Street, New York

How
do
you
solve
a
problem
that
requires
10
billion
calculations
?

Problems of this enormous complexity are so common in nuclear physics that the Atomic Energy Commission asked IBM for a computer 100 times faster

than
the fastest in existence. The result is the new IBM Stretch computer, the world's most powerful.

45.

Never serve the coffee without the Cream...Harvey's Bristol Cream

HARVEY'S BRISTOL CREAM®/©1963, HEUBLEIN, INC. HARTFORD, CONNECTICUT. SOLE IMPORTER, U.S.A.

46.

An after-dinner drink should be sweet, but Bristol Cream isn't sticky about it. Oh...you might enjoy it before dinner, too!
John Harvey and Sons, Ltd.

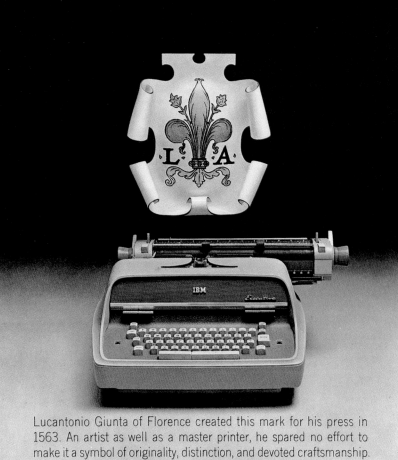

Lucantonio Giunta of Florence created this mark for his press in 1563. An artist as well as a master printer, he spared no effort to make it a symbol of originality, distinction, and devoted craftsmanship. A similar dedication produces today's IBM* typewriters. That is why the IBM "Executive"* Typewriter can add the unique quality of fine printing to your correspondence...create impressions beyond words.

48.

49.

JINGLE

47.

In 1502, this mark was created by master printer Aldus Manutius of Venice. It expressed his lifelong devotion to the principles of originality, artistry, and superb craftsmanship. A similar dedication to those high standards is reflected in today's IBM* typewriters. With the IBM "Executive"* Typewriter, your correspondence is enriched by the look of fine printing...to create impressions beyond words.

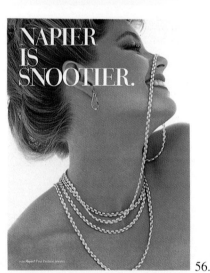

This was Louise Brooks. She made only twenty-four films, in a movie career that began in 1925 and ended, with enigmatic suddenness, in 1938. Two of them were masterpieces: "Pandora's Box" and its immediate successor, also directed by Pabst— "The Diary of a Lost Girl." Most, however, were assembly-line studio products. Yet around her, with a luxuriance that proliferates every year, a literature has grown up.

As an emblematic figure of the twenties, epitomizing the flappers, jazz babies, and dancing daughters of the boom years, Brooks has few rivals, living or dead. Moreover, she is unique among such figures in that her career took her to all the places—New York, London, Hollywood, Paris, and Berlin— where the action was at its height, where experiments in pleasure were conducted with the same zeal (and often by the same people) as experiments in the arts.

"Reminds me of the night when Buster Keaton drove me in his roadster out to Culver City, where he had a bungalow on the back lot of M-G-M. The walls of the living room were covered with great glass bookcases. Buster, who wasn't drunk, opened the door, turned on the lights, and picked up a baseball bat. Then, walking calmly round the room, he smashed every pane of glass in every bookcase."

"Here, inevitably, are Scott and Zelda. I met them in January, 1927, at the Ambassador Hotel in L.A. They were sitting close together on a sofa, like a comedy team, and the first thing that struck me was how *small* they were. I had come to see the genius writer, but what dominated the room was the blazing intelligence of Zelda's profile."

Of all the names that spilled out of Brooks's memories of America in the twenties, there was one for which she reserved a special veneration: that of Chaplin. "Do you know, I can't once remember him *still?* He was always standing up as he sat down, and going out as he came in. Except when he turned off the lights and went to sleep, without liquor or pills, like a child."

Despite the numerous men who have crossed the trajectory of her life, Brooks has pursued her own course. She has flown solo. The price to be paid for such individual autonomy is, inevitably, loneliness, and her loneliness is prefigured in one of the most penetrating comments she has ever committed to print: "The great art of films does not consist in descriptive movement of face and body, but in the movements of thought and soul transmitted in a kind of intense isolation."

From a Profile
of Louise Brooks
by Kenneth Tynan,
appearing in this week's issue
(June 11)
of The New Yorker.
Yes, The New Yorker.

59.

60.

The reason I had asked Frank about learning to tap-dance was that I had just turned fifty, was in much the same physical shape as Frank, and was taking a hard look at my life, narrowing my aspirations to realistic goals keyed to what little time I might have left. Two great dreams remained unfulfilled: (1) tap dancing, and (2) playing jai-alai.

"Watching a jai-alai match is exciting," the booklet notes, "but by simply placing a two-dollar bet the spectator becomes part of the actio... This ticket buys ten thrill-packed minutes of uncertainty." Since I feel I have experienced my share of thrill-packed minutes of uncertainty in life, I stay put. The players are warming up.

"Oh dear," said my mother when I told her on the phone about the posssibility of jai-alai lessons. "Do you think that's a good idea?" (She is eighty-three but still fascinated by separating the good ideas from the bad.) I assured her it was a splendid idea. My father—eighty-eight years old—was listening on the other phone. He said it sounded quite interesting to him.

We go through a cagelike entrance to the court, and then I am standing on the shiny concrete floor. The walls and ceiling seem very distant. It is exhilarating to be here at last. I swing the *cesta* this way and that, relishing its weight and shape, delighting in the grand space around me. Megalomania sets in: on this court, in my helmet, slashing about with my *cesta*, I am on the verge of being a *pelotari*. The rest of the world—abject non-players of jai-alai—must remain outside the fence.

From an article
by James Stevenson,
appearing in this week's issue
(June 4)
of The New Yorker.

61.

62.

A REPORTER AT LARGE
THE CLOSING CIRCLE –1

The First Law of Ecology: Everything Is Connected to Everything Else.

The Second Law of Ecology: Everything Must Go Somewhere.

The Third Law of Ecology: Nature Knows Best.

The Fourth Law of Ecology: There Is No Such Thing As a Free Lunch.

From a two-part article
by Barry Commoner about
the environmental crisis,
beginning this week
in The New Yorker.
Yes, The New Yorker.

REFLECTIONS
THE GREENING OF AMERICA

"There is a revolution under way. It is not like revolutions of the past. It has originated with the individual and with culture, and if it succeeds it will change the political structure only as its final act. It will not require violence to succeed, and it cannot be successfully resisted by violence. It is now spreading with amazing rapidity, and already our laws, institutions, and social structure are changing in consequence. Its ultimate creation could be a higher reason, a more human community, and a new and liberated individual. This is the revolution of the new generation."

From
"The Greening Of America,"
by Charles A. Reich,
an article appearing
this week in
The New Yorker.
Yes, The New Yorker.

63.

60 *Soixante.*

5:30 pm
5/21/76 *Friday.*
61 3 *Isle of Capri. Bicentstairs. Third Floor. New York City.*
1001
1001 *Cocktails Buffet.*
Songs and Sighs and Singing and Dancing and

R.S.V.P.   Joe McMahon
A.S.A.P.   172 61 *East Street.*
N.Y. 10021
Business.
(212) 421-6050
(212) 758-3528 *Home.*

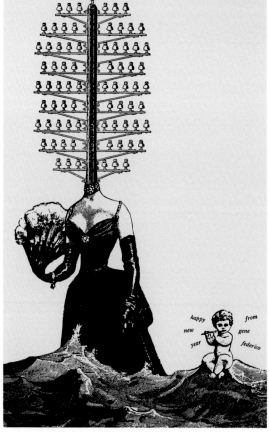

Astor Gallery   39th
Waldorf-Astoria   Annual Exhibition
Park Avenue   New York
and 50th Street   Art Directors Club
New York City   1960

April 12th 12 pm to 7 pm
April 13th 10 am to 7 pm
April 14th 10 am to 7 pm
April 15th 10 am to 7 pm
April 16th 10 am to 7 pm
April 17th 10 am to 7 pm
April 18th 10 am to 7 pm
April 19th 10 am to 7 pm
April 20th 10 am to 5 pm

65.

64.

call

A call for entries (to be postmarked by January 16, 1956) 14th Design and Printing for Commerce Exhibition 1955 + 50 Advertisements of the Year

66.

67.

co's most pleasing assignments is for Napier Jewelry, which for eighteen years he has done single-handedly, and whose basic format has not changed since the first ad. Of the format, a closeup photograph of the product on a model with the simple line, "Napier is...(with a descriptive word)," Federico says, "it's still fresh! And that to me, is the best advertising." In the early days of LGFE, he and Lord collaborated on a delightful campaign of full-page newspaper ads advertising *The New Yorker* using selected editorial contents from the product, with only one small advertising line at the bottom, "Yes, The New Yorker." Its message is as naturally timely and its design as fittingly timeless as the magazine itself.

As the firm grew, so did Federico's reputa-

tion. "He was called El Supremo," says Sam Antupit, vice president of design at Harry N. Abrams Inc. who as a student met Federico over thirty years ago. "Gene was, and is, considered the art director's art director. Even when he became a principal in a firm, he never renounced his creative role. His was also the first name on the list of important people to see when a young design student came to New York. And he actually made time to see you too."

With his mild, sometimes self-effacing manner, wry wit and palpable concern for good design and its creators, Federico is a bona fide elder statesman of this profession. What characterizes this eminence? Attitude is key, and *passion* is paramount. Respect, not only for his clients ("Finding the best solution for a client's

identity is not a matter or a means of self expression," he says) but deference for his audience dictates his practice. By not underestimating the consumer's intelligence, and by recognizing the constraints of this persuasive art, Federico continues to expand advertising's boundaries and set its standards.

by Steven Heller

68.

69.

70.

71.

72.

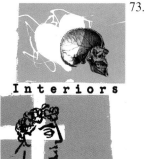

73.

74.

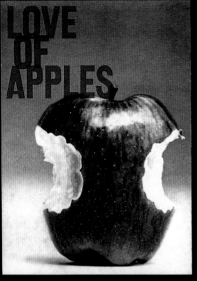
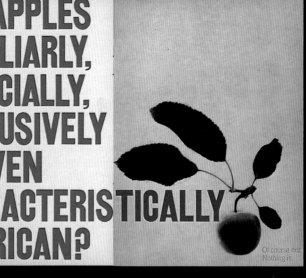

75.

76.

Oh, when the pioneers began to get smart about apples they did, indeed, pick out the best strains and learn how to propagate them. But an apple to them, was something that was good, not something that looked as though it ought to be. When we, in business, industrial America, began to get smart about apples **WE PACKAGED THEM AND PACKAGED THEM AND PACKAGED THEM**

UNTIL THE APPLE ITSELF

BECAME THE PACKAGE.

'Where is the knowledge we have lost in information?' wrote the American poet, T. S. Eliot (who has lived in England most of his life). Where is the wisdom we have lost in knowledge? Our pomologists know more about apples than the pioneers ever dreamed was possible. Yet, the wisdom of apples is

GRADUALLY BECOMING LOST.

Cryptographics:

79.

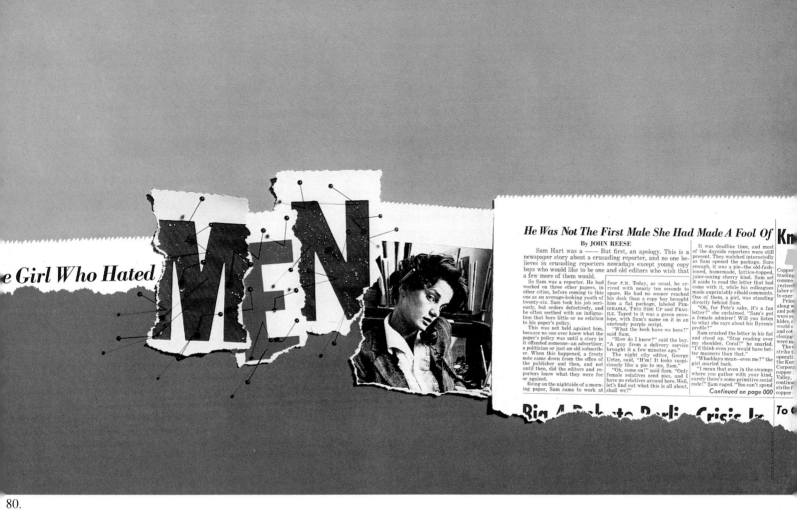

e Girl Who Hated **MEN**

He Was Not The First Male She Had Made A Fool Of
By JOHN REESE

Sam Hart was a ——— But first, an apology. This is a newspaper story about a crusading reporter, and no one believes in crusading reporters nowadays except young copy boys who would like to be one and old editors who wish that a few more of them would.

So Sam was a reporter. He had worked on three other papers, in other cities, before coming to this one as an average-looking youth of twenty-six. Sam took his job seriously, but orders defectively, and he often seethed with an indignation that bore little or no relation to his paper's policy.

This was not held against him, because no one ever knew what the paper's policy was until a story in it offended someone—an advertiser, a politician or just an old subscriber. When this happened, a frosty note came down from the office of the publisher and then, and not until then, did the editors and reporters know what they were for or against.

Being on the nightside of a morning paper, Sam came to work at four P.M. Today, as usual, he arrived with nearly ten seconds to spare. He had no sooner reached his desk than a copy boy brought him a flat package, labeled PERISHABLE, THIS SIDE UP and FRAGILE. Taped to it was a green envelope, with Sam's name on it in an unsteady purple script.

"What the heck have we here?" said Sam.

"How do I know?" said the boy. "A guy from a delivery service brought it a few minutes ago."

The night city editor, George Uetze, said, "H'm! It looks suspiciously like a pie to me, Sam."

"Oh, come on!" said Sam. "Only female relatives send pies, and I have no relatives around here. Well, let's find out what this is all about, shall we?"

It was deadline time, and most of the dayside reporters were still present. They watched interestedly as Sam opened the package. Sure enough, it was a pie—the old-fashioned, homemade, lattice-topped, juice-oozing cherry kind. Sam set it aside to read the letter that had come with it, while his colleagues made unprintably ribald comments. One of them, a girl, was standing directly behind Sam.

"Oh, for Pete's sake, it's a fan letter!" she exclaimed. "Sam's got a female admirer! Will you listen to what she says about his Byronic profile!"

Sam crushed the letter in his fist and stood up. "Stop reading over my shoulder, Coral!" he snarled. "I'd think even you would have better manners than that."

"Whaddaya mean—even me?" the girl snarled back.

"I mean that even in the swamps where you gather with your kind, surely there's some primitive social code!" Sam raged. "You can't spend

Continued on page 000

80.

Page

Gene Feder c

10.

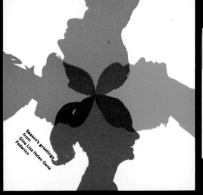

Gina,
Lisa,
Helen,
Gene
Federico
this year–
1964

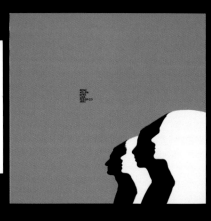

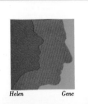

82.

HELEN GINA LISA GENE FEDERICO 1968

Helen Gina Lisa Gene Federico 1968.

HELEN, GENE, LIS

Gina
Lisa

Gene
Helen

Lisa
Helen
Gene
Gina
Federico 1977

Federico
1976

Gene
Helen
Lisa
Gina
Federico
1978

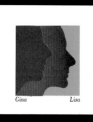

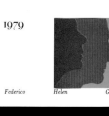

1979

Gina   Lisa   Federico   Helen   Gene

Gina Lisa Helen Gene and Federico
1981

Federico

HELEN
&GENE
FEDERICO

Pound Ridge, New York

The AIGA
Design Leadership
Award 1987:

Walker Art Center

1987 Awards Committee
Cheryl Heller, Committee Chairman
Chief Executive Officer and Creative Direct
Heller Breene

Alvin Eisenman
Director of Studies in Graphic Design
Yale School of Art

Douglass G. Scott
Senior Designer
WGBH Educational Foundation

Deborah Sussman
President
Sussman/Prezja & Co., Inc.

Past Recipients
IBM Corporation, 1980
Massachusetts Institute of Technology, 198
Container Corporation of America, 1982
Cummins Engine Company, Inc., 1983
Herman Miller, Inc., 1984
WGBH Educational Foundation, 1985
Esprit, 1986

POSTERS

Walker Art Center through January 31

Foirades/Fizzles

Prints of Jasper Johns

The Walker's terraces and roof decks constitute a series of sculpture pedestals; they welcome visitors and provide a preview of what is to be seen within the Art Center's walls. From an adjacent highway, drivers can easily read the exhibition banners on the building's north facade.

The museum's permanent collection includ twentieth-century painting, sculpture, prints drawings. Temporary exhibitions organize the Art Center staff may be thematic, as fo example *De Stijl* or *Tokyo: Form and Spirit*, g shows of living artists, or one-person retrospectives, and cover a wide range of disciplines including architecture, graphic

photo: Michael Moran

ustrial design, and photography, in addition
the traditional art museum fields of
ecialization. The Art Center also has active
ograms in new dance, theater, music, film and
ture series organized around topics that relate
current projects and programs in the museum,
well as guided tours and a variety of programs
children.

Located on the edge of Minneapolis's downtown
business district, the Walker is within walking
distance of the central city and several nearby
residential areas. The Art Center shares its site
with The Tyrone Guthrie Theater whose
playgoers often spend their pre-theater hours in
the Walker's galleries.

photo: Mark Hanauer

Although exhibitions and collections form the core of the Art Center's program, activities in the performing arts and film create lively platforms for expressions that relate to and interact with the visual arts. A variety of images (clockwise,

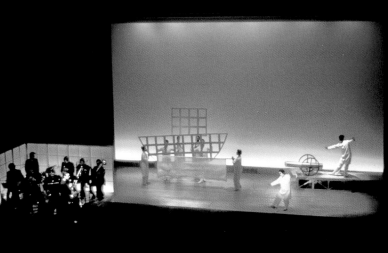

from top left) indicate the range and diversity of Walker programs: bannering in the upper lobby which joins the Art Center and The Guthrie Theater; David Hockney preparing works for his Walker retrospective, *Hockney Paints the Stage;* Concourse signing for the 1980 exhibition *Picasso from the Musée Picasso, Paris;* a scene from Robert Wilson's *Knee Plays,* commissioned by the Walker and premiered at the Art Center in 1984; films and concerts are Walker-sponsored summertime activities in a nearby city park; a koto player performing in the galleries as part of the 1986 exhibition *Tokyo: Form and Spirit;* choreographer-dancer Trisha Brown and Company in a 1985 performance of *Lateral Pass;* and children on Walker's roof terrace with Charles Ginnever's 1976 sculpture *Nautilus.*

De Stijl: 1917–1931, Visions of Utopia (1981) was a major exhibition of works from one of this century's most influential artistic movements. Initiated in the Netherlands by Piet Mondrian, Theo Van Doesburg, and Gerrit Rietveld, De Stijl participants included painters, architects and designers all over Europe, and its theoretical basis developed out of the same impulses that produced the Bauhaus School in Germany and the Constructivist movement in Russia.

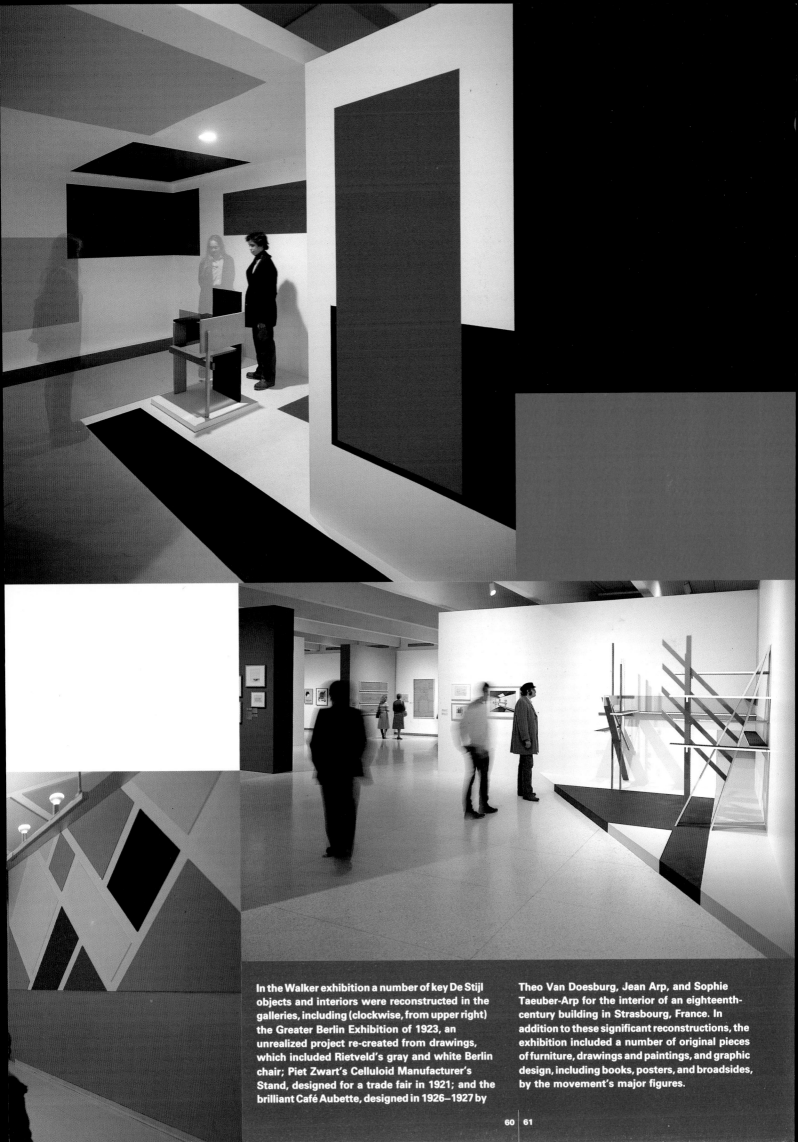

In the Walker exhibition a number of key De Stijl objects and interiors were reconstructed in the galleries, including (clockwise, from upper right) the Greater Berlin Exhibition of 1923, an unrealized project re-created from drawings, which included Rietveld's gray and white Berlin chair; Piet Zwart's Celluloid Manufacturer's Stand, designed for a trade fair in 1921; and the brilliant Café Aubette, designed in 1926–1927 by Theo Van Doesburg, Jean Arp, and Sophie Taeuber-Arp for the interior of an eighteenth-century building in Strasbourg, France. In addition to these significant reconstructions, the exhibition included a number of original pieces of furniture, drawings and paintings, and graphic design, including books, posters, and broadsides, by the movement's major figures.

Tokyo: Form and Spirit (1986), an extensive exhibition organized in association with Japan House Gallery, New York, dramatically illustrated the powerful traditions of Japanese design from the Edo period (1603–1868) to the present. Over 200 Edo-period objects were shown next to large-scale visionary environments created by some of today's most inventive architects and designers, including Arata Isozaki, Shiro Kuramata, Eiko Ishioka, Tadao Ando, Tadanori Yokoo, Hiroshi Hara, Shigeo Fukuda, Toyo Ito, and Fumuhiko Maki. All of the interiors created for the exhibition were constructed in Japan, taken apart for shipping, and then reconstructed

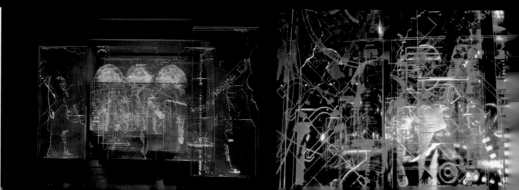

in the Walker's galleries. In conjunction with the exhibition, Japanese performing artists were brought to the U.S. for a series of dance and music events that took place in the galleries. The exhibition premiered in Tokyo before opening at the Walker, and later traveled to a number of venues, as do many exhibitions organized by the Walker Art Center.

The Architecture of Frank Gehry

The Architecture of Frank Gehry (1986) was first major museum exhibition of the work of the master builder. Gehry is renowned for his aesthetic vision and for his profound understanding of and original thinking within traditional vocabulary of architecture.

The Walker's examination of the work of the unorthodox form-giver includes many model drawings and photographs of his projects from 1964 to the present. His unique cardboard furniture, compelling fish and snake lamps, a series of full-scale structures, commissioned the exhibition, directly conveyed the principle Gehry's remarkable palette. As is the case with all Walker-originated exhibitions, the Gehry retrospective was accompanied by a book documenting the exhibition; it included critical articles on the architect's work by eminent architectural scholars and critics.

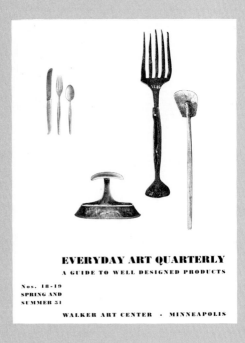

An issue of Walker Art Center's journal *Design Quarterly* is called "Julia Child's Kitchen: A Design Anatomy." It is not a glossy presentation of elegant utensils or stylish cabinetry but rather an analysis of a practical, continuously evolving work environment. The authors of the issue state that Child's kitchen is an excellent "research model" not because it is beautiful or conventionally well-designed, but because it is "Artless . . . Easily perceived . . . Small scale . . . Productive" (Bill Stumpf and Nicholas Polites, *DQ* 104, 1977). The essay reveals Child's personal system of "environmental graphics:" signage for the tools of the kitchen, written on masking tape or punched out on a dimestore Letramax machine, and a pegboard wall marked with the outlines of a hundred pots and pans. Rather than endorse specific "products" in Child's kitchen, *Design Quarterly* studied the manner in which such objects are used and arranged.

Organic and pragmatic rather than stylistically consistent or preplanned, Julia Child's kitchen exemplifies the kinds of subjects examined by Walker Art Center. Over the past twenty years the Walker's design department has moved away from traditional curatorial stances toward useful objects—it focuses neither on the precious, antique decorative arts collected by many museums, nor on the standards of contemporary good taste presented by some collections of modern design. Under design curator Mildred Friedman and museum director Martin Friedman, the Walker has broken down the concept of the individual, isolated "design object," which might be viewed with equal pleasure in a museum case or on a department store shelf. The Walker's exhibitions, publications, and educational programs view objects of art and design in terms of their broad cultural significance, rather than their intrinsic aesthetic qualities alone.

"When I joined the Walker in 1969, it wasn't a tangible 'museum' but rather a few offices in downtown Minneapolis," recalls Mildred Friedman. "The original 1927 building had been torn down, and a new one, designed by Edward Larrabee Barnes, was going up. For two years we organized exhibitions in schools, parks, and office lobbies—I think the experience being a museum without walls left a permanent mark on the Walker's psyche." The urban landscape, an accumulation of designed objects and systems (fences, factories, suburbs, shop signs, traffic lights, bus routes, zoning laws) has provided the Walker with a fruitful model of design's pervasiveness in daily life, and the way in which graphic and architectural forms continuously overlap.

Mildred Friedman, who had been a practicing interior designer, became both curator of the design department and designer of the new building's interiors in 1969; Martin Friedman had been the museum's director since 1961. The Walker does not split design and scholarly judgment into separate domains of authority, partly because the museum relatively small and partly because it understands that "design is not a clearly limited "discipline" like painting or sculpture. Mildred Friedman has functioned as a practicing exhibition designer as well as a curator—she succeeded Peter Seitz, who had served as both design curator and chief graphic designer. The design department is responsible for assembling exhibitions and events on architecture, urban planning, and graphic design; editing and producing the journal *Design Quarterly*; and designing the numerous exhibition graphics and

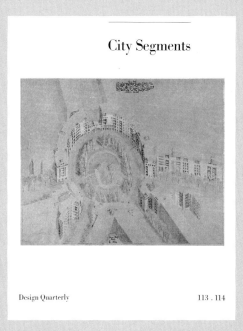

ublications of the institution at large, from signage and
atalogues to ticket stubs to the annual report. Designers James
ohnson and Robert Jensen preceded Lorraine Ferguson, who
 now chief graphic designer in what has always been a very
mall, very active department. The design staff presently
cludes graphic designer Craig Davidson, a design intern, a
pesetter, and Mrs. Friedman's assistant, Linda Krenzin.

In 1879 the art collection of T.B. Walker became the focus
f the Northwest's first art gallery free to the public, later named
Valker Art Center. By the late 1930s the museum was
ommitted to collecting modern European and American
ainting; an interest in contemporary design emerged around
940, when the first of two modernist "model houses" was built
ehind the museum. In 1946 the Walker began to publish
veryday Art Quarterly: A Guide to Well-Designed Products,
lited by Meg Torbert. During this early period the museum
as largely concerned with "good design," a critical concept
at focused on the quality of consumer products and became
concern of industrialized nations throughout the world in the
40s and 1950s.[1] The notion of "good design" examines an
ject in terms of its function, its use of materials, and its
stract, formal values. "Knife, Fork, and Spoon" was a
rticularly ambitious issue of Everyday Art Quarterly (1951),
arting the history of flatware. It accompanied an exhibition
the same title.

When Everyday Art Quarterly became Design Quarterly in
54, it continued to focus on high-quality products from the

international design community. Toward the end of the 1960s,
however, the Walker's approach to design began to expand.
Rather than presenting individual products as icons of good
taste, the museum began relating design to its broader urban
context. For example the exhibition and DQ issue "Mass Transit:
Problems and Promise" (1968) surveyed actual and
experimental vehicles, signage, roads, and railways, revealing
an untidy network of architectural, industrial, graphic, and
bureaucratic systems. The Design Quarterly issue "Making the
City Observable" (one of Mildred Friedman's first Walker
projects) is a compendium of maps, guide books, and aerial
photographs, selected and analyzed by information designer
Richard Saul Wurman (DQ 80, 1971). Wurman pinpointed an
intersection between graphic and urban design which would
later become the subject of numerous Walker programs and
publications, including Marc Treib's "Mapping Experience," a
history of cartography (DQ 115, 1980); John Chase's
"Unvernacular Vernacular: Contemporary American
Consumerist Architecture" (DQ 131, 1986); and the more
pristine exhibition and DQ issue "City Segments," which
assembled speculative drawings of the urban landscape (DQ
113.114, 1980).

An exhibition that exemplifies the Walker's interest in
crossing disciplinary boundaries and making design integral to
the curatorial process was Tokyo: Form and Spirit (1986).
According to director Martin Friedman, this project aimed to
relate Japanese art to urban life and to reveal the continuity
between traditional and contemporary design forms. The
exhibition was grouped according to such functions as Walking
(the street), Living (the house), Working (the shop and factory),

e Museum of Modern Art was particularly influential in establishing the
nciple of "good design." See Edgar J. Kaufman, Jr., What is Modern Design?
ew York: Museum of Modern Art, 1950).

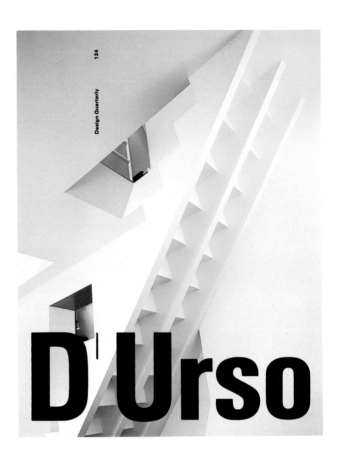

Unvernacular Vernacular

Design Quarterly 131

For over forty years, *Design Quarterly* has been a forum for design theory and practice. In its special role as the only design periodical produced by an American museum of contemporary art, *DQ* brings the design arts and the other visual arts together in articles that treat design in its broadest terms. Ranging from graphic design to architecture and industrial design, *DQ*'s central concern is with design th creates increasingly humane, stimulating and creative public and private environments. Designers, critics and theorists who have

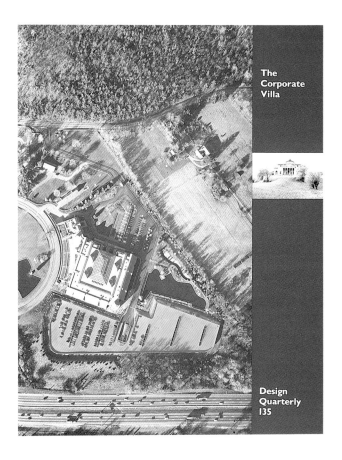

The
Corporate
Villa

Design
Quarterly
135

The Flower Gardens of Gertrude Jekyll
Design Quarterly 137

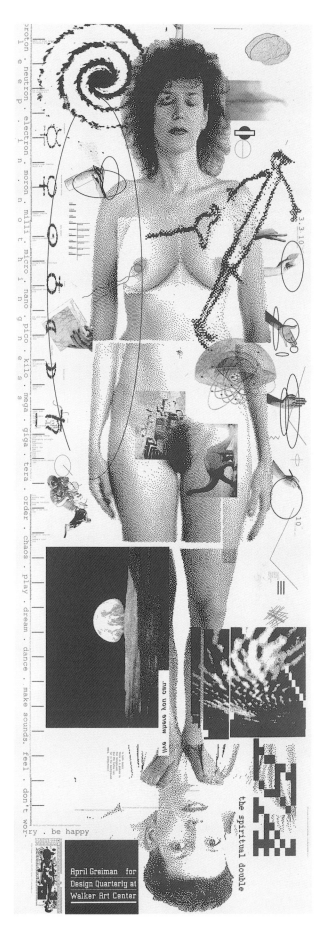

ntributed words and images to recent issues f *DQ* include: Joe D'Urso, Fred Koetter, Michael an Valkenburgh, Steven Holl; several graphic esigners have created issues of the agazine—providing the design as well as the say: "Signs" by Inge Druckrey; "A Paul Rand Miscellany," a much delayed follow-up to Rand's singular "Thoughts on Design;" and "Does It Make Sense?" by April Greiman, in which the computer is put to a variety of marvelous, unexpected uses. *Design Quarterly* is co-published with MIT Press Journals.

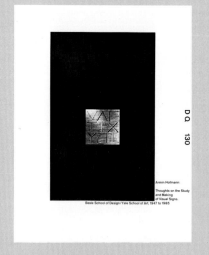

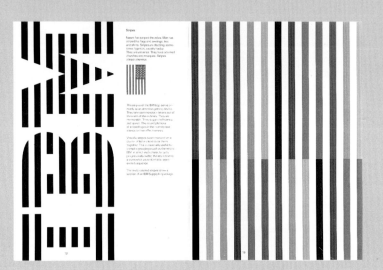

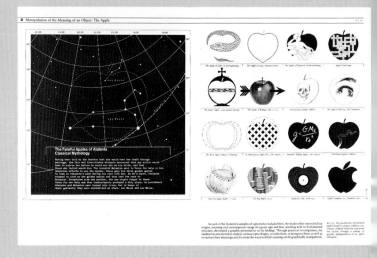

Performing (the theater), and Reflecting (the temple); each section displayed Edo-period Japanese objects—from street signs to Kabuki costumes—in juxtaposition with "visionary environments" created by contemporary Japanese architects and designers.

The 1981 exhibition *De Stijl: 1917–1931, Visions of Utopia* also brought together objects from many disciplines: painting, architecture, interior design, and graphic design. It was the first major exhibition on the De Stijl movement to be organized in America since 1952.

Some of the Walker's projects focus exclusively on graphic design, such as the issues of *DQ* by Paul Rand (*DQ* 123, 1984), April Greiman (*DQ* 133, 1986), Armin Hofmann and Wolfgang Weingart (*DQ* 130, 1985); or the exhibition and book *The Twentieth Century Poster: Design of the Avant-Garde* (1984). Currently, in collaboration with the AIGA, Mildred Friedman is organizing *Graphic Design in America: A Visual Language History,* an exhibition to premiere at the Walker in fall 1989 and

then travel to other institutions. Whereas the twentieth-century poster show stayed inside the limits of a recognizably "artistic" genre, the American graphic design exhibition will cover a varied range of activities, many of which bear little resemblance to "art:" advertising, packaging, newspapers, magazines, world's fairs, corporate identity, film credits, and electronic text and graphics. Mildred Friedman explains, "We want to present graphic design in terms of its social functions as well as its purely aesthetic qualities. This is a challenging job, because large segment of the public is unaware of 'graphic design' as a major discipline, and many designers are unprepared to look at their work in broad terms."

The Walker's location in a moderately sized Midwestern city distinguishes it from an institution like The Museum of Modern Art in New York. Whereas MoMA focuses on a relativel sophisticated urban audience, the Walker addresses a more heterogeneous group, some of whose members may enter the museum with little prior affection for contemporary art. The

The Twentieth Century Poster: Design of the Avant-Garde (1984), was an exhibition of primarily European posters that came from a number of major museum collections including that of the Victoria and Albert Museum, London, The Museum of Modern Art, New York, and the collection of Merrill Berman in New York. Widely seen, but little understood, the poster in this century has generally not received the attention it deserves from scholars or collectors, and the exhibition was an effort to alleviate that situation by calling attention to distinguished examples of the genre. Works of a variety of scales were shown, and a kiosk was created in the Walker Concourse to display the Wolfgang Weingart poster that was commissioned for the exhibition. Behind the kiosk, a twenty-four sheet billboard by Robert Cuzin for Michelin tires filled the Concourse entry wall.

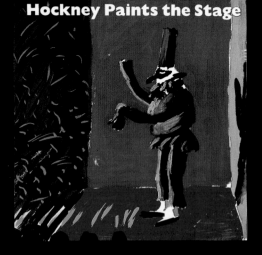

The 20th-Century Poster : Design of the Avant-Garde

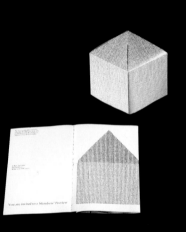

Jennifer Bartlett

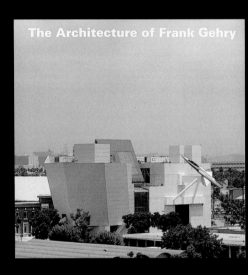

The Architecture of Frank Gehry

STIJL

1917-1931

DE

Visions of Utopia

IMAGES AND

IMPRESSIONS

Because Walker's exhibition catalogues are co-published with various tradebook publishers, a wide, international audience is now aware of the museum's catalytic role in twentieth-century art and design. As part of the Walker's program to commission works by significant artists, a poster commemorating Merce Cunningham's 1981 dance residency in Minneapolis was designed by the American painter Jasper Johns, who at that time was artistic advisor to the Cunningham Company.

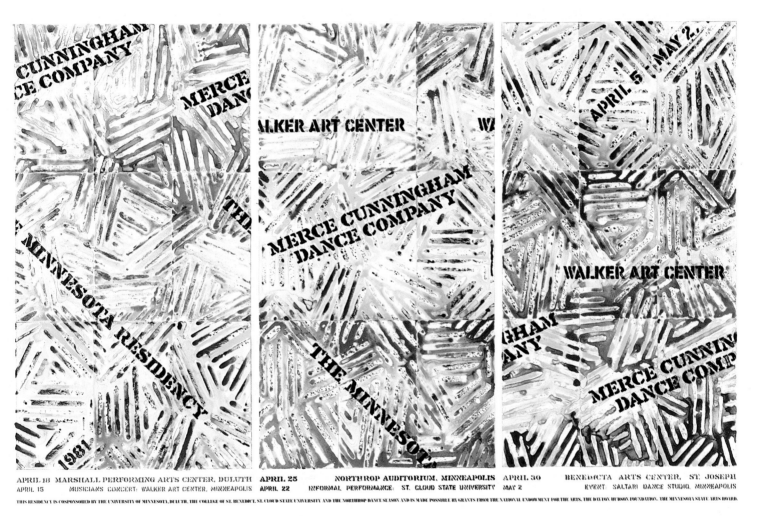

APRIL 18 MARSHALL PERFORMING ARTS CENTER, DULUTH   APRIL 25   NORTHROP AUDITORIUM, MINNEAPOLIS   APRIL 30   BENEDICTA ARTS CENTER, ST. JOSEPH
APRIL 15   MUSICIANS CONCERT: WALKER ART CENTER, MINNEAPOLIS   APRIL 22   INFORMAL PERFORMANCE: ST. CLOUD STATE UNIVERSITY   MAY 2   EVENT: SALTARI DANCE STUDIO, MINNEAPOLIS

THIS RESIDENCY IS COSPONSORED BY THE UNIVERSITY OF MINNESOTA, DULUTH, THE COLLEGE OF ST. BENEDICT, ST. CLOUD STATE UNIVERSITY AND THE NORTHROP DANCE SEASON AND IS MADE POSSIBLE BY GRANTS FROM THE NATIONAL ENDOWMENT FOR THE ARTS, THE DAYTON HUDSON FOUNDATION, THE MINNESOTA STATE ARTS BOARD.

Walker has therefore elected to use its exhibitions, publications, and educational programs to illuminate cultural and social issues, rather than as a neutral background for tasteful objects.

The museum's education department is one of its most active divisions, engaging children of all ages as well as professionals and the general public: for example, a whole series of events evolved out of the 1986 exhibition *The Architecture of Frank Gehry*. In a seminar led by Gehry and his sister Doreen Nelson, a specialist in urbanism and education, a group of children designed and built an "ideal city," which Gehry critiqued; the project later served as a model in a workshop for local teachers. "House and Home," a lecture series on the politics and aesthetics of domestic design, also stemmed from the Gehry show, as did the follow-up issue of *DQ*, in which several of the lectures were published. Adam Weinberg, director of the Walker's education department, explains, "You don't have to be in college to look at the designed environment critically and historically—you can be fully grown-up or in grade school. The education department responds spontaneously to contemporary issues in local and national design. There's no fixed menu. The fare changes from week to week, reflecting the desires of the chefs."

Every design exhibition, publication, or program involves many creative people, and the Walker's unique curatorial and editorial approach to design is the result of the judgment, wit, and hard work of a devoted staff. Over the past twenty years they have brought together a remarkable number of innovative architects, designers, and critics, developing one of America's most influential forums for design.

—Ellen Lupton

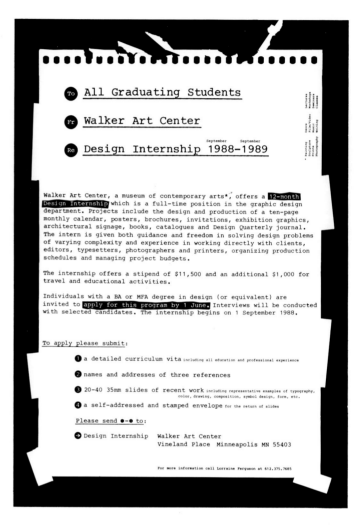

Walker Art Center   Educational Resources and Services 1987-88

The 1987–1988 education department brochure celebrates the Minneapolis Sculpture Garden, a joint project of Walker Art Center and the Minneapolis Park and Recreation Board. Opening in the fall of 1988, the garden's central element is *Spoonbridge and Cherry,* a pool and fountain by Claes Oldenburg and Coosje van Bruggen, seen here in an Oldenburg sketch.

In addition to its major publications, the Walker produces a monthly calendar, many small catalogues, brochures, and broadsides, all designed to bring the creative arts of our time to a continually expanding audience.

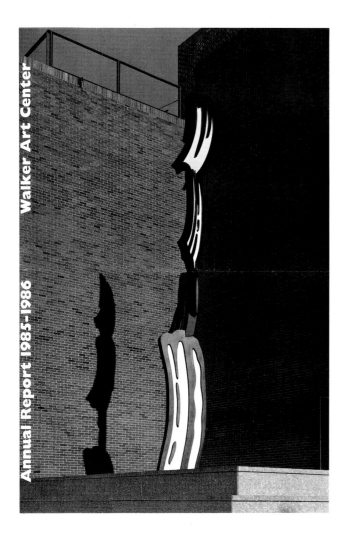

Walker Art Center Director
Martin Friedman, from 1961

Design Curator
Mildred Friedman, from 1969

Chief Graphic Designers
Lorraine Ferguson, from 1985
Robert Jensen, 1979 –1985
James E. Johnson, 1970 –1978
Peter Seitz, 1964 –1969

Graphic Designers
Craig S. Davidson, from 1987
Jeffrey Cohen, 1984 –1987
Donald Bergh, 1982–1984
Nancy Allen, 1981–1983

Design Interns
Mona Marquardt, 1987–1988
Jeanne Lee, 1986 –1987
Tori Wilke, 1985 –1986
Henry A. Kugeler III, 1984 –1985
Lorene Lee, 1983 –1984
William M. Ayres, Jr., 1981–1982
Michael Cervantes, 1980 –1981

Support Staff
Linda Krenzin, from 1974
Glenn Halvorson, from 1977
Gloria Philippi, from 1987
Lucinda Gardner, 1984 –1987

Communication Graphics

This year's show contained 207 pieces which were selected from about 5,650 entries. One third of those selected were submitted by individuals who had not been represented in AIGA shows in the past. Designers from every possible problem-solving context and region of the United States are represented in this show.

Most judges felt there was a fairly good level of competence. Five or ten years ago, one could certainly tell whether a piece had a regional look, but today that is not true. This change is occurring not only in graphics, but in all the applied arts as people become more design-conscious and technologically advanced. Roslyn Eskind from Toronto stated there seemed to be

"no difference between a piece from New York or Toronto." Michael Cronan commented, "The level of design is continuing to improve. People are getting better each year which makes these kinds of competitions harder and harder to judge. Things that were considered the cutting edge are becoming commonplace." Steven Fabrizio said, "It was hard finding pieces that went beyond being just good, which made judging difficult. When we did find them, it was a unanimous response."

My thanks to the judges.

Diana Graham
President
Diagram Design and
Marketing Communications, Inc.

Call for Entry:
Communication Graphics
Designer:
Debra Thompson, Ivy Li,
and Wing Chan
Illustrator:
Roy Wieman
Photography:
David Perry
Typography:
JCH Graphics Ltd.
Paper:
Bulkley Dunton and
S. D. Warren Co.
Printing:
Dolan/Wohlers Company

The American Institute of Graphic Arts Communication Graphics 1987–1988

The extensions, "the tools, are changing with relentless advance of technology,

but the essence of graphic design remains unchanged. That essence is the ability to

translate ideas and concepts into a visual form and bring order to information."

S
N
O
I
S
S

Jury

Seymour Chwast
President and Partner
The Pushpin Group

Michael Cronan
President
Cronan Design

Bob Dion
Senior Vice President
Chiat/Day

Joe Duffy
Partner and Senior Designer
The Duffy Design Group

Roslyn Eskind
Principal
Eskind Waddell

Steven Fabrizio
Senior Designer
Gips + Balkind + Associates
Inc./The GBA Group

Diana Graham
President
Diagram Design and
Marketing Communications, Inc.

Rachel Katzen
Partner
Inc Design

Ron Manzke
Executive Vice President
Siegel & Gale

Richard Poulin
Principal
de Harak & Poulin Associates

John Van Dyke
Principal
Van Dyke Company

Christina Weber
Partner
Weber Design

Lowell Williams
President and Owner
Lowell Williams Design Inc.

Bus Poster:
Anything Goes
Art Director:
James Russek
Artist:
James McMullan
Design Firm:
Russek Advertising
New York, NY
Client:
Vivian Beaumont Theater
Printer:
Triumph Productions

Bus Poster:
WNCN Radio
Art Director:
James Russek
Artist:
Paul Davis
Design Firm:
Russek Advertising
New York, NY
Client:
WNCN Radio
Printer:
Winston Network

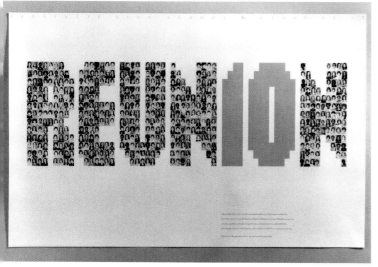

Poster Invitation:
Reun10n
Art Director:
Ron Sullivan
Designer:
Willie Baronet
Design Firm:
Sullivan Perkins
Dallas, TX
Client:
Lafayette High School Class
of '77
Typographer:
Robert J. Hilton Co., Inc.
Printer:
Padgett Printing Co.

Table Cover/Poster:
Wallaby's Restaurant
Art Director/Designer:
Ross Carron
Artist:
Ken Orvidas
Design Firm:
Ross Carron Design
San Francisco, CA
Client:
Wallaby's Restaurant
Typographer:
Letset
Printer:
Venture Graphics

Poster:
Chart Good Courses
Art Director:
McRay Magleby
Artist:
McRay Magleby
Design Firm:
Brigham Young University
Graphics
Provo, UT
Client:
Brigham Young University
Printer:
Rory Robinson

Poster:
Jerry Uelsmann
Art Director:
Lori Siebert
Designers:
Lori Siebert and Lisa Gavin
Photographer:
Jerry Uelsmann
Design Firm:
Siebert Design
Cincinnati, OH
Client:
American Society of
Magazine Photographers
Typographer:
Harlan Typographic
Printer:
The Hennegan Company

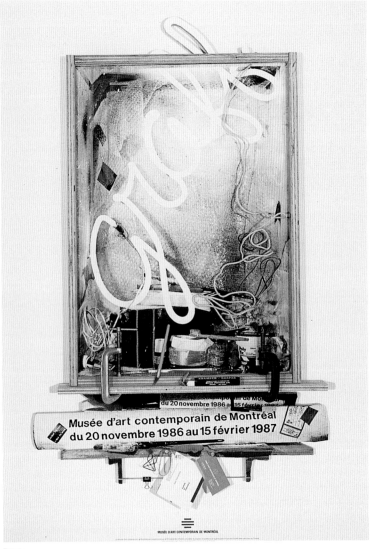

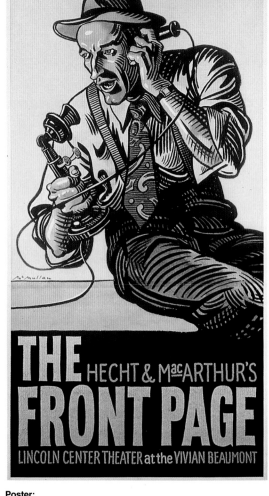

Poster:
Graff
Art Director:
Pierre Amyot
Designer:
Jean Quirion
Artist:
Pierre Amyot
Design Firm:
Bélanger, Legault
Designers, Ltée.
Montréal, CAN
Client:
Musée d'Art
Contemporaine Montréal
Typographer:
Typo Express
Printer:
Imprimerie Wiko

Poster:
The Front Page
Art Director:
James Russek
Artist:
James McMullan
Design Firm:
Russek Advertising
New York, NY
Client:
Vivian Beaumont Theater
Printer:
Stevens/Bandes Printing
Corp.

Poster:
Anything Goes
Art Director:
James Russek
Artist:
James McMullan
Design Firm:
Russek Advertising
New York, NY
Client:
Vivian Beaumont Theater
Printer:
Triumph Productions

Poster:
Death and the King's
Horseman
Art Director:
James Russek
Artist:
James McMullan
Design Firm:
Russek Advertising
New York, NY
Client:
Vivian Beaumont Theater
Printer:
Edison Lithographers

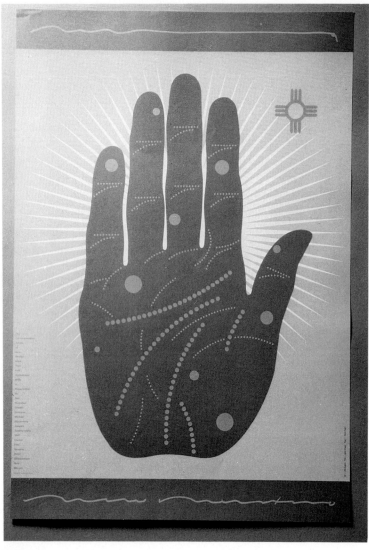

Poster:
New Mexico
Art Director/Designer:
Michael Manwaring
Design Firm:
The Office of Michael
Manwaring
San Francisco, CA
Client:
New Mexico
Communicating Artists
Printer:
Academy Printers

**Quarterly
Calendar/Poster:**
Spring
Art Director/Designer:
Paula Scher
Artist:
Paula Scher
Design Firm:
Koppel & Scher
New York, NY
Client:
Ambassador Arts
Printer:
Ambassador Arts

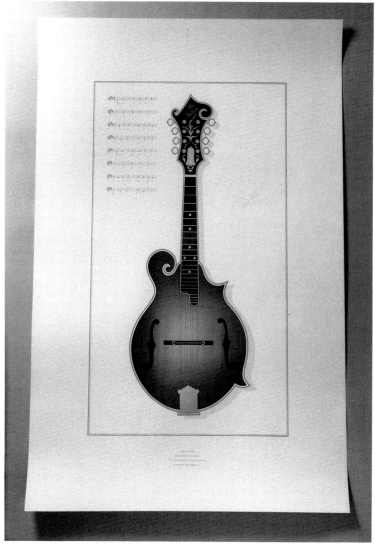

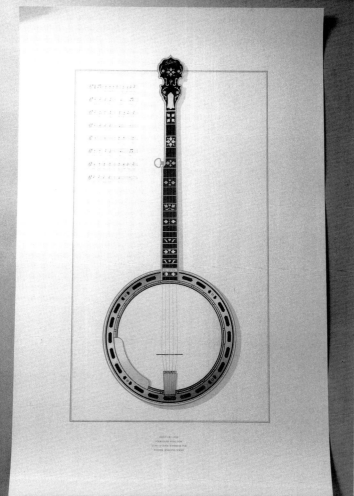

Poster Series:
Guitar, Mandolin, Banjo
Art Director:
McRay Magleby
Artist:
McRay Magleby
Design Firm:
Brigham Young University
Graphics
Provo, UT
Client:
Brigham Young University
Typographer:
Jonathan Skousen
Printer:
Rory Robinson

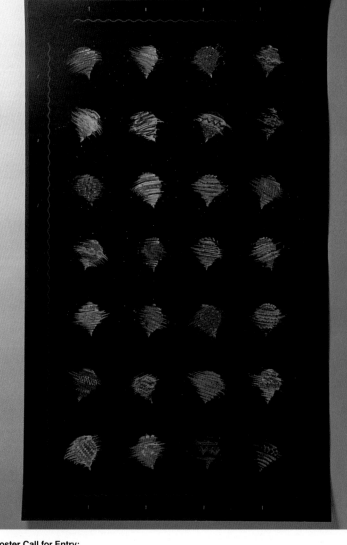

Poster and Wheel of Fortune:
10 San Francisco Designers
Art Director (Poster):
Craig Frazier
Designers (Wheel):
Craig Frazier and Conrad Jorgenson
Writer:
Craig Frazier
Design Firm (Poster):
Frazier Design
San Francisco, CA
Design Firm (Wheel):
Frazier Design
Jorgenson Design Associates
San Francisco, CA
Client:
AIGA, San Francisco Chapter
Typographers:
Display Lettering + Copy (Poster)
Eurotype (Wheel)
Printers:
Graphic Arts Center (Poster)
James H. Barry Co. (Wheel)

Poster Call for Entry:
TOPS
Art Director/Designer:
Brian Boyd
Artist:
Brian Boyd
Design Firm:
Richards Brock Miller Mitchell & Associates/The Richards Group
Dallas, TX
Client:
Dallas Advertising League
Typographer:
Image Type
Printer:
Color Dynamics

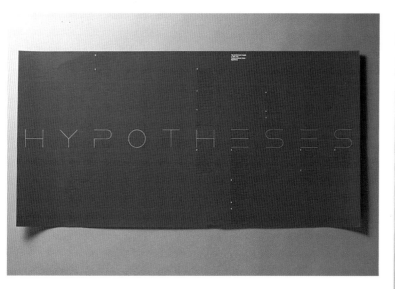

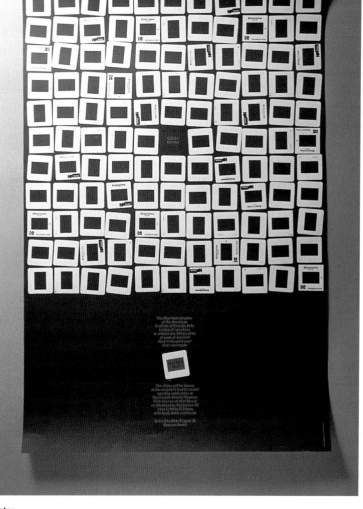

Poster:
Hypotheses
Designer:
Michael Bierut
Design Firm:
Vignelli Associates
New York, NY
Client:
Architectural League of
New York
Typographer:
Concept Typographic
Services
Printer:
Combine Graphics

Poster:
Classic 1948 Plymouth
Station Wagon
Art Director:
Cheryl Heller
Designer:
David Lopes
Photographer:
Clint Clemens
Design Firm:
Heller Breene
Boston, MA
Client:
S.D. Warren Paper Co.
Typographer:
Typographic House
Printer:
Lebanon Valley Offset Co.

Poster:
Your Best Shot
Designer:
Michael Bierut
Design Firm:
Vignelli Associates
New York, NY
Client:
AIGA, New York Chapter
Typographer:
Typogram
Printer:
Combine Graphic

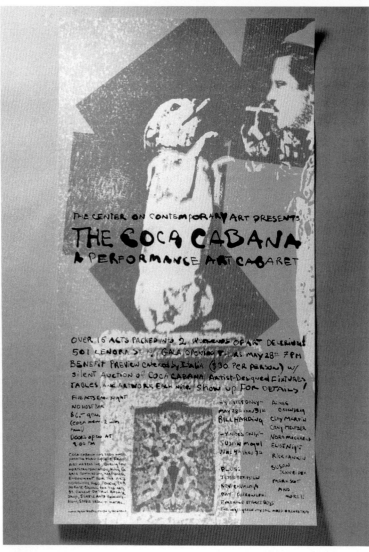

Poster:
Coca Cabana
Art Director/Designer:
Art Chantry
Artist:
Art Chantry
Design Firm:
Art Chantry Design
Seattle, WA
Client:
COCA (Center on
Contemporary Art)
Letterer:
Art Chantry
Printer:
Art Garcia

Poster:
Born to Roam
Art Director/Designer:
Sharon Werner
Artists:
Sharon Werner and Lynn
Schulte
Design Firm:
The Duffy Design Group
Minneapolis, MN
Client:
Donaldson's
Typographer:
Typeshooters
Printer:
R.S.I.

Self-Promotional Item:
Wrap-Rap Christmas
Wrapping Paper
Art Directors:
John Parham and Maruchi
Santana
Design Firm:
Parham-Santana, Inc.
New York, NY
Client:
Parham-Santana, Inc.
Typographer:
Viner Graphics
Printer:
Water Street Press

**Self-Promotion Poster
Series:**
Mirko Ilić
Art Director:
Mirko Ilić
Designer:
Nicky Lindeman
Artist:
Mirko Ilić
New York, NY
Client:
Yugoslav Cultural Center
Typographer:
David Shapiro
Printer:
NENAD

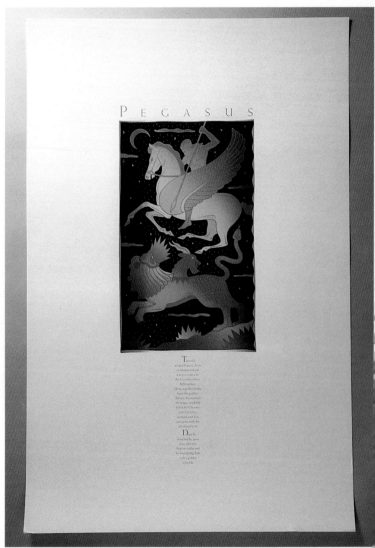

Poster Call for Entry:
Simpson Printed Paper
Competition
Art Director:
Michael Vanderbyl
Artist:
Michael Vanderbyl
Design Firm:
Vanderbyl Design
San Francisco, CA
Client:
Simpson Paper Company
Printer:
Mastercraft Press

Poster Series:
Sphinx, Minotaur, Medusa,
Cerberus, Pegasus
Art Director:
McRay Magleby
Artist:
McRay Magleby
Design Firm:
Brigham Young University
Graphics
Provo, UT
Publisher:
Brigham Young University
Typographer:
Jonathan Skousen
Printer:
Rory Robinson

Poster:
New Dutch Graphic Design
Art Director:
Cheryl A. Brzezinski
Design Firm:
Minor Design Group, Inc.
Houston, TX
Typographer:
Characters, Inc.
Printer:
Drake Printing Co.

Poster Call for Entry:
2nd International Exhibition
Art Director/Designer:
Milton Glaser
Artist:
Milton Glaser
Design Firm:
Milton Glaser, Inc.
New York, NY
Client:
The Art Directors Club
Typographer:
Cardinal Type Service Inc.

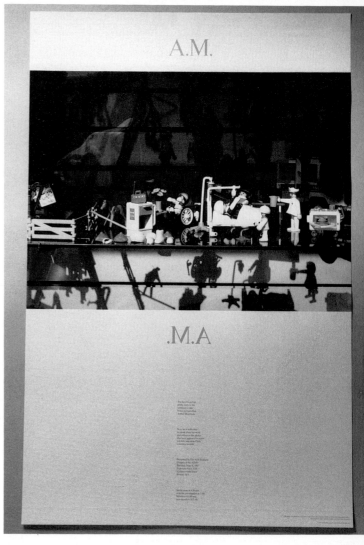

Poster:
Ray's Heterosexual Dance
Hall
Art Director/Designer:
Scott A. Mednick
Illustrator:
Greg Martin
Design Firm:
Scott Mednick and
Associates
Los Angeles, CA
Client:
A Chanticleer Film
Typographer:
Andresen Typography
Printer:
George Rice & Sons

Poster:
MIA.M:I
Art Director/Designer:
Bill Carson
Photographer:
Arthur Meyerson
Design Firm:
Lowell Williams Design, Inc.
Houston, TX
Client:
Arthur Meyerson
Typographer:
Typeworks
Printer:
Grover Printing Co.

Poster:
AM MA
Art Director/Designer:
Bill Carson
Photographer:
Arthur Meyerson
Design Firm:
Lowell Williams Design, Inc.
Houston, TX
Client:
Arthur Meyerson
Typographer:
Typeworks
Printer:
Williamson Printing Co.

Poster:
Limn (A progressive and modern classic furniture store)
Designer/Artist:
Michael Mabry
Design Firm:
Michael Mabry Design
San Francisco, CA
Client:
Limn
Typographer:
Petrographics Typeworld
Printer:
Cory Brixen

Poster:
The New World String Quartet
Art Director/Designer:
Susan Turner
Photographer:
Jeff Coolidge
Design Firm:
Clifford Selbert Design, Inc.
Cambridge, MA
Client:
Harvard University
Department of Music
Typographer:
Monotype Composition
Printer:
Eusey Press

Poster:
First Bank Work
Art Director/Designer:
Charles S. Anderson
Artists:
Charles S. Anderson and
Lynn Schulte
Design Firm:
The Duffy Design Group
Minneapolis, MN
Client:
First Bank System
Typographer:
Great Faces
Printer:
Litho Specialties

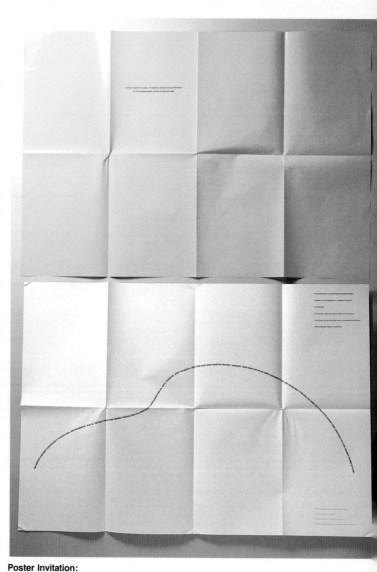

Poster:
AAAI '87
Art Director:
Jeff Hurn
Designer:
Craig Frazier
Design Firm:
Frazier Design
San Francisco, CA
Client:
1987 Conference on
Artificial Intelligence
Typographer:
Display Lettering + Copy
Printer:
Jeff Hurn

Poster Invitation:
DSVC-Helmut Krone
Evening
Art Directors:
Ed Zahra and Tom Lout
Designers:
Kent Anderson and Mike
Arthur
Design Firm:
Zahra/Lout Advertising
Designers, Inc.
Dallas, TX
Client:
Dallas Society of Visual
Communications
Typographer:
Southwestern Typographics
Printer:
Jewel Printing

Poster:
The Rocky Horror Show 2
Art Director/Designer:
Art Chantry
Photographer:
Fred Andrews
Design Firm:
Art Chantry Design
Seattle, WA
Client:
Beth Brooks and Empty
Space Theatre
Typographer:
Eclipse Typography
Printer:
Display Products, Ltd.

Poster:
Brodnax Color
Art Director/Designer:
Jack Summerford
Design Firm:
Summerford Design, Inc.
Dallas, TX
Client:
Brodnax Printing
Typographer:
Southwestern Typographics
Printer:
Brodnax Printing

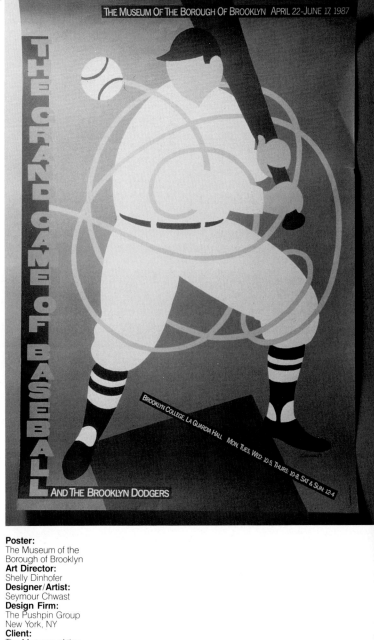

Poster:
American Ballroom Theater
Art Director:
James Russek
Designer:
James Sarfati
Artist:
Javier Romero
Design Firm:
Russek Advertising
New York, NY
Client:
American Ballroom Theater
Typographer:
The Graphic Word
Printer:
Eastern Press

Poster:
The Museum of the
Borough of Brooklyn
Art Director:
Shelly Dinhofer
Designer/Artist:
Seymour Chwast
Design Firm:
The Pushpin Group
New York, NY
Client:
The Museum of the
Borough of Brooklyn
Typographer:
Cardinal Type Service
Printer:
Sterling Roman Press Inc.

Poster:
Smarty Cats
Art Director:
Bill Freeland
Designer/Artist:
Seymour Chwast
Design Firm:
The Pushpin Group
New York, NY
Publisher:
LaGuardia Community
College
Long Island City, NY
Lettering:
Seymour Chwast
Printer:
The Adams Group

Poster Call for Entry:
Last stop before the real
world.
Art Director:
Douglas May
Photographer:
Black Box Studio
Design Firm:
Douglas May Design
Dallas, TX
Client:
Dallas Society of Visual
Communication
Typographer:
Characters
Printer:
Williamson Printing Co.

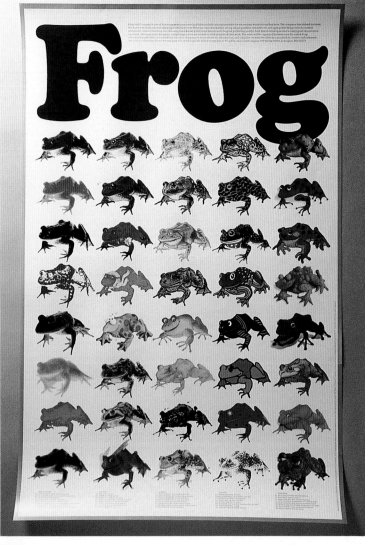

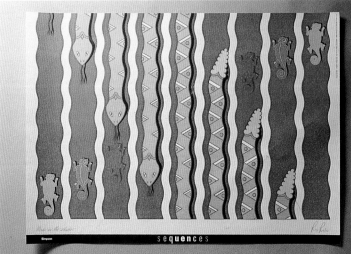

Poster:
Frog
Art Director/Designer:
Peter Bradford
**Artists and
Photographers:**
Various
Design Firm:
Peter Bradford Publishers
New York, NY
Client:
Ginn & Co.
Typographer:
Concept Typographics
Printer:
Lehigh Press, Inc.

Poster:
Sequences
Art Director/Designer:
Michael Manwaring
Design Firm:
The Office of Michael
Manwaring
San Francisco, CA
Client:
Simpson Paper Co.
Printer:
Simpson Paper Co.

Poster:
Sequences
Art Director:
James Cross
Artist:
Rex Peteet
Design Firm:
Sibley/Peteet Design, Inc.
Dallas, TX
Client:
Simpson Paper Co.
Typographer:
Robert J. Hilton Co., Inc.

Poster:
Cooper Union Design
Lecture Series—Fall 1987
Art Director:
Richard Poulin
Designers:
Richard Poulin and Mieko
Oda
Design Firm:
de Harak & Poulin
Associates, Inc.
New York, NY
Client:
Cooper Union School of
Architecture & Art
Typographer:
Ultratype
Printer:
Rapoport Printing Corp.

Advertisement:
Precious Cargo
Art Director:
Mark Fennimore
Designer:
William Wondriska
Photographer:
Jay Maisel
New York, NY
Design Firm:
Ogilvy & Mather
Client:
United Technologies Corp.

Poster:
Advertising Photography in
Japan '86
Art Director:
Vance Studley
Photographer:
Yukihiro Ichinose
Design Firm:
Art Center College of
Design
Pasadena, CA
Publisher:
Art Center Exhibitions
Typographer:
dee Typographers
Printer:
ColorGraphics

Poster:
The Lincoln Tunnel 50th
Anniversary
Art Director:
Van W. Carney
Photographer:
Jerry Rosen
Design Firm:
The Port Authority of NY &
NJ General Services
Department
New York, NY
Client:
Alice Kee/Tunnels, Bridges
and Terminals Department
Typographer:
Graphic Technology
Printer:
Beaumont Offset Corp.

I WILL NEVER
ENTER DESIGN
SHOWS AGAIN

Poster:
AIGA Minnesota
Art Director:
Timothy L. Eaton
Designers:
T. Eaton, P. Swenson, and B.
Pederson
Photographer:
Paul Shambroom
Design Firm:
Eaton & Associates
Minneapolis, MN
Client:
AIGA, Minnesota Chapter
Typographer:
TypeMasters, Inc.
Printer:
Litho Specialties

Poster:
I Will Never . . .
Art Director/Designer:
Jack Summerford
Design Firm:
Summerford Design, Inc.
Dallas, TX
Client:
Art Directors and Artists
Club of Sacramento
Typographer:
Southwestern Typographics
Printer:
Brodnax Printing

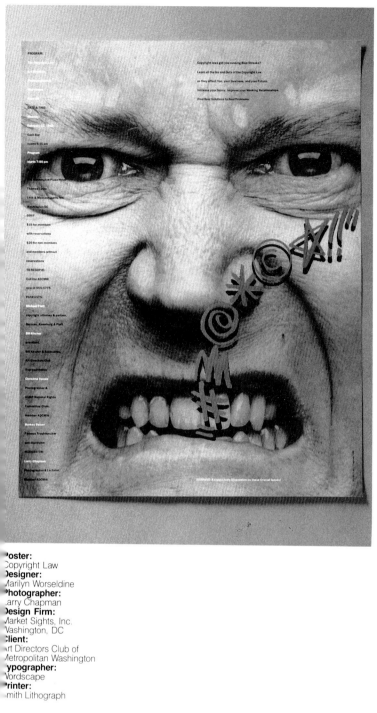

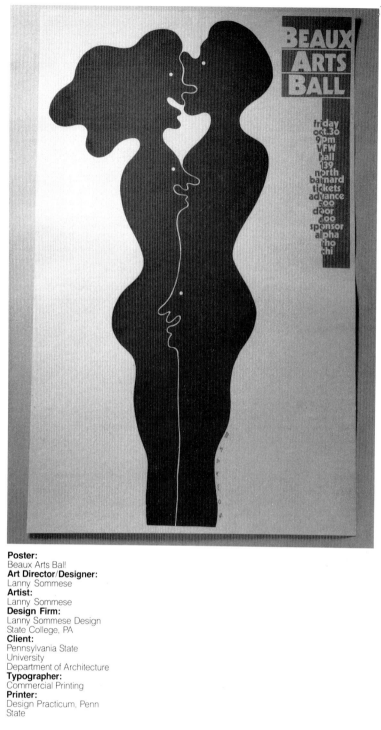

Poster:
Copyright Law
Designer:
Marilyn Worseldine
Photographer:
Larry Chapman
Design Firm:
Market Sights, Inc.
Washington, DC
Client:
Art Directors Club of
Metropolitan Washington
Typographer:
Wordscape
Printer:
Smith Lithograph

Poster:
Beaux Arts Ball
Art Director/Designer:
Lanny Sommese
Artist:
Lanny Sommese
Design Firm:
Lanny Sommese Design
State College, PA
Client:
Pennsylvania State
University
Department of Architecture
Typographer:
Commercial Printing
Printer:
Design Practicum, Penn
State

Newsletter:
Art Center Review,
September 1987
Art Director:
Kit Hinrichs
Designers:
Kit Hinrichs and Lenore
Bartz
Photographers:
Steven A. Heller, Henrik
Kam, Gary Meyer, and Joe
Henninger
Illustrators:
Walid Saba and John
Mattos
Design Firm:
Pentagram
San Francisco, CA
Client:
Art Center College of
Design
Typographer:
Eurotype
Printer:
Color Graphics

Newsletter:
Art Center Review, May
1987
Art Director:
Kit Hinrichs
Designers:
Kit Hinrichs and Lenore
Bartz
Photographers:
Steven A. Heller, Henrik
Kam, John Blaustein, and
Jeffery Dunn Studios
Illustrators:
Gerard Huerta and John
Mattos
Design Firm:
Pentagram
San Francisco, CA
Client:
Art Center College of
Design
Typographer:
Eurotype
Printer:
Color Graphics

Brochure:
Esprit Bath & Bed
Art Director:
Michael Vanderbyl
Photographers:
Phil Hunt Studio and
Roberto Carra
Design Firm:
Vanderbyl Design
San Francisco, CA
Client:
Esprit De Corp
Typographer:
Hester Typography
Printer:
Tannagraphics

Packaging:
Esprit Portfolio
Art Director:
Michael Vanderbyl
Design Firm:
Vanderbyl Design
San Francisco, CA
Client:
Esprit De Corp

Brochure:
Esprit Kids
Art Director:
Michael Vanderbyl
Photographer:
Roberto Carra
Design Firm:
Vanderbyl Design
San Francisco, CA
Client:
Esprit De Corp
Typographer:
Hester Typography
Printer:
George Rice & Sons

In-House Booklet:
South China Seas
Art Director:
John C. Jay
Photographer:
Herb Ritts
Design Firm:
Bloomingdale's Design
New York, NY
Client:
Bloomingdale's
Printer:
Zarrett Graphics

Brochure:
Directory of Guest Services
Art Director:
David Carter
Designer:
Gary LoBue Jr.
Artist:
Gary LoBue Jr.
Design Firm:
David Carter Design
Dallas, TX
Client:
The Catamaran Resort
Hotel
Typographer:
Robert J. Hilton
Typographers
Printer:
Sprueill & Co.

Brochure:
Kodak Road
Art Director:
Woody Pirtle
Designers:
Jeff Weithman and Woody
Pirtle
Photographer:
Phil Branner
Design Firm:
Pirtle Design
Dallas, TX
Client:
Phil Branner
Typographer:
Robert J. Hilton Co., Inc.
Printer:
Heritage Press

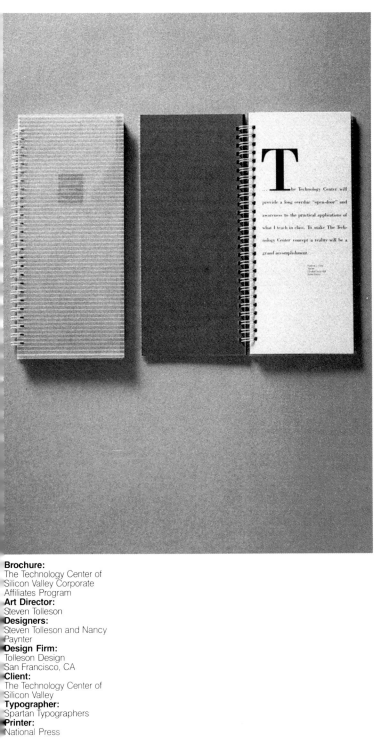

Brochure:
The Technology Center of
Silicon Valley Corporate
Affiliates Program
Art Director:
Steven Tolleson
Designers:
Steven Tolleson and Nancy
Paynter
Design Firm:
Tolleson Design
San Francisco, CA
Client:
The Technology Center of
Silicon Valley
Typographer:
Spartan Typographers
Printer:
National Press

Brochure:
Ramses II
Art Director:
McRay Magleby
Designer:
McRay Magleby and Linda
Sullivan
Photographer:
John Snyder
Design Firm:
Brigham Young University
Graphics
Provo, UT
Publisher:
Brigham Young University
Typographer:
Jonathan Skousen
Printer:
Brigham Young University
Print Services

Catalogue:
Esprit Europe Spring '88
Art Director:
Tamotsu Yagi
Image Photographer:
Oliviero Toscani
Still Photographer:
Roberto Carra
Design Firm:
Esprit Graphic Design
Studio
San Francisco, CA
Publisher:
Esprit De Corp
Typographer:
Display Lettering + Copy

Promotional Brochure:
Color Vision
Art Director:
Woody Pirtle
Designers:
Jeff Weithman and Woody
Pirtle
Photographers:
Various
Design Firm:
Pirtle Design
Dallas, TX
Client:
Colordynamics
Typographer:
Southwestern Typographics,
Inc.
Printer:
Colordynamics

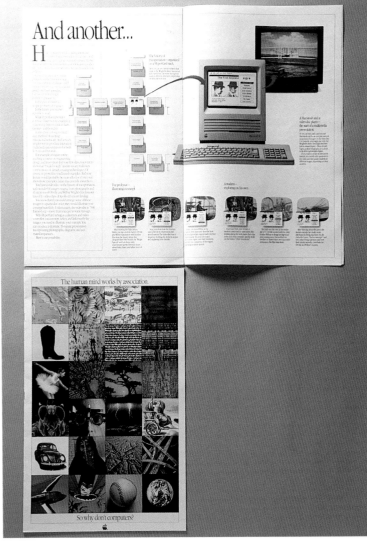

Promotional Magazine:
Photo Metro/September
1987
Art Director:
Henry Brimmer
Designer:
Henry Brimmer + Guests
Photographers:
Charly Franklin (cover) and
others
Design Firm:
Henry Brimmer
San Francisco, CA
Publisher:
Photo Metro
Typographer:
Metro Type
Printer:
Singer Printing

Brochure:
The human mind works by
association . . .
Art Directors:
Clement Mok and Hugh
Dubberly
Designers:
Clement Mok and Steve
Sieler
Artist:
Doris Mitsch
Design Firm:
Apple Creative Services
Cupertino, CA
Publisher:
Apple Computer, Inc.

Brochure:
Trammell Crow
Art Director:
Don Sibley
Illustrator:
Mark Domiteaux
Photographer:
Joe Aker
Design Firm:
Sibley/Peteet Design, Inc.
Dallas, TX
Client:
Trammell Crow Company
Printer:
Heritage Press

Brochure:
Menkes Developments Inc.
Art Directors:
Scott Taylor and Mike
Malloy
Designer:
Jean Page
Photographer:
Hedrich Blessing
Design Firm:
Taylor & Browning Design
Associates
Toronto, CAN
Client:
Menkes Developments Inc.
Typographer:
Cooper & Beatty, Ltd.
Printer:
Arthurs-Jones
Lithographing Ltd.

Brochure:
Benson, Hlavaty &
Associates
Art Director/Designer:
Don Sibley
Artists:
Don Sibley, Martti Benson,
Judy Dolim, and Greg
Hlavaty
Photographer:
Burt Pritzker
Design Firm:
Sibley/Peteet Design, Inc.
Dallas, TX
Client:
Benson, Hlavaty &
Associates
Typographer:
Robert J. Hilton Co., Inc.
Printer:
Phoenix Press

Catalogue:
California College of Arts &
Crafts 1988-89
Art Director:
Michael Mabry
Designers:
Michael Mabry and Piper
Murakami
Photographers:
Leslie Flores and Monica
Lee
Design Firm:
Michael Mabry Design
San Francisco, CA
Client:
California College of Arts &
Crafts
Typographer:
On Line Typography
Printer:
Cal Central Press

Promotional Book:
Catalyst
Art Director/Designer:
John Casado
Photographer:
Rudi Legname
Design Firm:
Casado, Inc.
San Francisco, CA
Client:
G.B. Cox for Haworth, Inc.
Typographer:
Display Lettering + Copy
Printer:
George Rice & Sons

Annual Report:
Expeditors International
Annual Report 1986
Art Director/Designer:
John Van Dyke
Photographer:
Cliff Fiess
Design Firm:
Van Dyke Company
Seattle, WA
Client:
Expeditors International
Typographer:
Typehouse
Printer:
Graphicolor

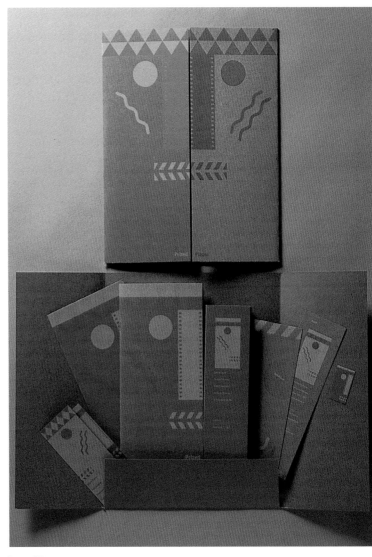

Brochure:
Annual Report Trends: 6
Art Director/Designer:
John T. Cleveland
Photographers:
Various
Design Firm:
John Cleveland, Inc.
Los Angeles, CA
Client:
S.D. Warren Co.
Typographer:
Phototype House
Printer:
Anderson Lithograph Co.

Press Kit:
Prized Pieces
Art Director:
Davina Davies Beck
Designers:
Chris Prater, Davina Davies
Beck, and Bob Thomas
Design Firm:
RichardsonSmith, Inc.
Worthington, OH
Client:
National Black
Programming Consortium

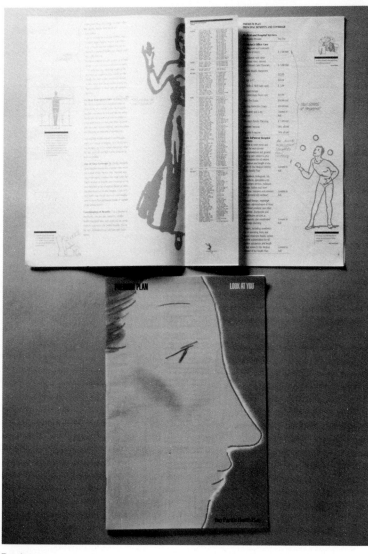

Brochure:
Look at You
Art Directors:
Bob Manley and Bruce
Crocker
Designer:
Bruce Crocker
Artist:
Merle Nacht
Design Firm:
Altman & Manley Design
San Francisco, CA
Client:
Bay Pacific Health Plan
Typographer:
Typographic House

Catalogue Series:
Generra Collection Story
Art Directors:
David Edelstein, Nancy
Edelstein and Lanny French
Designers:
David Edelstein, Nancy
Edelstein, Lanny French,
Carol Davidson, and D.
Thom Bisset
Photographers:
Jim Cummins and Karl
Bischoff
Design Firm:
Edelstein Associates
Advertising, Inc.
Seattle, WA
Client:
Generra
Typographer:
Thomas & Kennedy
Printer:
Unicraft Printing Control

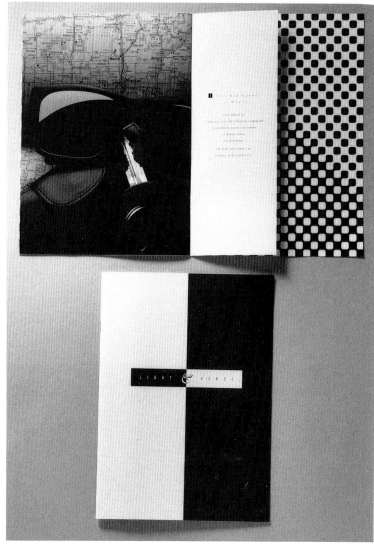

Catalogue Series:
Generra "After A Fashion"
Art Directors:
David Edelstein, Nancy
Edelstein and Lanny French
Designers:
David Edelstein, Nancy
Edelstein, Lanny French,
and Carol Davidson
Photographer:
Sara Rossingnol
Design Firm:
Edelstein Associates
Advertising, Inc.
Seattle, WA
Client:
Generra
Typographer:
Thomas & Kennedy
Printer:
Atomic Press and Unicraft
Printing Control

Promotional Booklet:
Light & Verse
Art Director/Designer:
John Van Dyke
Photographer:
Terry Heffernan
Design Firm:
Van Dyke Company
Seattle, WA
Client:
Weyerhaeuser Paper
Company
Typographer:
Typehouse
Printer:
Graphicolor

Brochure:
Audi 80/90 Series 1988
Art Director:
Barry Shepard
Designers:
Barry Shepard, Steve Ditko,
Karin Burklein Arnold, and
Douglas Reeder
Artists:
Roland Dahlquist and Rick
Kirkman
Photographers:
Rick Rusing and Rick Gayle
Design Firm:
SHR Communications
Planning and Design
Scottsdale, AZ
Client:
Audi of America, Inc.
Typographer:
Andresen Typographics
Printer:
Bradley Printing Co.

Capabilities Brochure:
Castrol: The Standard of
Performance
Art Director/Designer:
Rachel Katzen
Artist:
Steven Guarnaccia
Photographers:
Gabe Palmer and NASA
Design Firm:
Corporate Graphics, Inc.
New York, NY
Client:
Castrol Corporation
Typographer:
Typogram
Printer:
L.P. Thebault Co.
Parsippany, NJ

Brochure:
Graphic Coating Company:
Coatings for Survival
Art Director:
Craig Frazier
Designers:
Craig Frazier and Scott
Brown
Writer:
John Frazier
Illustrators:
Craig Frazier, Barron Storey,
Max Seabaugh, Mark
Hriksen, and Nicholas
Wilton
Design Firm:
Frazier Design
San Francisco, CA
Client:
Graphic Coating Co.
Typographer:
Display Lettering + Copy
Printer:
James H. Barry Co.

Dealer Kit:
Steelcase: The Office
Environment Company
Art Directors:
Craig Frazier and Kirk
Hinshaw
Designer:
Craig Frazier
Writers:
Michael Wright and David
Hill
Photographers:
Jock McDonald and Rudi
Legname
Design Firm:
Frazier Design
San Francisco, CA
Clients:
Saatchi & Saatchi/DFS and
Steelcase, Inc.
Typographer:
Display Lettering + Copy
Printer:
Pacific Lithograph Co.

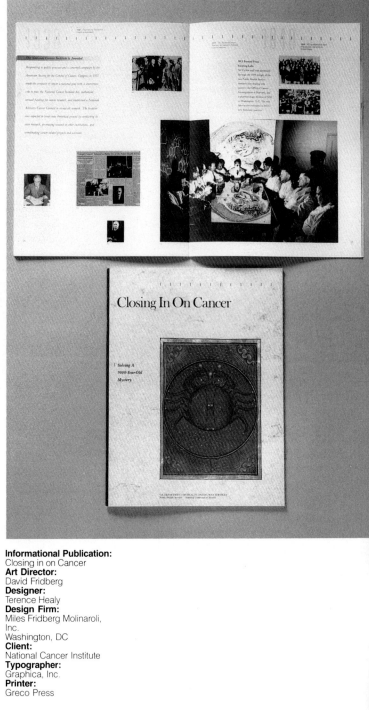

Brochure:
Mergers and Acquisitions:
The Smith Barney
Difference
Art Director:
Leslie Smolan
Designer:
Alyssa Adkins
Photographers:
Various
Design Firm:
Carbone Smolan
Associates
New York, NY
Client:
Smith Barney
Typographer:
Typogram
Printer:
Daniels Printing Co.

Informational Publication:
Closing in on Cancer
Art Director:
David Fridberg
Designer:
Terence Healy
Design Firm:
Miles Fridberg Molinaroli,
Inc.
Washington, DC
Client:
National Cancer Institute
Typographer:
Graphica, Inc.
Printer:
Greco Press

Promotional Booklet:
James McDermott
Art Director:
Diana Graham
Designers:
Debra Thompson and Wing
Chan
Photographer:
John McDermott
Design Firm:
Diagram Design &
Marketing Communications,
Inc.
New York, NY
Client:
John McDermott
Typographer:
CH Graphics Ltd.
Printer:
Overseas Printing Co.

Advertisement:
Restaurant
Florent/November
Art Director:
Tibor Kalman
Photographer:
Kelly Campbell
Design Firm:
M&Co.
New York, NY
Client:
Restaurant Florent

Catalogue:
Martex Spring '88
Art Director:
James Sebastian
Designers:
James Sebastian and
Junko Mayumi
Photographer:
Bruce Wolf
Interior Designer:
William Walter
Design Firm:
Designframe Inc.
New York, NY
Clients:
Martex and West Point
Pepperell
Typographer:
Typogram
Printer:
The Hennegan Co.

Catalogue:
Esprit Fall 1987
Art Director:
Tamotsu Yagi
Image Photographer:
Oliviero Toscani
Still Photographer:
Roberto Carra
**Architectural
Photographer:**
Sharon Risedorph
Design Firm:
Esprit Graphic Design
Studio
San Francisco, CA
Publisher:
Esprit De Corp
Typographer:
Display Lettering + Copy
Printer:
Graphic Arts Center

Brochure:
Rancho California
Art Director:
Michael Vanderbyl
Photographer:
Thomas Heinser Studio
Design Firm:
Vanderbyl Design
San Francisco, CA
Client:
Bedford Properties, Inc.
Typographer:
Hester Typography
Printer:
Mastercraft Printing

Promotional Brochure:
Fish Stories
Art Director/Designer:
Cheryl Heller
Photographer:
Herb Ritts
Design Firm:
Heller Breene
Boston, MA
Client:
S.D. Warren Paper Co.
Typographer:
Typographic House
Printer:
Acme Printing Co.

Advertisement:
Restaurant Florent/June
Art Director:
Tibor Kalman
Designer:
Timothy Horn
Photographer:
Frederick Lewis Stock Photo
Design Firm:
M&Co.
New York, NY
Client:
Restaurant Florent
Typographer:
Tru-Font Typographers Inc.

Promotional Folder:
Japan: The New Tradition
Art Director:
James Cross
Designer:
Yee-Ping Cho
**Artists and
Photographers:**
Various
Design Firm:
Cross Associates
Los Angeles, CA
Client:
Simpson Paper Co.
Typographer:
Central Typesetting Co.
Printer:
Lithographix

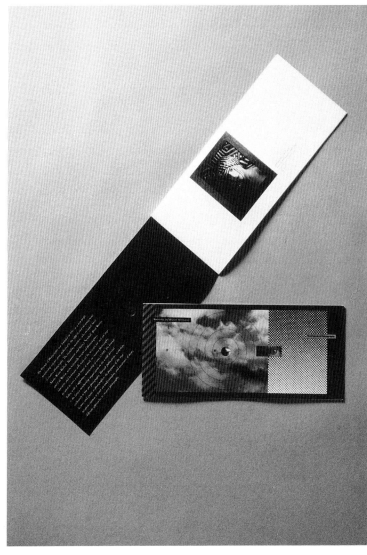

Folder:
Levi's Shirts
Art Director:
Bill Cahan
Designers:
Liz Miranda and Patricia
McShane
Design Firm:
Cahan & Associates
San Francisco, CA
Client:
Levi Strauss & Co.
Typographer:
EuroType
Printer:
Minute Men Press

Membership Brochure:
The Friends of Photography
Art Director:
Michael Mabry
Designers:
Michael Mabry and Margie
Chu
Design Firm:
Michael Mabry Design
San Francisco, CA
Client:
The Friends of Photography
Typographer:
Reardon & Krebs
Printer:
James H. Barry Co.

Campaign Booklet:
The Centennial Campaign
for Agnes Scott College
Art Director/Designer:
Domenica Genovese
Photographer:
Jeremy Green
Design Firm:
The North Charles Street
Design Organization
Baltimore, MD
Client:
Agnes Scott College
Typographer:
Charles Street Graphics
Printer:
Schmitz Printers

Casebooks:
Art Center College of
Design
Why Design? Why Art
Center?
Art Directors:
Neil Shakery and Kit
Hinrichs
Photographers:
Jim Blakely and Steven A.
Heller
Design Firm:
Pentagram
San Francisco, CA
Client:
Art Center College of
Design
Typographer:
Reardon & Krebs
Printer:
Color Graphics

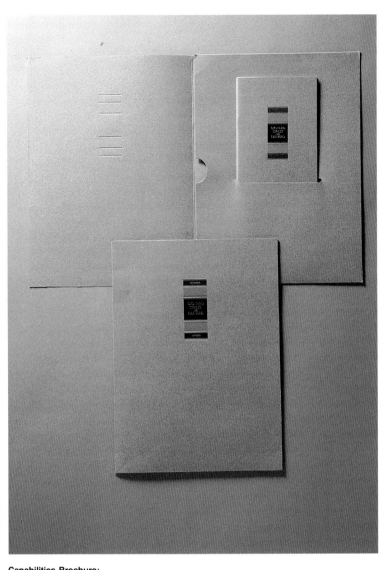

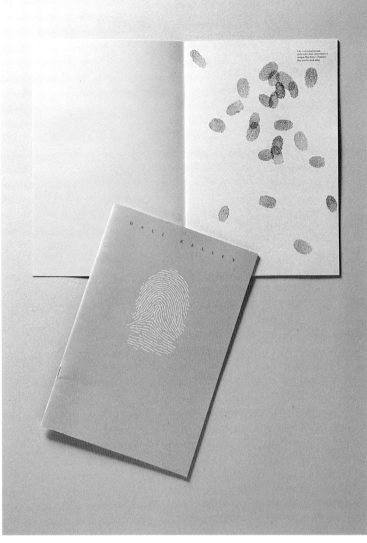

Capabilities Brochure:
Leonard, Street & Deinard
Art Director/Designer:
Laurie Jacobi
Logo Designer:
Eric Madsen
Photographer:
Tom Berthiaume
Design Firm:
Avchen & Jacobi, Inc.
Minneapolis, MN
Client:
Leonard, Street & Deinard
Typographer:
TypeShooters
Printer:
Wallace Carlson Co.

**Self-Promotional
Brochure:**
Hall Kelley
Art Director/Designer:
Michael Hall
Artists:
Michael Hall and Martin
Lawler
Design Firm:
Hall Kelley, Inc.
Minneapolis, MN
Publisher:
Hall Kelley, Inc.
Typographer:
TypeShooters
Printer:
Wallace Carlson Print

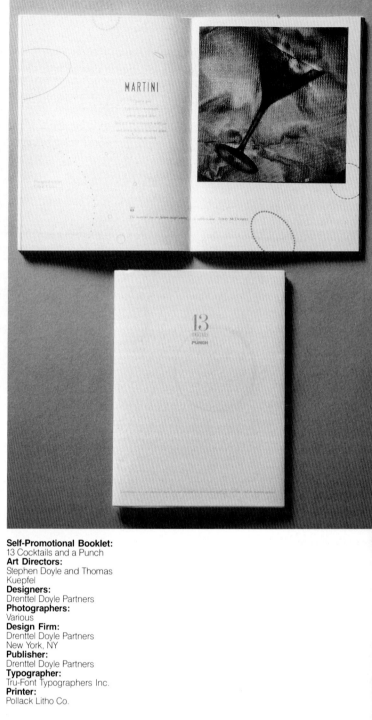

Brochure:
The Earth Technology
Corporation
Art Director:
Lowell Williams
Designers:
Lowell Williams and Bill
Carson
Photographer:
Jeff Corwin
Design Firm:
Lowell Williams Design, Inc.
Houston, TX
Client:
The Earth Technology
Corporation
Typographer:
Typeworks
Printer:
Williamson Printing Co.

Self-Promotional Booklet:
13 Cocktails and a Punch
Art Directors:
Stephen Doyle and Thomas
Kuepfel
Designers:
Drenttel Doyle Partners
Photographers:
Various
Design Firm:
Drenttel Doyle Partners
New York, NY
Publisher:
Drenttel Doyle Partners
Typographer:
Tru-Font Typographers Inc.
Printer:
Pollack Litho Co.

Catalogue:
Louis; Boston, Spring
Art Director/Designer:
Tyler Smith
Photographer:
Aldo Fallai
Design Firm:
Tyler Smith
Providence, RI
Client:
Louis, Boston
Typographer:
M Productions
Printer:
National Bickford Foremost

Direct Mail Poster Series:
Kitchell Contractors
Art Director/Designer:
Ann Morton Hubbard
Photographer:
Studio Shots: Rick Gayle
Location Shots: Bill
Zimmerman
Writer:
Barbara Bean
Design Firm:
Hubbard and Hubbard
Design
Phoenix, AZ
Client:
Kitchell Contractors
Typographer:
Andresen Typographics
Printer:
Heritage Graphics Inc.

Annual Report:
The Canada Council 30th
Annual Report
Art Director:
Malcolm Waddell
Designer:
Peter Scott
Design Firm:
Eskind Waddell
Toronto, CAN
Client:
The Canada Council
Typographer:
Fleet Typographers
Printer:
Arthurs-Jones
Lithographing, Ltd.

Annual Report:
H.J. Heinz Co. 1987 Annual
Report
Art Director:
Bennett Robinson
Designers:
Bennett Robinson and Erika
Siegel
Photographer:
Rodney Smith
Design Firm:
Corporate Graphics, Inc.
New York, NY
Client:
H.J. Heinz Co.
Typographer:
Typogram
Printer:
Anderson Lithograph Co.

Promotional Packet:
Wish you were here
Art Director:
Steve Gibbs
**Artists and
Photographers:**
Various
Design Firm:
Gibbs Design
Dallas, TX
Client:
VMS
Typographer:
Typographics
Printer:
Williamson Printing Co.

Annual Report:
Hechinger 1987 Annual
Report
Art Director:
Ivan Chermayeff
Designer:
Bill Anton
Artist:
Ivan Chermayeff
Photographer:
Alan Shortall
Design Firm:
Chermayeff & Geismar
Associates
New York, NY
Client:
Hechinger Company
Typographer:
Print & Design
Printer:
Watt-Peterson

Promotional Kit:
International Paper Presents
Famous Coverups
Art Director:
Rex Peteet
Artists:
Rex Peteet and Tom Curry,
Jack Unruh, Jerry
Jeanmard, and John Evans
Design Firm:
Sibley/Peteet Design, Inc.
Dallas, TX
Client:
International Paper Co.
Typographer:
Robert J. Hilton Co., Inc.
Printer:
Williamson Printing
Corporation

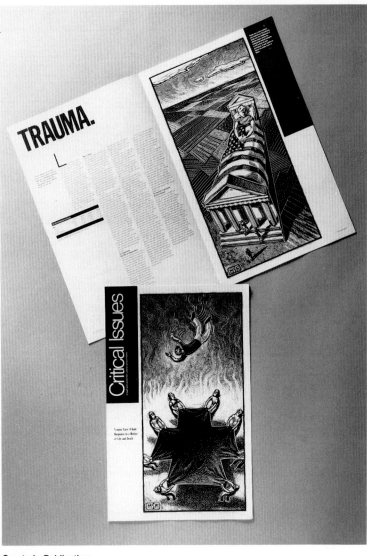

Quarterly Publication:
Critical Issues: Trauma Care
Art Director:
Kym Abrams
Designer:
Barry Deck
Photographer:
Erik Hausman
Artist:
Mary Flock
Design Firm:
Kym Abrams Design
Chicago, IL
Client:
Lutheran General Hospital
Typographer:
Paul Baker Typography
Printer:
Printing Arts

Promotional Booklet:
Reflections of Inspiration
Designer:
Steven Liska
Photographer:
Charles Shotwell
Design Firm:
Liska and Associates, Inc.
Chicago, IL
Client:
Bradley Printing Co.
Typographer:
Master Typographers
Printer:
Bradley Printing Co.

Annual Report:
Blue Cross, Blue Shield of
Delaware 1986 Annual
Report
Art Director:
Michael Gunselman
Photographer:
Ed Eckstein
Design Firm:
Michael Gunselman, Inc.
Wilmington, DE
Client:
Blue Cross, Blue Shield of
Delaware
Typographer:
Composing Room, Inc.,
Philadelphia
Printer:
Lebanon Valley Offset Co.

Annual Report:
Network Equipment
Technologies 1987 Annual
Report
Art Director/Designer:
Steven Tolleson
Photographer:
David Martinez
Design Firm:
Tolleson Design
San Francisco, CA
Client:
Network Equipment
Technologies
Typographer:
Spartan Typographers
Printer:
George Rice & Sons, Inc.

Promotional Kit:
Partners in Performance
Art Director/Designer:
Charles S. Anderson
Artists:
Charles S. Anderson and
Lynn Schulte
Design Firm:
The Duffy Design Group
Minneapolis, MN
Client:
First Bank Systems
Typographer:
Typeshooters
Printer:
Litho Specialties

Promotional Book:
Speckletone/New Hues
from Afar
Art Director:
Charles S. Anderson
Designers:
Charles S. Anderson and
Joe Duffy
Photographer:
Dave Bausman
Artists:
Charles S. Anderson, Joe
Duffy, and Sharon Werner
Design Firm:
The Duffy Design Group
Minneapolis, MN
Client:
French Paper Co.
Typographer:
Typeshooters
Printer:
Williamson Printing Co.

Menu & Wine List:
Cocolezzone
Art Director/Designer:
Haley Johnson
Artist:
Haley Johnson
Design Firm:
The Duffy Design Group
Minneapolis, MN
Client:
Cocolezzone Restaurant
Typographer:
Typeshooters
Printer:
Haley's Mill

Catalogue:
Generra Spring Summer
Fashion System Box
Art Directors:
David Edelstein, Nancy
Edelstein and Lanny French
Designers:
David Edelstein, Nancy
Edelstein, Lanny French,
and Carol Davidson
Photographer:
Peter Gravelle
Design Firm:
Edelstein Associates
Advertising, Inc.
Seattle, WA
Client:
Generra
Typographer:
Thomas & Kennedy
Printers:
NW Paper Box and Atomic
Press

Brochure:
The Inside Story
Art Directors:
Paul Huber and Bob
Manley
Designer:
Paul Huber
Artists:
Various
Photographer:
Steve Marsel
Design Firm:
Altman & Manley Design
San Francisco, CA
Client:
Tristar Sports
Typographer:
Typographic House
Printer:
Dynagraf, Inc.

Catalogue:
Bernhardt Furniture
Catalogue
Art Director:
Michael Vanderbyl
Photographer:
Alderman Company
Design Firm:
Vanderbyl Design
San Francisco, CA
Client:
Bernhardt Furniture
Company
Typographer:
Hester Typography
Printer:
Clay Printing Co.

Promotional Book:
Dickson's
Art Directors:
Joe Duffy and Charles S.
Anderson
Designers:
Joe Duffy, Charles S.
Anderson, Sharon Werner,
and Lynn Schulte
Artists:
Joe Duffy, Charles S.
Anderson, and Sharon
Werner
Design Firm:
The Duffy Design Group
Minneapolis, MN
Client:
Dickson's Inc.
Typographer:
Dickson's Inc.
Printer:
Dickson's Inc.

Self-Promotional Booklet:
Portfolio of Lowell Williams
Design, Inc.
Art Director:
Lowell Williams
Designers:
Lowell Williams and Bill
Carson
Photographer:
Ron Scott
Design Firm:
Lowell Williams Design, Inc.
Houston, TX
Client:
Lowell Williams Design, Inc.
Typographer:
Typeworks
Printer:
Heritage Press

Self-Promotional
Cookbook:
Samata Associates Holiday
Recipes
Art Directors:
Pat and Greg Samata
Portrait Photographer:
Mark Joseph
Design Firm:
Samata Associates
Dundee, IL
Publisher:
Samata Associates
Typographer:
Paul Thompson
Printer:
Great Northern Design
Printing Company

Promotional Booklet:
Lotus Week
Art Director/Designer:
Tom Hughes
Artist:
Lonnie Sue Johnson
Photographer:
Bill Gallery
Design Firm:
Lotus Creative
Cambridge, MA
Publisher:
Lotus Development Corp.
Typographer:
Lotus Graphic Services
Printer:
Anderson Lithograph Co.

Promotional Kit:
Creativity begins with a
white page
Art Director:
Robert Frankle
Designer:
Robert Llewellyn
Photographer:
Robert Llewellyn
Design Firm:
Cook & Shanosky
Associates, Inc.
Princeton, NJ
Client:
Mead Paper
Typographer:
Tristin Type
Printer:
Lebanon Valley Offset (4
color brochure)
Glasgow Printing (Paper
dummies)

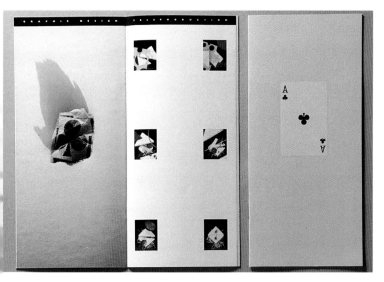

Announcement Booklet:
Clubs
Art Directors:
Brent Croxton and Paul
Huber
Designer:
Brent Croxton
Artists:
Mark Fisher and Ron Pearl
Photographer:
William Huber
Design Firm:
Altman & Manley Design
Boston, MA
Client:
Creative Club of Boston
Typographer:
Typographic House
Printer:
Dynagraf, Inc.

Holiday Booklet:
International Paper
Holiday Picture Puzzlers
Art Director/Designer:
Rex Peteet
Artists:
Rex Peteet and Judy Dolim
Design Firm:
Sibley/Peteet Design, Inc.
Dallas, TX
Client:
International Paper Co.
Typographer:
Robert J. Hilton Co., Inc.
Printer:
Williamson Printing
Corporation

**Self-Promotional
Catalogue:**
25 Good Posters
Art Director:
Peter Good
Artist:
Peter Good
Photographers:
Various
Design Firm:
Peter Good Graphic Design
Chester, CT
Publisher:
Peter Good Graphic Design
Typographer:
Comp One, Inc.
Printer:
The Hennegan Co.

Booklet:
Bloomie's Bear
Art Director:
Robert Valentine
Artist:
Dave Calver
Design Firm:
Bloomingdale's Design
New York, NY
Client:
Bloomingdale's
Typographer:
Photo Lettering
Printer:
Zarrett Graphics

Promotional Book:
Dimensions 87: An
American Reader
Art Director/Designer:
Jerry Herring
Illustrators:
Various
Design Firm:
Herring Design
Houston, TX
Publisher:
Simpson Paper Co.
Typographer:
Characters, Inc.
Printer:
Grover Printing Co.

Self-Promotional Booklet:
On Your Mark
Art Director/Designer:
Margi Denton
Design Firm:
Denton Design Associates
Pasadena, CA
Publisher:
Denton Design Associates
Typographer:
Central Typesetting
Printer:
McPherson Printing

Promotional Booklet:
A Guide to the New York
City Design Scene
Art Director:
Colin Forbes
Designer:
Michael Gericke
Illustrator:
Mel Calman
Design Firm:
Pentagram
New York, NY
Client:
Steelcase, Inc.
Typographer:
Typogram
Printer:
L. P. Thebault Co.

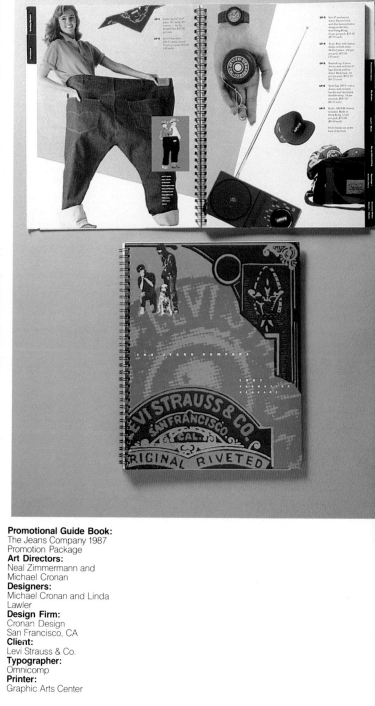

Promotional Book:
So Far: The First Ten Years
of A Vision
Art Directors:
Thom Marchionna and Jill
Savini
**Artists and
Photographers:**
Various
Design Firm:
Apple Creative Services
Cupertino, CA
Publisher:
Apple Computer, Inc.
Typographer:
Vicki Takla and Donna
Helliwell
Printer:
George Rice & Sons

Promotional Guide Book:
The Jeans Company 1987
Promotion Package
Art Directors:
Neal Zimmermann and
Michael Cronan
Designers:
Michael Cronan and Linda
Lawler
Design Firm:
Cronan Design
San Francisco, CA
Client:
Levi Strauss & Co.
Typographer:
Omnicomp
Printer:
Graphic Arts Center

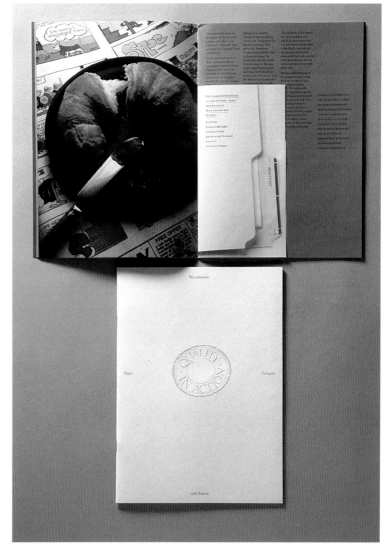

Self-Promotional Calendar
Series:
Sametz Blackstone
Associates: Bembo,
Bodoni, Akzidenz,
Garamond, Baskerville, Gill
Sans, Caslon, Memphis,
Helvetica, Century, Futura
and Univers
Art Director:
Roger Sametz
Artists/Designers:
Roger Sametz, John Kane,
Dan Gallagher, Andre
Secours, Stuart Darsch, and
Abby Gladstone
Design Firm:
Sametz Blackstone
Associates
Boston, MA
Publisher:
Sametz Blackstone
Associates
Typographer:
Monotype Composition Co.
Printer:
Reynolds DeWalt Printing,
Inc.

Annual Report:
Weyerhaeuser Paper
Company 1986 Report
Art Director/Designer:
John Van Dyke
Photographer:
Terry Heffernan
Design Firm:
Van Dyke Company
Seattle, WA
Client:
Weyerhaeuser Paper
Company
Typographer:
Typehouse
Printer:
Graphicolor

Annual Report:
BEI Electronics
Art Director:
Steven Tolleson
Designers:
Steven Tolleson and Nancy
Paynter
Photographer:
Steven Unze
Design Firm:
Tolleson Design
San Francisco, CA
Client:
BEI Electronics
Typographer:
Spartan Typographics
Printer:
Graphic Arts Center

Symbol Use Guidelines:
Pacific Gas and Electric
Company
Creative Director:
David Canaan
Design Director:
Tracy Moon
Designers:
Tracy Moon, Tony Hyun,
Rob Hugel, and Chuck
Adsit
Photographer:
R.J. Muna
Design Firm:
S&O Consultants
San Francisco, CA
Client:
Pacific Gas and Electric Co.
(PG&E)
Typographer:
Eurotype
Printer:
Cannon Press

Annual Report:
U.S. Healthcare Annual
Report
Art Director:
Michael Gunselman
Designer:
Ralph B. Billings, Jr.
Photographer:
Ed Eckstein
Design Firm:
Michael Gunselman, Inc.
Wilmington, DE
Client:
U.S. Healthcare Inc.
Typographer:
Composing Room, Inc.,
Philadelphia
Printer:
Revere Press, Inc.

Annual Report:
Nellcor Incorporated 1987
Annual Report
Art Directors:
Richard Klein and Paul
Schulte
Designer:
Paul Schulte
Photographers:
Raja Muna and Richard
Leach
Design Firm:
RKD, Inc.
Palo Alto, CA
Client:
Nellcor, Inc.
Typographer:
Drager & Mount
Printer:
George Rice & Sons

Promotional Brochure:
Street Dreams
Art Director:
Cheryl Heller
Designers:
Cheryl Heller and David Lopes
Photographer:
Clint Clemens
Design Firm:
Heller Breene
Boston, MA
Client:
S.D. Warren Paper Co.
Typographer:
Typographic House
Printer:
Lebanon Valley Offset

Catalogue:
The Alliance: Reebok Professional Instructor; Fall 1987, Winter 1988
Art Director/Designer:
Carole Bouchard
Photographer:
Christopher Harting
Design Firm:
Heller Breene
Boston, MA
Client:
Reebok

Sales Catalogue:
Levi's Street Jeans
Art Director:
Jennifer Morla
Photographer:
Jeffrey Newbury
Design Firm:
Morla Design
San Francisco, CA
Client:
Levi Strauss & Co.
Typographer:
Spartan Typographers
Printer:
Sales Print, Inc.

Advertisement Series:
Now Available: Colors of
Your Mind; Pigments of the
Imagination; True Color . . . .
Art Director/Designer:
Tyler Smith
Artist:
Tyler Smith
Photographers:
Myron, Clint Clemens, and
Anthony Russo
Design Firm:
Tyler Smith
Providence, RI
Client:
CCS/Toyo Printing Inks
Typographer:
TM Productions

Poster:
"88"
Art Director:
Robert Valentine
Designer:
Neville Brody
Artist:
Neville Brody
Design Firm:
Bloomingdale's Design
New York, NY
Client:
Bloomingdale's
Typographer:
Neville Brody
Printer:
Diversified Graphics

Invitation:
Juste pour rire, Juste pour
Ritz
Art Directors:
Danielle Roy and Serge
Cassan
Designer:
Serge Cassan
Design Firm:
Danielle Roy Design et
Communication
Montreal, CAN
Client:
Le Festival Juste pour Rire
Typographer:
M&H Ltée.
Printer:
O'Keefe Printing Co.

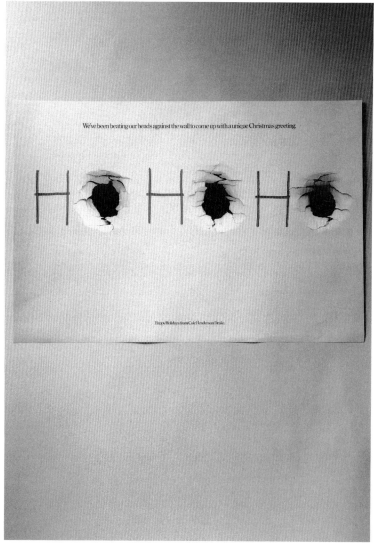

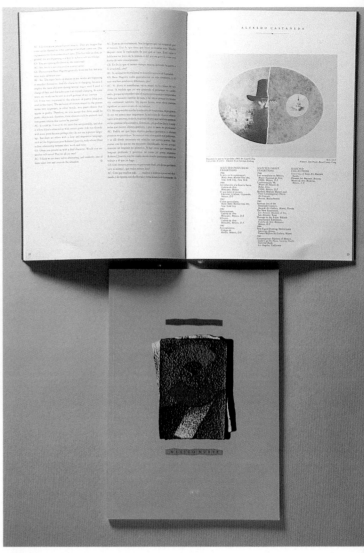

Catalogue:
Martex/Special Places 1987
Art Director:
James Sebastian
Designers:
James Sebastian and
Junko Mayumi
Photographer:
Bruce Wolf
Interior Designer:
William Walter
Design Firm:
Designframe Inc.
New York, NY
Client:
Martex and West Point
Pepperell
Typographer:
Typogram
Printer:
The Hennegan Co.

Brochure:
Mexico Nine
Art Director/Designer:
Steven Wedeen
Artists:
Various
Cover Artist:
Mark Chamberlain
Design Firm:
Vaughn/Wedeen Creative,
Inc.
Albuquerque, NM
Client:
Tamarind Institute
Typographer:
Starline Printing
Printer:
Albuquerque Printing Co.

Self-Promotional Booklet:
Broomshtick
Art Director:
Woody Pirtle
Designers:
Woody Pirtle and Jeff
Weithman
Artist:
Woody Pirtle
Design Firm:
Pirtle Design
Dallas, TX
Client:
Pirtle Design
Typographer:
Robert J. Hilton Co., Inc.
Printer:
Heritage Press

Promotional Folder:
Beautiful Faces
Art Director/Designer:
Paula Scher
Artist:
Paula Scher
Design Firm:
Koppel & Scher
New York, NY
Client:
Champion International
Typography:
Collection of Paula Scher
Printers:
L.P. Thebault and
Young & Klein

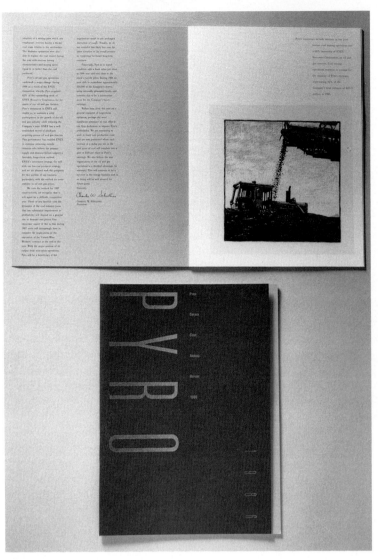

Annual Report:
Pyro Energy Corporation
Annual Report 1986
Art Director:
Thomas Ryan
Designer:
David Wariner
Illustrator:
David Wariner
Design Firm:
Thomas Ryan Design
Nashville, TN
Client:
Pyro Energy Corp.
Typographer:
Dixie Graphics
Printer:
Color Graphics

Brochure:
Specie Mesa at Telluride,
Colorado
Art Director/Designer:
Richard A. DeOlivera
Photographer:
Lindsay Walker
Design Firm:
DeOlivera Creative, Inc.
Denver, CO
Client:
Telluride Prospect, Ltd.
Printer:
Communigraphics, Inc.

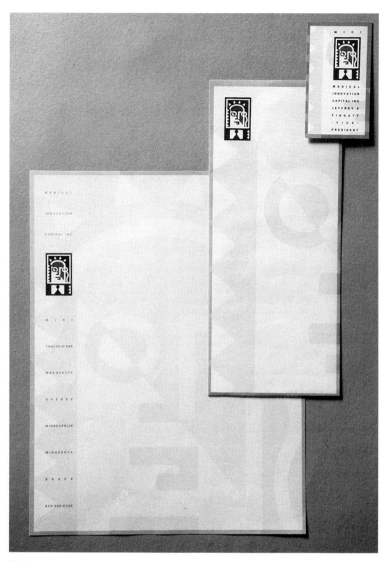

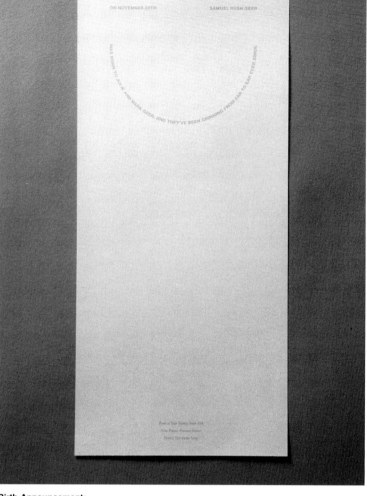

Stationery:
Medical Innovation Capital
Inc.
Art Director:
Charles S. Anderson
Designers:
Charles S. Anderson and
Sharon Werner
Artists:
Charles S. Anderson and
Lynn Schulte
Design Firm:
The Duffy Design Group
Minneapolis, MN
Client:
Medical Innovation Capital
Inc.
Typographer:
Typeshooters
Printer:
Watt Peterson

Birth Announcement:
On November 24th, Samuel
Rush Geer
Art Director:
Mark Geer
Design Firm:
Kilmer/Geer Design
Houston, TX
Client:
Julie and Mark Geer
Typographer:
Typographiks, Inc.
Printer:
Specialty Press

Brochure:
Maeser
Art Director:
McRay Magleby
Designers:
McRay Magleby and Linda
Sullivan
Photographer:
John Snyder
Design Firm:
Brigham Young University
Graphics
Provo, UT
Client:
Brigham Young University
Typographer:
Jonathan Skousen
Printer:
Brigham Young University
Print Services

Marketing Brochure:
Euro-Disneyland
Art Directors:
James Cross and Jay
Novak
Designer:
Joseph Jacquez
Photographers:
Warren Faubel and Charles
Imstepf
Design Firm:
Cross Associates
Los Angeles, CA
Client:
The Walt Disney Corp.
Typographer:
Central Typographer
Printer:
Anderson Lithograph Co.

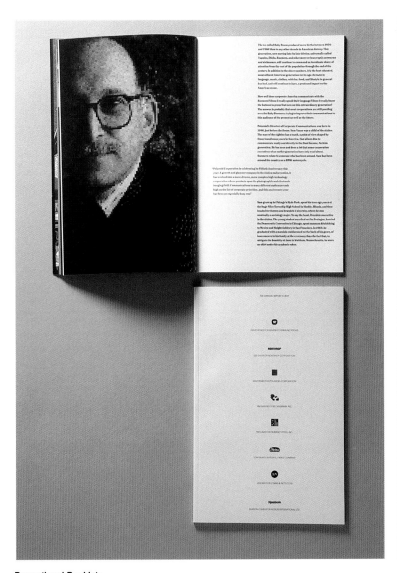

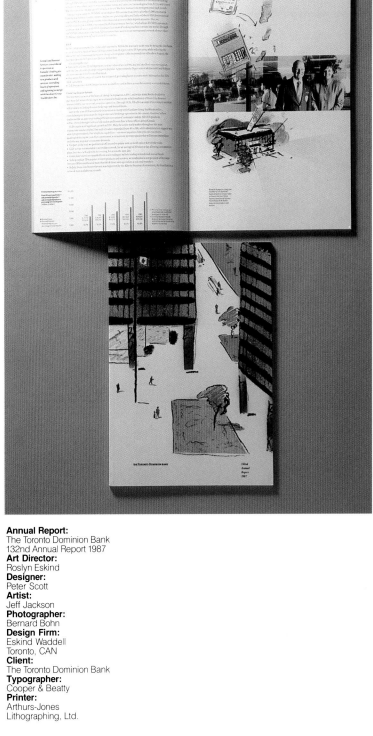

Promotional Booklet:
The Annual Report Client
Art Director:
Bennett Robinson & others
Designers:
Bennett Robinson and Erika
Siegel
Photographers:
Various
Design Firm:
Corporate Graphics, Inc.
New York, NY
Client:
Simpson Paper Co.
Typographer:
Typogram
Printer:
Anderson Lithograph Co.

Annual Report:
The Toronto Dominion Bank
132nd Annual Report 1987
Art Director:
Roslyn Eskind
Designer:
Peter Scott
Artist:
Jeff Jackson
Photographer:
Bernard Bohn
Design Firm:
Eskind Waddell
Toronto, CAN
Client:
The Toronto Dominion Bank
Typographer:
Cooper & Beatty
Printer:
Arthurs-Jones
Lithographing, Ltd.

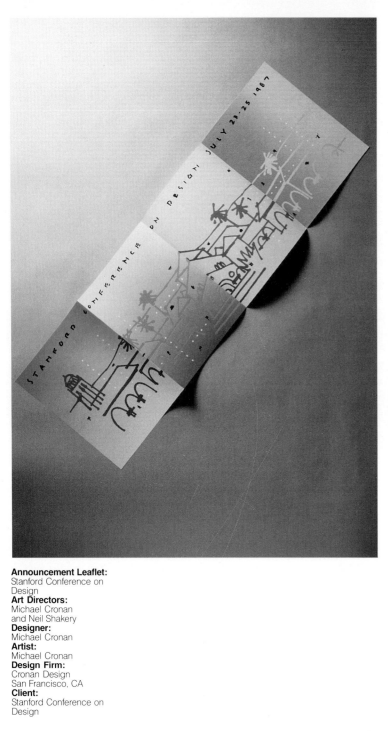

Announcement Leaflet:
Stanford Conference on
Design
Art Directors:
Michael Cronan
and Neil Shakery
Designer:
Michael Cronan
Artist:
Michael Cronan
Design Firm:
Cronan Design
San Francisco, CA
Client:
Stanford Conference on
Design

Brochure:
A Passion for Silk
Art Director:
James Sebastian
Designers:
Margaret Wollenhaupt,
Michael McGinn and
Gretchen Grace
Photographer:
Peter Bosh
Illustrators:
David Monteil, Seymour
Chwast, Paul Yalowitz, and
Michael McGinn
Writer:
David Konigsberg
Design Firm:
Designframe Inc.
New York, NY
Client:
Hopper Papers and
Georgia Pacific
Typographer:
Typogram
Printer:
Tanagraphics

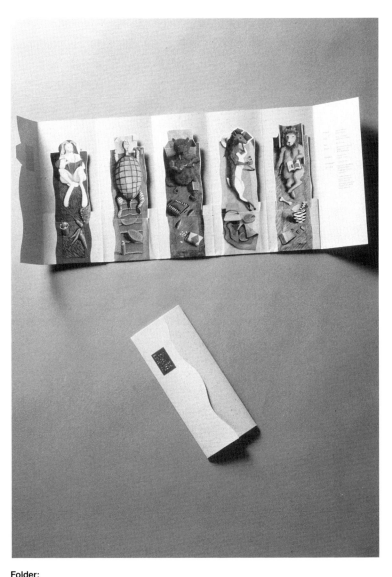

Folder:
Bookmark Poems
Art Director:
Patricia Belyea
Artist:
Brian Holtzinger
Design Firm:
Belyea Design
Seattle, WA
Publisher:
Impression Northwest
Typographer:
Thomas & Kennedy
Printer:
Impression Northwest

Promotional Booklet:
Rolling Stone's 20th
Art Directors/Designers:
Charles S. Anderson and
Joe Duffy
Artists:
Charles S. Anderson and
Joe Duffy
Design Firm:
The Duffy Design Group
Minneapolis, MN
Client:
Rolling Stone
Typographer:
Typeshooters
Printer:
Litho Specialties

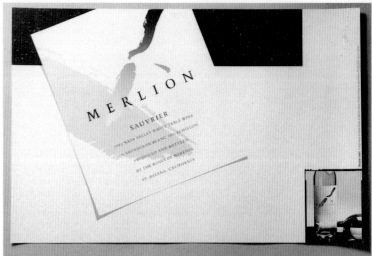

Self-Promotional Poster Series:
Frazier Design
Art Director:
Craig Frazier
Writer:
Craig Frazier
Photographers:
Various
Design Firm:
Frazier Design
San Francisco, CA
Publisher:
Frazier Design
Typographer:
Display Lettering + Copy
Printer:
Technigraphics

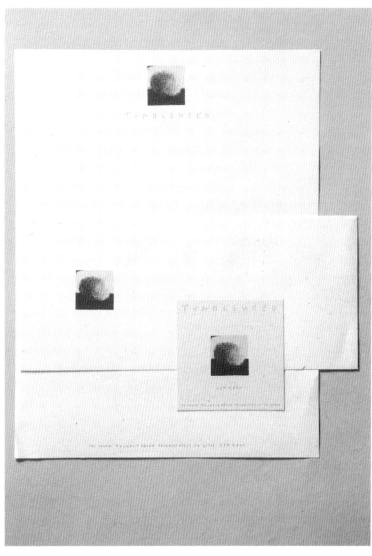

Stationery:
Tumbleweed
Art Director:
Michael Brock
Designer:
Gaylen Braun
Photographer:
Tom Keller
Design Firm:
Michael Brock Design
San Francisco, CA
Client:
Tumbleweed Restaurant
Typographer:
Michael Brock Design
Printer:
Charlie Chan Printing

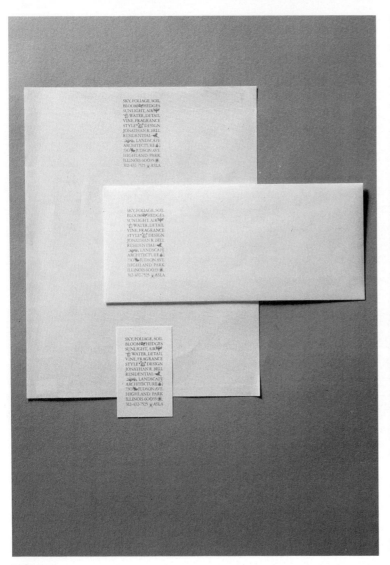

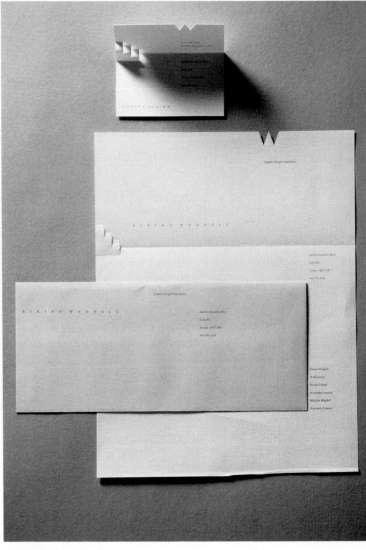

Stationery:
Jonathan R. Bell
Art Director/Designer:
Julia Lapine
Artist:
Julia Lapine
Design Firm:
Lapine/O'Very Inc.
Salt Lake City, UT
Client:
Jonathan R. Bell
Printer:
Graphic Reproductions,
Inc.

Stationery:
Eskind Waddell
Art Directors:
Roslyn Eskind, Malcolm
Waddell, and Christopher
Campbell
Design Firm:
Eskind Waddell
Toronto, CAN
Client:
Eskind Waddell
Typographer:
Cooper & Beatty, Ltd.
Printer:
MacKinnon Moncur, Ltd.

Stationery:
The Arizona Portfolio
Art Director/Designer:
Ann Morton Hubbard
Design Firm:
Hubbard and Hubbard
Design
Phoenix, AZ
Client:
The Arizona Portfolio
Typographer:
Andresen Typographics
Printer:
Panoramic Press

Stationery:
Linda R. Price, Doctor of
Optometry
Art Director:
Dick Mitchell
Design Firm:
Richards Brock Miller
Mitchell & Associates/The
Richards Group
Dallas, TX
Client:
Dr. Linda R. Price
Typographer:
Southwestern Typographics
Printer:
Monarch Press

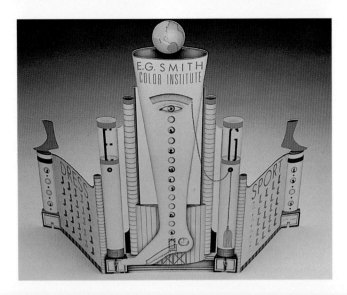

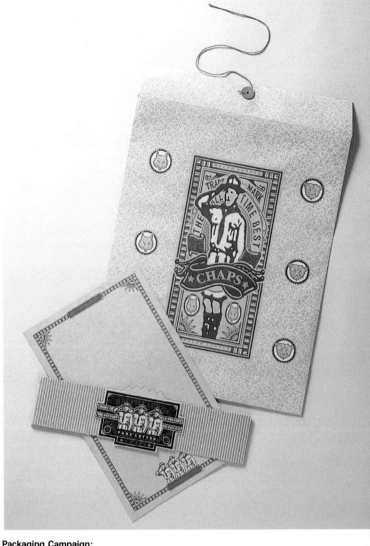

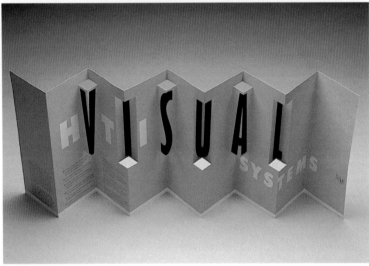

Counter Display:
E.G. Smith Color Institute
Building
Art Director/Designer:
Seth Jaben
Artist:
Seth Jaben
Design Firm:
Seth Jaben Studio
New York, NY
Client:
E.G. Smith, Inc.
Typographer:
Boro Typographers
Printer:
Sterling Roman Press Inc.

Foldout Announcement:
HTI Visual Systems
Art Director:
Ken Carbone
Designer:
Eric A. Pike
Design Firm:
Carbone Smolan
Associates
New York, NY
Client:
HTI Visual Systems, Inc.

Packaging Campaign:
Chaps-Scout Tags
Art Director:
Charles S. Anderson
Designers:
Charles S. Anderson and
Sara Ledgard
Artists:
Charles S. Anderson and
Lynn Schulte
Design Firm:
The Duffy Design Group
Minneapolis, MN
Client:
Chaps and Ralph Lauren
Typographer:
Typeshooters
Printer:
Litho Specialties

Packaging/Tin Box:
Chaps Golf
Art Director:
Joe Duffy
Designers:
Joe Duffy and Sara
Ledgard
Artists:
Joe Duffy and Lynn Schulte
Design Firm:
The Duffy Design Group
Minneapolis, MN
Client:
Chaps and Ralph Lauren
Printer:
Metal Box Co.

Packaging/Wooden Box:
Chaps, Ralph Lauren
Art Director:
Charles S. Anderson
Designers:
Charles S. Anderson and
Haley Johnson
Artists:
Charles S. Anderson and
Lynn Schulte
Design Firm:
The Duffy Design Group
Minneapolis, MN
Client:
Chaps and Ralph Lauren
Typographer:
Typeshooters
Printer:
Process Displays

157

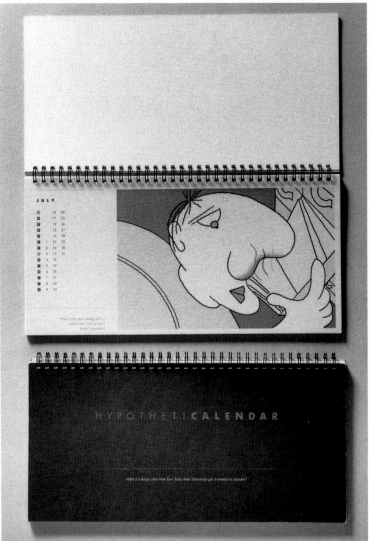

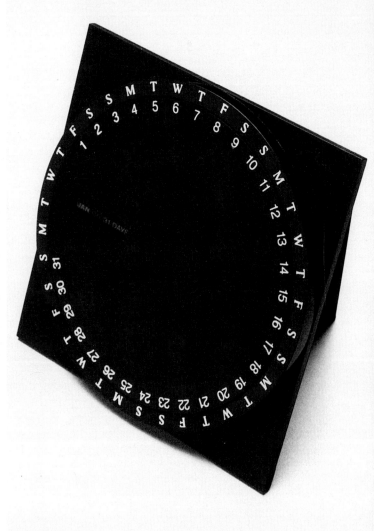

Calendar:
HypothetiCalendar
Art Director:
David Beck
Dallas, TX
**Artists and
Photographers:**
Ellen Alva Hales, David
Beck, Brad Sims, John
Peterson, Bruce
Wynne-Jones, Mark Smith,
Robert Shniderson, Cary
Trout, Paul Munsterman,
David Lerch, Linda Martin,
Tad Giffin, Morgan Bomar,
Haesun Kim, John Norman,
Karla Campalans, and Allen
Weaver
Client:
East Texas State University
Typographer:
Southwestern Typographics
Printer:
Heritage Press

**Self-Promotional
Calendar:**
Year 'Round
Art Director/Designer:
Patrick Florville
Design Firm:
Florville Design & Analysis,
Inc.
New York, NY
Client:
Florville Design & Analysis,
Inc.
Plastic Molding:
Bennett Plastics

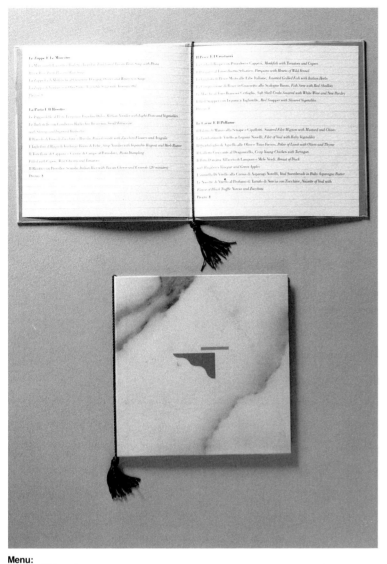

Menu:
Toscana Ristorante
Art Director:
Massimo Vignelli
Designer:
Mark Randall
Photographer:
Reven T.C. Wurman
Design Firm:
Vignelli Associates
New York, NY
Client:
Toscana Ristorante
Typographer:
Concept Typographic
Services
Printer:
L.S. Graphic

Menu:
China Grill
Art Director:
Tibor Kalman
Designer:
Douglas Riccardi
Artist:
Maira Kalman
Design Firm:
M&Co.
New York, NY
Client:
China Grill
Typographer:
Tru-Font Typographers Inc.
Printer:
Waverly Graphics

Shopping Bag:
Down Under
Art Director:
Joe Duffy
Designers:
Joe Duffy and Sharon
Werner
Artists:
Joe Duffy and Lynn Schulte
Design Firm:
The Duffy Design Group
Minneapolis, MN
Client:
Donaldson's
Printer:
Rainbow Signs

Packaging:
E.G. Smith Open Mind
Remedie Box
Art Director/Designer:
Seth Jaben
Artist:
Seth Jaben
Design Firm:
Seth Jaben Studio
New York, NY
Client:
E.G. Smith, Inc.
Typographer:
Boro Typographers
Printer:
Sterling Roman Press Inc.

Self-Promotional Item:
Happy Holiday
Art Director/Designer:
Kurt Meinecke
Design Firm:
Group/Chicago, Inc.
Chicago, IL
Client:
Group/Chicago, Inc.
Typographer:
CAPS
Printer:
Elgin Printing

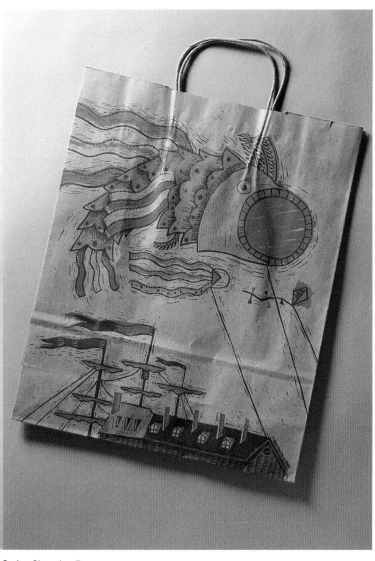

Spring Shopping Bag:
South Street Seaport
Art Director:
Ron Sullivan
Designer:
Linda Helton
Artist:
Linda Helton
Design Firm:
Sullivan Perkins
Dallas, TX
Client:
The Rouse Co. and South
Street Seaport
Printer:
Champion International

Shopping Bag:
San Francisco Clothing
Art Director:
George Tscherny
Artist:
George Tscherny
Design Firm:
George Tscherny, Inc.
New York, NY
Client:
San Francisco Clothing
Printer:
Champion Paper,
Packaging Division

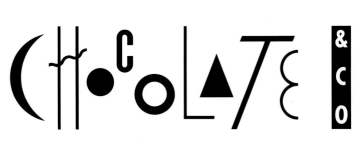

Logo:
Harmony Business Systems
Art Director/Designer:
Alan Mickelson
Design Firm:
Mickelson Design & Assoc.
Ames, IA
Client:
Harmony Business Systems
Typographer:
Alan Mickelson

Logo:
CHICAIGA
Art Director:
Bart Crosby
Designer:
Carl Wohlt
Design Firm:
Crosby Associates
Chicago, IL
Client:
AIGA, Chicago Chapter

Logo:
Chocolate & Co.
Art Director:
Pat Hansen
Design Firm:
Pat Hansen Design
Seattle, WA
Client:
Chocolate & Co.
Letterers:
Jesse Doquilo and Pat
Hansen

Logo:
Details Hair Salon
Art Director:
Jim Feldman
Design Firm:
Resource Manhattan
New York, NY
Client:
Capri Associates, Inc.

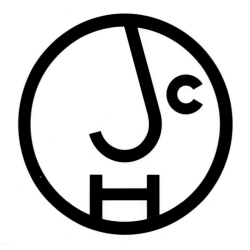

Logo:
J.C.H. Telegraphics
Art Directors:
Takaaki Matsumoto and
Michael McGinn
Designer:
Michael McGinn
Design Firm:
M Plus M Inc.
New York, NY
Client:
J.C.H. Telegraphics
Typographer:
J.C.H. Telegraphics
Printer:
C.G.S. Inc.

Advertisement:
What counts are the things
we believe . . .
Art Director:
Rob Hugel
Artist:
Rob Hugel
Design Firm:
XXX Design
San Francisco, CA
Client:
Herman Miller, Inc.
Typographer:
Display Lettering + Copy

Logo:
Baxter Arabian Farms
Art Director:
Mike Schroeder
Artist:
Mike Schroeder
Design Firm:
Schroeder Design
Dallas, TX
Client:
Brenda Baxter

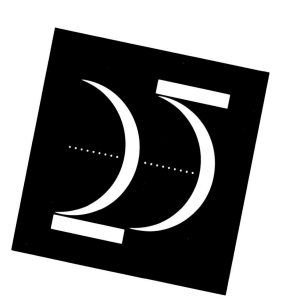

Logo:
IBM 25th Anniversary
Art Directors:
Richard Kilmer and Mark
Geer
Designer:
Richard Kilmer
Design Firm:
Kilmer/Geer Design
Houston, TX
Client:
IBM and Federal Systems
Division

Promotional T-Shirt:
Jump Street
Designers:
Steven Guarnaccia and
Susan Hochbaum
Artist:
Steven Guarnaccia
Design Firm:
Studio Guarnaccia
New York, NY
Client:
Jump Street Records

Promotional T-Shirts:
Swatch Watch USA, Inc.
Art Director:
Cheryl Chung
Designer/Artist:
Steven Guarnaccia
Design Firm:
Studio Guarnaccia
New York, NY
Client:
Swatch Watch USA, Inc.
Printer:
Adtees

T-Shirt:
Square One Preschool
Art Director:
Valerie Richardson
Designer:
Rosemary Connelly
Artists:
Various Images by Children
Design Firm:
Richardson or Richardson
Phoenix, AZ
Client:
Square One Preschool
Typographer:
DigiType
Printer:
Surf & Ski

T-Shirt:
Pacific Wave Museo:
Fortuny
Art Director/Designer:
Michael Cronan
Artist:
Michael Cronan
Design Firm:
Cronan Design
San Francisco, CA
Client:
Pacific Wave Museo

Environmental Graphics:
J&J Industries Showroom
Art Director:
Shelley Evenson
Designers:
David W. Williams, Shelley
Evenson, John McCulley,
Keith Kresge, and Deecy
Porro
Design Firm:
RichardsonSmith, Inc.
Worthington, OH
Client:
J&J Industries, Inc.

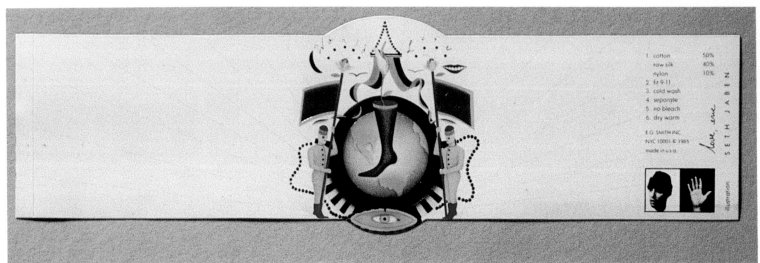

Packaging Label:
E.G. Feet
Art Director/Designer:
Seth Jaben
Artist:
Seth Jaben
Design Firm:
Seth Jaben Studio
New York, NY
Client:
E.G. Smith, Inc.
Typographer:
Boro Typographers
Printer:
Sterling Roman Press Inc.

Packaging Label:
World Love
Art Director/Designer:
Seth Jaben
Artist:
Seth Jaben
Design Firm:
Seth Jaben Studio
New York, NY
Client:
E.G. Smith, Inc.
Typographer:
Boro Typographers
Printer:
Sterling Roman Press Inc.

**Environmental
Graphics/Color Plastic
Ribbon Tubing:**
Ameritech 1987
Pan-American Games
Art Directors:
Kenneth Jay Riha, Barry
Slavin and Larry Klein
Designers:
RSK Collaborative, Inc. with
Capatain Balloon
Design Firm:
RSK Collaborative, Inc.
Client:
Ameritech

Environmental Graphics:
712 Fifth Avenue
Construction Bridge
Art Director:
Massimo Vignelli
Designers:
Rebecca Rose, Michael
Leone, and Stephen
Magner
Design Firm:
Vignelli Associates
New York, NY
Client:
Solomon Equities
Typographer:
Typogram
Fabricator:
Evergreen Studio

Environmental Graphics:
Hasbro, Inc. Showrooms
Pawtucket, RI & NYC
Art Director:
Deborah Sussman
Design Team:
Deborah Sussman, Paul
Prejza, Mark Nelsen, Susan
Hancock, Fernando
Vazquez, Chuck Milhaupt,
Stephen Silvestri, James
Barkley, Kyoko Tsuge, and
Kristin Dietrich
Design Firm:
Sussman/Prejza & Co., Inc.
Santa Monica, CA
Client:
Hasbro, Inc.

Signage:
Karl's Bus
Art Director:
John Sayles
Design Firm:
Sayles Graphic Design, Inc.
Des Moines, IA
Clients:
Spoerl Advertising and
Karl's Chevrolet

Signage:
Dallas Museum of Art Van
Gogh Van
Art Director:
Rex Peteet
Design Firm:
Sibley/Peteet Design, Inc.
Dallas, TX
Client:
Dallas Museum of Art
Van Signage:
Horton Design
Window Art:
American Porcelain

Point of Purchase
Display:
Crayon
Art Director:
Joanne Biron
Designers:
Joanne Biron and Julie
Edwards
Design Firm:
Heller Breene
Boston, MA
Client:
Reebok
Fabricator:
Carlton Display Corp.

Environmental Graphics:
IDCNY Signage Program
Art Director:
Massimo Vignelli
Designers:
Rebecca Rose and Janice
Carapellucci
Design Firm:
Vignelli Associates
New York, NY
Client:
The International Design
Center, New York (IDCNY)

Environmental Graphics:
35 West Wacker
Building Barricade
Art Director:
Ronald Kovach
Designers:
Ronald Kovach and Angie
Weitz
Fabricator:
C.K. Doty & Associates
Design Firm:
Mobium Corporation for
Design & Communication
Chicago, IL
Clients:
Leo Burnett and The John
Buck Co.
Typographer:
Typographic Resource

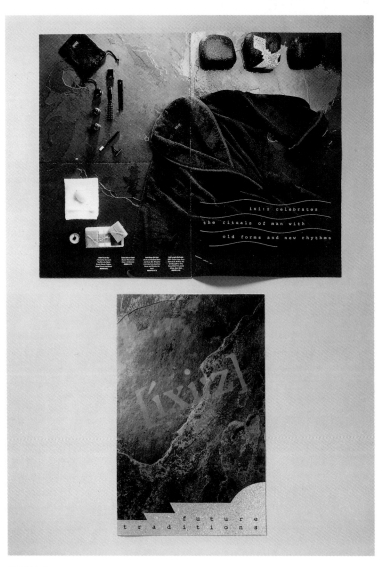

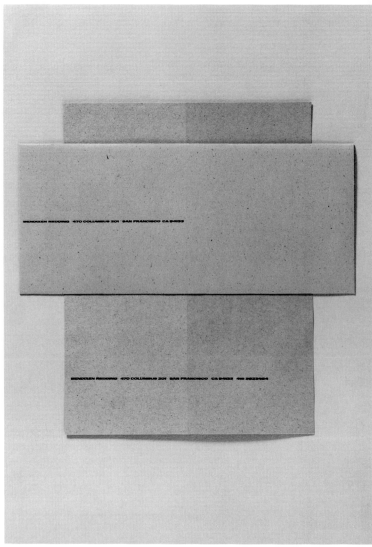

Catalogue:
ixi:z Fall Catalogue
Art Director:
Gerald Reis
Photographer:
John Clayton
Design Firm:
Gerald Reis & Company
San Francisco, CA
Client:
IDD/International Division of
Durban
Typographer:
MetroType
Printer:
George Rice & Sons

Stationery:
Bendixen Redding
Art Directors/Designer:
Ursula Bendixen and Sue
Redding
Design Firm:
Bendixen Redding
San Francisco, CA
Client:
Bendixen Redding
Typographer:
Mastertype
Printer:
T & J Printing Co.

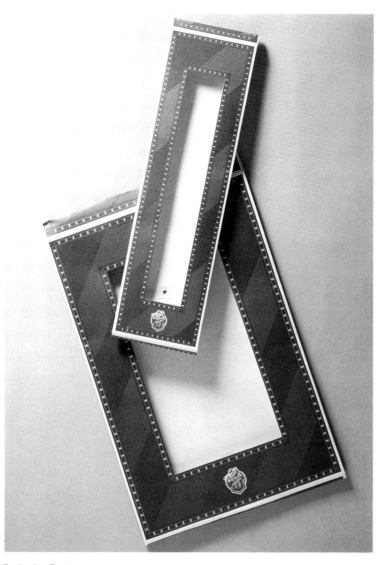

Packaging/Bags:
Golf Tie and Shirt Packages
Art Director:
Joe Duffy
Designers:
Joe Duffy and Sara
Ledgard
Artists:
Joe Duffy and Lynn Schulte
Design Firm:
The Duffy Design Group
Minneapolis, MN
Client:
Chaps and Ralph Lauren
Typographer:
Typeshooters
Printer:
Litho Specialties

Packaging, Shoe Box:
Brooks for Women
Art Director:
Charles S. Anderson
Designer:
Charles S. Anderson
Artists:
Charles S. Anderson and
Lynn Schulte
Design Firm:
The Duffy Design Group
Minneapolis, MN
Client:
Brooks Shoes
Typographer:
Typeshooters
Printer:
Process Displays

Juries
The Book Show

David Barich
Art and Production Director
Chronicle Books

Elaine Lustig Cohen
Artist and President
Ex Libris Books

Louise Fili
Art Director
Pantheon Books

Lance Hidy
Book and Poster Designer

Fred Marcellinc
Designer and Illustrator

Gael Towey
Art Director
Clarkson N. Potter, Inc.

Book Jacket and
Paperback Covers Show

Louise Fili
Art Director
Panthcon Books

Steven Guarnaccia
Illustrator

Rita Marshall
Designer

Krystyna Skalski
Art Director
Grove Press and
Weidenfeld & Nicholson

Lucille Tenazas
Principal
Tenazas Design

Call for Entry:
The Book Show and Book Jacket and
Paperback Covers Show
Designer:
Louise Fili
Illustrator:
Philippe Weisbecker
Typography:
Maxwell Photographics and
Photo-Lettering
Paper:
Allan & Gray
Printing:
Longacre Press

CALL FOR ENTRIES · AIGA BOOK SHOW 1987 & BOOK JACKET & PAPERBACK COVERS SHOW 1984-87

The books, jackets, and covers that survived the scrutiny of these juries tended to be of the more popularly stylized variety. Unanimity of opinion was had only for books like *Miniature Golf*, *Read Yourself Raw*, and *Stay Up Late*, which had high production values, whereas the elegant, classically designed books that were modestly produced, without benefit of production gimmickry, were often passed by. Approximately one quarter of the books and about the same percentage of jackets were selected from New York-area entries.

Louise Fili
Chairperson
Pantheon Books

Book Title:
Seasons at Eagle Pond
Author:
Donald Hall
Designer:
Anne Chalmers
Illustrator:
Thomas W. Nason
Publisher:
Ticknor & Fields
New York, NY
Typographer:
Heritage Printers, Inc.
Printer:
The Book Press, Inc.
Production Manager:
Albert Bachand
Paper:
Glatfelter Ivory laid 70#
Binder:
The Book Press, Inc.
Slipcase Manufacturer:
A. F. French Co.
Slipcase Panel Printer:
Prospect Park Press, Inc.
Slipcase Designer:
Anne Chalmers
Slipcase Illustrator:
Thomas W. Nason

Book Title:
The Ninth Street Show
Author:
Robert Pincus-Witten
Art Director/Designer:
Michael Torosian
Photographer:
Timothy Greenfield-Sanders
Publisher:
Lumiere Press
Toronto, CAN
Typographer:
Michael Torosian
Printer:
Michael Torosian
Production Manager:
Michael Torosian
Paper:
Mohawk Letterpress Text
Binder:
Michael Torosian

Robert Rauschenberg

Book Title:
Passion by Design: The Art and Times of Tamara de Lempicka
Authors:
Baroness Kizette de Lempicka-Foxhall and Charles Phillips
Editor:
Alan Axelrod
Art Director:
James Wageman
Designer:
Renée Khatami
Publisher:
Robert E. Abrams
Abbeville Press
New York, NY
Production Manager:
Dana Cole

up he did find himself rich, and it is more than likely that he found himself captivating.

I have found a glass like the one in the photograph and have poured out the last of the tequila.

From the foot of the bed it is possible to look into a wall of mirrors and see the photograph of my brother in the Japanese robe and the display of mannequins across the street mirrored together in such a way that Nicholas appears to be among them.

He does not appear to be one of them. The mannequins across the street do not hold cigarettes at angles to feature their hands, and the mannequins across the street do not wear Japanese robes. The mannequins across the street are grouped around stationary bicycles and chrome masses of exercise equipment. Only a few of the mannequins across the street wear anything that Nicholas would have called a frock. Those that do, those in cashmere or angora, are displayed in the process of taking those clothes off. The mannequins across the street shrug themselves from coat sleeves; they pull belts through loops; they bend down to untie shoes, all of this in order, presumably, to join the other mannequins, the shirtless ones in gym shorts bunched up at the crotch.

The shirtless mannequins across the street in the

windows that Nicholas could see from his bed are hanging from chin-up bars, or they are wedged into apparatus to give the impression of straining for all that they are worth.

I look at Nicholas among the mannequins.

Nicholas is posing for all that he is worth.

Nicholas never spoke about his body. Nicholas spoke about his figure. I think that Nicholas's idea of physical exertion, if he had one, would have been to take a taxi to a gym and smoke a cigarette in the locker room. I wonder if it ever occurred to him, at any time since the photograph was taken, the years that he could look out and see the standards change from season to season in the windows, that the ideal young beauty captured in the pose, even if he could have kept it, had ceased to be ideal. I wonder if it crossed his mind that being captivating had ceased to be the fashion, or sufficient.

I study the angle of the cigarette and the bare feet crossed under the border of the Japanese robe. Even the feet are posed. It must have killed Nicholas that he did not have beautiful feet. Nicholas had, in fact, enormous feet. Nothing else was wrong with them, but they were enormous for the rest of him, and I expect they are the reason for the champagne bottle positioned on the grass. I expect that the bottle is there to hide the feet as much as possible.

I am trying to be sure about the setting, to know

Book Title:
I Look Divine
Author:
Christopher Coe
Designer:
Anne Chalmers
Publisher:
Ticknor & Fields
New York, NY
Typographer:
D.K. Graphics
Printer:
Arcata/Fairfield Graphics
Production Manager:
Albert Bachand
Paper:
Antique Cream white 55#
Binder:
Arcata/Fairfield Graphics
Jacket Designer:
Lascove
Jacket Painting:
Lascove

Book Title:
Four Miles from Ear
Mountain
Author:
A.B. Guthrie, Jr.
Art Director/Designer:
Emily Strayer
Illustrator:
Kathy Bogan
Publisher:
Kutenai Press
Missoula, MT
Typographer:
Emily Strayer
Printer:
Emily Strayer
Production Manager:
Emily Strayer
Paper:
Frankfurt White
Binder:
Emily Strayer

VOW

I will not kowtow to the tribal chief
that man has made of God,
that self-lover, hot for homage,
that lasher with the rod.

If it ever fell to me
to change this dismal scam,
I swear to God I'd make of God
a better God than man.

1986

TWIN LAKES RHYMES

FOUR
MILES
FROM EAR
MOUNTAIN

Book Title:
Four Miles from Ear
Mountain
Author:
A.B. Guthrie, Jr.
Art Director/Designer:
Emily Strayer
Illustrator:
Kathy Bogan
Publisher:
Kutenai Press
Missoula, MT
Typographer:
Emily Strayer
Printer:
Emily Strayer
Production Manager:
Emily Strayer
Paper:
Frankfurt White
Binder:
Emily Strayer

Book Title:
Burning Patience
Author:
Antonio Skarmeta
Art Director:
Susan Mitchell
Designer:
Guenet Abraham
Publisher:
Pantheon Books
New York, NY
Typographer:
PennSet Inc.
Printer:
Arcata/ Fairfield Graphics
Production Manager:
Diane Ward
Paper:
Sebago 21¼" 50#
Binder:
Arcata/ Fairfield Graphics
Jacket Designer:
Louise Fili
Jacket Photographer:
Christine Rodin

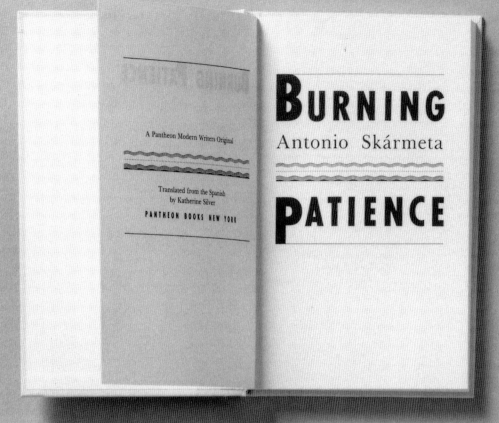

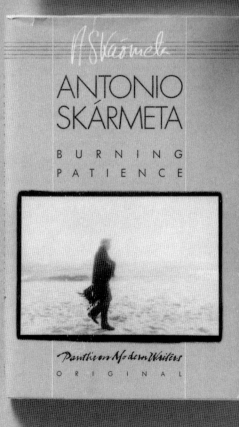

Book Title:
Nick Vaughn: Selected
Work 1978-1987
Author:
Phyllis Lutjeans
Art Director/Designer:
Byron Jacobs
Artist:
Nick Vaughn
Design Firm:
Byron Jacobs Design
San Diego, CA
Publisher:
University of California,
Irvine
Typographer:
Orange County Type
Printer:
Crest Printers
Production Manager:
Byron Jacobs
Papers:
Topkote 100 cover
Topkote 100 text
Jacket Designer:
Byron Jacobs

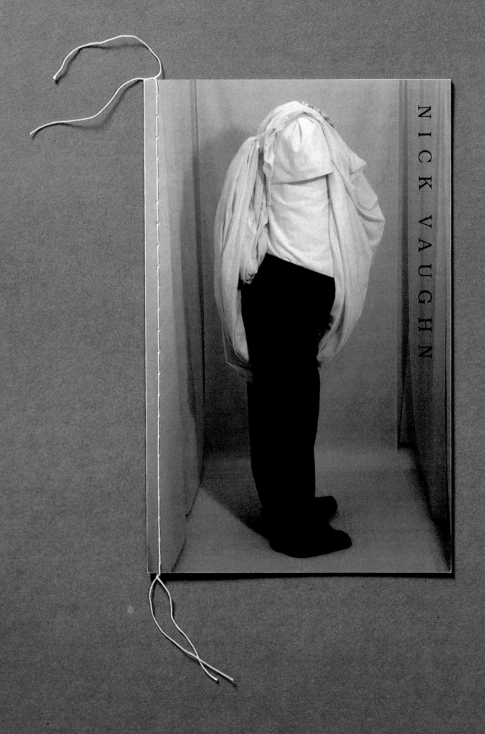

Book Title:
Portrayals
Authors:
Charles Stainback and
Carol Squiers
Art Directors:
Bill Kobasz and Arlene
Lappen
Design Firm:
Reliable Design Studios,
Inc.
Photographer:
Various
Publisher:
International Center of
Photography
Typographers:
Text: Satellite Typesetters,
Inc.
Title: Solotype
Printer:
Canfield & Tack, Inc.
Papers:
Cover: Kroydon-flex Cover,
Spanish overtone
Text: Sterling Litho 80#
Binder:
Canfield & Tack, Inc.

Book Title:
On Home Ground
Author:
Alan Lelchuk
Art Director:
Joy Chu
Designer:
Michael Farmer
Illustrator:
Merle Nacht
Publisher:
Gulliver Books/Harcourt
Brace Jovanovich,
Publishers
San Diego, CA
Typographer:
PennSet Typographers, a
division of Maryland
Linotype Composition Co.
Printer:
R.R. Donnelley & Sons Co.
Production Manager:
Rebecca Miller
Paper:
Lyon's Fall Antique Book
Binder:
R.R. Donnelley & Sons Co.
Jacket Designer:
Michael Farmer
Jacket Illustrator:
Merle Nacht

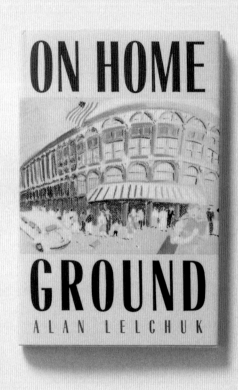

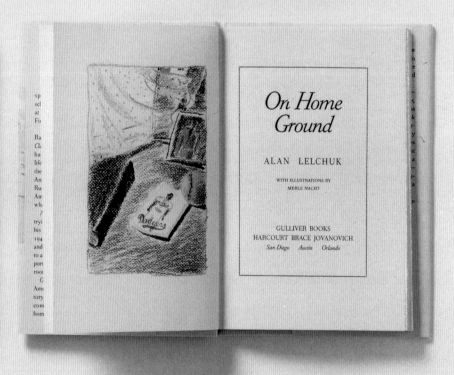

Book Title:
Mad Love (L'Amour Fou)
Author:
André Breton
Art Director/Designer:
Richard Eckersley
Publisher:
University of Nebraska
Press
Lincoln, NE
Typographer:
B. Vader Design/Production
Printer:
Edwards Brothers, Inc.
Production Manager:
Debra K. Turner
Paper:
Glatfelter Text 55#
Binder:
Edwards Brothers, Inc.
Jacket Designer:
Richard Eckersley
Jacket Montage:
Richard Eckersley

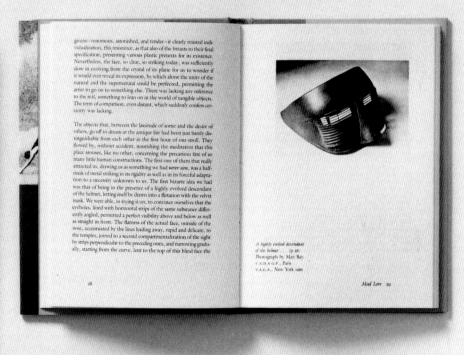

givers—venomous, astonished, and tender—it clearly resisted individualization, this resistance, as that also of the breasts to their final specification, presenting various plastic pretexts for its existence. Nevertheless, the face, so clear, so striking today, was sufficiently slow in evolving from the crystal of its plane for us to wonder if it would ever reveal its expression, by which alone the unity of the natural and the supernatural could be perfected, permitting the artist to go on to something else. There was lacking any reference to the real, something to lean on in the world of tangible objects. The term of comparison, even distant, which suddenly confers certainty was lacking.

The objects that, between the lassitude of some and the desire of others, go off to dream at the antique fair had been just barely distinguishable from each other in the first hour of our stroll. They flowed by, without accident, nourishing the meditation that this place arouses, like no other, concerning the precarious fate of so many little human constructions. The first one of them that really attracted us, drawing us as something we had *never seen*, was a half-mask of metal striking in its rigidity as well as in its forceful adaptation to a necessity unknown to us. The first bizarre idea we had was that of being in the presence of a highly evolved descendant of the helmet, letting itself be drawn into a flirtation with the velvet mask. We were able, in trying it on, to convince ourselves that the eyeholes, lined with horizontal strips of the same substance differently angled, permitted a perfect visibility above and below as well as straight in front. The flatness of the actual face, outside of the nose, accentuated by the lines leading away, rapid and delicate, to the temples, joined to a second compartmentalization of the sight by strips perpendicular to the preceding ones, and narrowing gradually, starting from the curve, lent to the top of this blind face the

A highly evolved descendant of the helmet . . . (p. 28) Photograph by Man Ray. © A.D.A.G.P., Paris V.A.G.A., New York 1986

28

Mad Love 29

Book Title:
Seashells & Sunsets
Author:
Nan Chalat
Art Director/Designer:
Don Weller
Photographers:
Seashells: Michael
Schoenfeld
Sunsets: Don Weller
Publisher:
The Weller Institute for the
Cure of Design, Inc.
Park City, UT
Typographer:
Alpha Graphix
Printer:
Paragon Press
Production Manager:
Don Weller
Paper:
Photographs: Centura
Gloss book 100#
Text/End Papers: Simpson
Paper's Teton 80#
Binder:
Paragon Press
Jacket Designer:
Don Weller
Jacket Photographers:
Michael Schoenfeld and
Don Weller

Book Title:
Stars and Stripes
Author:
Kit Hinrichs
Editing:
Delphine Hirasuna
Art Director:
Kit Hinrichs
Design Firm:
Pentagram
San Francisco, CA
Illustrators:
Various
Photographers:
Michele Clement, Barry
Robinson, and Terry
Heffernan
Publisher:
Chronicle Books
Typographer:
On Line Typography
Printer:
Dai Nippon Printing Co.,
Ltd.
Production Manager:
Tanya Stringham
Papers:
Cover: Bone Ivory 310 gsm
115#
Text: Glossy Coated
157gsm 106#

Book Title:
The Faithless
Author:
Marge Piercy
Art Director/Designer:
Cecelia A. Conover
Design Firm:
Evans & Conover
Illustrator:
David Diaz
Publisher:
David Diaz
Carlsbad, CA
Typographer:
Ed Blount Typesetting
Printers:
Letterpress: E. P. Wilson
Four-Color: Conklin Litho.
Co.
Paper:
Crane White Parchment
56#
Hand Binder:
Cecilia Diaz
Jacket Designer:
David Diaz
Jacket Illustrator:
David Diaz

Book Title:
Ogden Nash's Zoo
Author:
Ogden Nash
Editor:
Roy Finamore
Designer:
Rita Marshall
Illustrator:
Etienne Delessert
Publisher:
Stewart Tabori & Chang
New York, NY
Typographers:
Trufont Typographers, Inc.
Printer:
Toppan Printing Co., Inc.
Production Manager:
Kathy Rosenbloom
Paper:
Sun fantasy 105#
Binder:
Toppan Printing Co., Inc.
Jacket Designer:
Rita Marshall
Jacket Illustrator:
Etienne Delessert

Book Title:
Thirty Centuries of Graphic
Design
Authors:
James Craig and Bruce
Barton
Art Director:
James Craig
Design Firm:
Craig Graphics
New York, NY
Publisher:
Watson-Guptill Publications,
Inc.
New York, NY
Typographer:
Trufont Typographers, Inc.
Printer:
Arcata Graphics/Halliday
Lithographers
Production Manager:
Ellen Greene

1700-1800

GRAPHIC ARTS

Printing in England

By the 1700s, printing had become a major industry throughout Europe with no particular nation in a position of dominance. With the increased demand for printed matter and a more discriminating reading public, printers and publishers became aware of the need for better typefaces, paper, and presswork.

New forms of printed matter appeared: JOSEPH ADDISON and RICHARD STEELE wrote and published the first successful periodic journals, the *Tatler* in 1709 and the *Spectator* in 1711. The English novel developed as a popular literary form.

With the increased volume of printing and a heightened sense of national pride, English printers sensed the need for native English typeface designs. Until this time England had been content to import the matrices for typefaces from Holland and have the type cast at local foundries. But Holland was a rival for markets and colonies around the world and not a reliable source.

A first step in independence came in 1720, when WILLIAM BOWYER, a London printer, advanced the sum of £500 to enable WILLIAM CASLON, an engraver, to set up his own foundry. By 1725 Caslon had designed, cut, and cast his first roman and italic typefaces.

Although strongly influenced by Dutch designs, *Caslon* became the quintessential English typeface and dominated English printing throughout the century (5). Caslon is considered the last of the major *old style* type designs.

The man who probably did the most for English printing, JOHN BASKERVILLE, was considered in his time to be an amateur. He began his career as a writing master, but gave that up as a young man to make his fortune at the japanning business in Birmingham. After retiring at the age of forty-four, Baskerville returned to his first love, letterforms, and began printing as a wealthy amateur.

Extremely dissatisfied with the state of English printing and typography, Baskerville set out to do something about it.

The City of London replaced Amsterdam as Europe's major financial and printing center. In England printing flourished, stimulated by the newly won freedom of the press in 1694.

He decided to print his own books to show by example what could be done when one took pains with every stage of production. To achieve the best possible results, Baskerville designed his own typefaces, experimented with inks and paper, and, above all, demanded excellence in presswork.

In 1757, Baskerville published his first book, the works of Virgil (7), and went on to publish many more books including the Juvenal satires (6).

At first Baskerville's books received a mixed response. Many felt that the high contrast created by the intense black ink and brilliant white paper Baskerville used in his books dazzled the eyes and made reading difficult. Much of the criticism has been attributed to professional jealousy. Today, both Baskerville's types and books are universally acclaimed.

Baskerville also experimented with various printing surfaces and is credited by some with being the first printer to use wove paper.

For centuries handmade paper was produced on a parallel wire screen supported by stronger wires, called chains. This produced a sheet of paper, referred to as *laid*, with an uneven surface that retained the impression of the screen, especially the chain marks.

Baskerville realized that a finely woven screen would produce a smoother paper and eliminate the wire and chain impression. This new type of paper was called *wove*. To make the surface of the paper even smoother and glossier, the paper was pressed between hot copper plates, a process we now call *calendering*.

Baskerville first used wove paper on his *Virgil* of 1757 and later for his *Paradise Regained* in 1759.

ABCD
ABCDE
ABCDEFG
ABCDEFGHI
ABCDEFGHIJKL
ABCDEFGHIJKL
ABCDEFGHIKLMN

DOUBLE PICA ROMAN.
Quousque tandem abutere, Catilina, patientia nostra? quamdiu nos etiam furor iste tuus eluder? quem ad finem sese effrenata jac-
ABCDEFGHJIKLMNOP

GREAT PRIMER ROMAN.
Quousque tandem abutere, Catilina, patientia nostra? quamdiu nos etiam furor iste tuus eluder? quem ad finem sese effrenata jactabit audacia? nihilne te nocturnum præsidium palatii, nihil urbis vigilia, nihil timor populi, nihil con-
ABCDEFGHJIKLMNOPQRS

ENGLISH ROMAN.
Quousque tandem abutere, Catilina, patientia nostra? quamdiu nos etiam furor iste tuus eluder? quem ad finem sese effrenata jactabit audacia? nihilne te nocturnum præsidium palatii, nihil urbis vigilia, nihil timor populi, nihil con-
ABCDEFGHJIKLMNOPQRSTVUWX

PICA ROMAN.
Melum, novis vitae Padorem, novis fui necide, Fiat, fuit ibi quandam in hac regia, virtus, ut viri fortes acioribus supplicis coercerent civem, quam acerbissimum hostem coherent. Habemus enim fenatusconsultum in te, Catilina, vehemens, & grave; non deeft reip. confilium, neque auctoritas hujus ordinis: nos, nos dico aperte, confules defumus. De-
ABCDEFGHJIKLMNOPQRSTVUWX

SMALL PICA ROMAN N0.1
At iste egeftatem pari furor patriae funefare conate fuerunt, bellum excitare fædifragus; ha provinciam, Catilina, meritis, fitheliter,

French Canon.
Quousque tandem abutere, Catilina, patientia nostra?

Quousque tandem abutere, Catilina, patientia nostra?

JUVENALIS SATYRA VI. 73

Jamque eadem summis pariter, minimisque libido:
Nec melior pedibus silicem qua conterit atram;
Quam quæ longorum vehitur cervice Syrorum.
Ut spectet ludos, conducit Ogulnia redem.
Conducit comites, sellam, cervical, amicas,
Nutricem, et flavam, cui det mandata, puellam.
Hæc tamen argenti superest quodcunque paterni
Levibus athletis, ac vasa novissima donat.
Multis res angusta domi est: sed nulla pudorem
Paupertatis habet; nec se metitur ad illum,
Quem debet sibi prodidque modum. Tamen utile quidfit,
Prospiciunt aliquando viri; frigidque, famesque,
Formica tandem quidam expavere magistra,
Prodiga non sentit pereuntem femina censum.
At velut exhausta redivivus pullulet arca
Nummus, et e pleno semper tollatur acervo,
Non unquam reputat, quanti sibi gaudia constent.
Sunt quas eunuchi imbelles, ac mollia semper
Oscula delectent, et desperatio barbæ,
Et quod abortivo non est opus. Illa voluptas
Summa tamen, quod jam calida et matura juventa
Inguina traduntur medicis, jam pectine nigro.

K   Ergo

PUBLII VIRGILII
MARONIS
BUCOLICA.
GEORGICA,
ET
AENEIS.

BIRMINGHAMIÆ
Typis JOHANNIS BASKERVILLE
MDCCLVII.

5 Detail from a Caslon specimen sheet with type sizes specified not in points, but by names such as canon, primer, and pica. Caslon is considered the last of the old style faces.

6 The clear, open forms of Baskerville's type, as seen in this page from Juvenal's Satires, demonstrates why Baskerville has remained a popular book typeface. Baskerville is now classified as a transitional typeface.

7 Title page from Baskerville's first book, a Virgil, which was published in 1757. It was received with mixed reviews; many found the paper too white, the ink too black, and the type too dazzling.

104   105

JAMES CRAIG
BRUCE BARTON

THIRTY
CENTURIES
OF
GRAPHIC
DESIGN

AN ILLUSTRATED SURVEY

Book Title:
Souvenir Collection of the
Postage Stamps of Canada
1986
Authors:
Louise Ellis and Guy
Patenaude
Editing:
Josette Guiguere and David
Jewellyn
Art Directors:
Rolf Harder and Louise
Maffett
Designers:
Rolf Harder and Leo
Schweizer
Cover Photographer:
Russell Proulx
Design Firm:
Rolf Harder & Associates
Montreal, CAN
Publisher:
Canada Post Corp.
Typographer:
Precicomp, Inc.
Printer:
Ashton-Potter Ltd
Production Manager:
George dePassillé
Papers:
Cover: Kromekote Cover
188m
Inside: Michigan Matte
Cover 130m
Binder:
Bindery Services

Molly Brant – woman of two worlds

Molly Brant has been overlooked by history. Although her brother, the Mohawk war chief Joseph Brant, has a well documented life, in reality Molly's influence far outstripped that of her more illustrious brother.

Molly Brant : une femme, deux mondes

Molly Brant a certes été négligée par l'histoire. On connaît pourtant la renommée de son frère, le chef mohawk Joseph Brant, mais en fait, l'influence de Molly dépasse largement celle de son illustre cadet.

To mark the 250th anniversary of Molly Brant's birth, a unique task was posed to Sara Tyson, the stamp's illustrator. In the first place, there were no extant drawings or paintings from which to create a portrait of Brant. But even if there had been, how could one portrait do justice to her multifaceted life? By piecing together historical information and portraits of Molly's brother, Joseph Brant, and amalgamating three faces which represent three distinctive roles, Ms. Tyson arrived at a very inventive solution.

The left profile, with a bear claw necklace, symbolizes the Mohawk roots and authority of Molly Brant, or Koñwatsi tsiaiéñni (meaning "someone lends her a flower" in Iroquoian). Her assimilation into aristocratic British culture is represented by the profile with a ruffled lace collar. And in the centre appears the face of not only a Loyalist and mediator between two cultures, but a woman of prominence in her own right.

Créer un timbre pour le deux cent cinquantième anniversaire de la naissance de Molly Brant constituait un défi de taille pour Sara Tyson. En effet, il n'existe aucun portrait de Molly Brant. Même s'il en avait existé, comment rendre justice à cette femme aux multiples visages? Madame Tyson a trouvé une solution ingénieuse. À partir de renseignements historiques et de portraits de Joseph, le frère de Molly, elle a conçu une illustration qui témoigne des trois vies de Molly Brant.

Le profil gauche de Molly Brant (en iroquois Koñwatsi tsiaiéñni, «on lui prête une fleur») porte un collier de griffes d'ours, symbole de ses origines mohawks et de l'autorité qu'elle a exercée sur son peuple. Le profil droit revêt un jabot plissé, indice de son appartenance à l'aristocratie britannique. Entre les deux, on devine non seulement la loyaliste qui a contribué au rapprochement des deux cultures, mais également la femme qui s'est imposée par son seul talent.

Specifications
Denomination: 34¢
Date of issue: 14 April 1986
Design: Sara Tyson
Printer: Ashton-Potter Limited
Quantity: 15,000,000
Dimensions: 30 mm x 36 mm (vertical)
Perforation: 13+
Printing process: Lithography in five colours
Pane layout: 50 stamps

Données techniques
Valeur: 0,34 $
Date d'émission: 14 avril 1986
Design: Sara Tyson
Imprimeur: Ashton-Potter Limited
Tirage: 15 000 000
Format: 30 mm sur 36 mm (vertical)
Dentelure: 13+
Procédé d'impression: lithographie en cinq couleurs
Présentation de la feuille: 50 timbres

These was to her ever increasing family, of whom eight survived childhood. As head of the Six Nations Society of Matrons, she lavishly bestowed on hundreds of Indians everything from blankets to sound advice. A Stewart Loyalist, she was invaluable in cementing the often tenuous alliance between the Indians and the British. Widowed just before the American Revolution and then driven from her home by Rebels, she settled in Kingston after the war, where she died in 1796.

Molly Brant's power was more than just the result of both birth and circumstance. It was a product of her high-spirited devotion and magnetic personality.

mes responsabilités. D'abord, elle a plusieurs enfants, dont huit survivront. Ensuite, à titre de chef des Aînées de la Ligue des Six Nations, elle fait preuve d'une grande générosité, produisant à ses frères et sœurs de sang des objets de première nécessité et des conseils éclairés. Enfin, loyaliste fervente, elle contribue, de façon inestimable, à l'affermissement des liens souvent fragiles entre Amérindiens et Britanniques. Veuve à l'aube de la Révolution américaine, elle est chassée de chez elle par les rebelles. Après la guerre, elle s'établit à Kingston, où elle meurt en 1796.

L'influence de Molly Brant n'est pas uniquement reliée à ses origines ou à d'heureuses circonstances. Elle est plutôt le résultat d'un engagement fidèle, d'une forte personnalité et d'un magnétisme indéniable.

Souvenir Collection
of the Postage Stamps
of Canada 1986

Collection-souvenir des
timbres-poste
du Canada de 1986

Canada Post Corporation

Société canadienne des postes

Book Title:
A Design for Living:
Vienna in the Twenties
Author:
Lillian Langseth-
Christensen
Design Director:
Amy Hill
Designer:
Francesca Belanger
Photographer:
Various
Publisher:
Viking Penguin, Inc.
New York, NY
Typographer:
N.K. Graphics
Printer:
Arcata Graphics
Production Manager:
Roni Axelrod
Paper:
Glatfelter smooth offset 70#
Binder:
Arcata Graphics
Jacket Designer:
Maggie Payette

Book Title:
A Scrap of Time
Author:
Ida Fink
Art Director/Designer:
Susan Mitchell
Publisher:
Pantheon Books
New York, NY
Typographer:
Maryland Linotype
Composition Co.
Printer:
The Haddon Craftsmen
Production Manager:
Marlene Zack
Paper:
Sebago Antique #55
Binder:
The Haddon Craftsmen
Jacket Designer:
Louise Fili
Jacket Illustrator:
Melanie Marder Parks

the trucks didn't stop nor were there any shots. The rumbling of the motors was drowned out by the wailing of the spectators. The crowd broke up and angrily dispersed, loudly discussing what had happened.

He could barely contain himself until his peasant arrived that evening; he was trembling with excitement.

"What happened?"

"What happened was . . . ," the peasant responded in his singsong Volhynian accent, "the devil take them! They ran over a pig!"

That evening he did not touch his food, that night he didn't close his eyes.

There was one more attic, then a forest; he endured the last months of the war buried in a hole beneath a pigsty. The woman was poor but she gave him food, protected him, and when he was very ill, she swore from the goodness of her heart that she would bury him under the most beautiful apple tree in her orchard. It was at her place that he survived the war. When she pulled him—filthy, covered with lice, unable to walk—from his underground hiding place, he said, "You know, when they ran over that pig, I didn't believe there were any human beings left . . ."

"Yes, yes," she answered him, as if talking to a child. And being a sober, sensible woman, she thought to herself, "The poor thing has gone crazy from happiness. He's babbling about pigs!"

82

TITINA

Perhaps because Ludek was the youngest, the commandant ordered him, "Bring Titina." That's all, he didn't give him a list like he gave the others who had just left the *Judenrat* building and scattered through the town. Ludek asked, "By myself?" but the short, bald commandant didn't answer and slammed the door in his face. A storm of voices was raging behind the door.

It was a warm, windy night. The ice was breaking up on the river, and the sound of the water could be heard everywhere in town. There wasn't a single light in the houses, just thick darkness, sleep.

He walked quickly. The river's voice grew stronger. Titina lived next to the bridge. "Good evening," he imagined himself saying, and heard Titina answer, "*Bonsoir, jeune homme.*"

"*Bonsoir, Madame,*" he corrected himself—she insisted he speak to her only in French. The little desk under the window, the worn volume from Larousse, the gilded binding of *Letters from My Windmill*. And the smell of mold from the dark room. Even back then she showed signs of becoming a madwoman. That mustiness. She never opened the windows. Dark, slender spruce trees outside. She referred to her little house as "Spruce Manor," and rolled her r's as befits a teacher of French.

"*Comment va ta maman?*"

"*Merci, elle va bien.*"

83

Book Title:
Close Cover Before Striking:
The Golden Age of
Matchbook Art
Authors:
H. Thomas Steele, Jim
Heimann, and Rod Dyer
Art Direction:
H. Thomas Steele and Jim
Heimann
Editor:
Walton Rawls
Designers:
Rod Dyer and Harriet Baba
Design Firm:
Dyer/Kahn, Inc.
Publisher:
Robert E. Abrams
Abbeville Press
New York, NY
Production Manager:
Hope Koturo

Book Title:
Fit to be Tied: Vintage Ties
of the Forties and Early
Fifties
Authors:
Rod Dyer and Ron Spark
Art Director/Designer:
Rod Dyer
Los Angeles, CA
Photographer:
Steve Sakai
Publisher:
Robert E. Abrams
Abbeville Press
New York, NY
Typographer:
Andresen
Production Manager:
Jo Sayama
Jacket Designer:
Rod Dyer
Jacket Photographer:
Steve Sakai

Book Title:
Phantom Silver
Author:
William Kittredge
Art Director/Designer:
Emily Strayer
Illustrator:
Dirk Lee
Publisher:
Kutenai Press
Missoula, MT
Typographer:
Emily Strayer
Printer:
Emily Strayer
Paper:
Mohawk Letterpress Text
Binder:
Emily Strayer

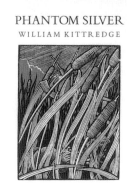

Book Title:
The Scholar Adventurer:
A Tribute to John D. Gordan
Author:
Dr. John D. Gordan
Art Director/Designer:
Sean Adams
Design Firm:
Graphics Office
New York Public Library
Publisher:
New York Public Library
New York, NY
Typographer:
Meriden-Stinehour Press
Printer:
Meriden-Stinehour Press
Production Manager:
Tony Pizzo
Paper:
Mohawk Superfine Soft
white text 80#
Eggshell finish
Binder:
Meriden-Stinehour Press
Jacket Designer:
Sean Adams

The
SCHOLAR
ADVENTURER

A Tribute to John D. Gordan (1907–1968)

With Six of His Essays

A Legend Revisited:
Elinor Wylie

"SHE WAS A LEGEND before she was a fact," Carl Van Doren wrote of Elinor Wylie after her death on December 15, 1928. Legends have a way of disappearing even from the scandal sheets of the national press that once made so free with her name. Changes in literary fashion have taken all but one of her four mannered novels out of print and obscured the power and beauty of the last of her four volumes of poetry, *Angels and Earthly Creatures*. The facts of her life, from which her poetry grew, were only imperfectly established in her sole biography, *The Portrait of an Unknown Lady*, 1935, by her younger sister, the novelist Nancy Hoyt. Yet her story has the fascination of classical tragedy, and a reexamination of literary values will inevitably bring her work back to public attention.

The legend of Elinor Wylie is recorded in the work and in the reminiscences of her friends and enemies, eminent figures of the 1920s. She is sympathetically delineated by Kathleen Coyle in *Immortal Ease* as Victoria Rising and by Isa Glenn in *East of Eden* as Eva Littlefield. Nancy Hoyt treated her frivolously as Athene in *Bright Intervals* and Anne Parrish maliciously as Christabel Caine in *All Kneeling*. She described herself with a detachment remarkable for

· *11* ·

Book Title:
Miniature Golf
Authors:
Nina Garfinkel and Maria
Reidelbach
Editor:
Walton Rawls
Art Director:
James Wageman
Designer:
Helene Silverman
Photographer:
John Margolies
Publisher:
Robert E. Abrams
Abbeville Press
New York, NY
Production Manager:
Hope Koturo

Book Title:
South of the Fork
Author:
Ana Kehoe
Art Director/Designer:
Linda Eissler
Dallas, TX
Illustrator:
Linda Eissler
Photographers:
Jim Olvera and Sally
Larroca
Design Assistant:
Randall Hill
Publisher:
The Junior League of
Dallas, Inc.
Typographer:
Typographics
Printer:
Heritage Press
Production Manager:
Sissy Alsabrook
Papers:
LOE gloss book white 100#
Natural Speckletone Text
70#
Binder:
Raymer Bookbindery

Book Title:
Growing up with Canada
Authors:
Ewa Jarmicka and Bernard
Legaré
Designer:
Wanda Lewicka
Design Firm:
Axion Design Inc.
Montreal, CAN
Photographs:
CN Photo Library and
Public Archives, Canada
Publisher:
Canadian National
Printer:
Imprimerie RBT Lte.
Papers:
J.B.R. coated offset cover
160m .007
Silverblade Matte 155m

William Mackenzie (1) and Donald
Mann (2).

William Mackenzie (1) et Donald
Mann (2).

The Canadian Northern Railway

The first railway to seize the opportunity was the Canadian Northern, led by two imaginative and courageous Ontario men, William Mackenzie and Donald Mann. They began by building a line in Manitoba from Portage la Prairie northwest to Dauphin. In 1902, only six years after their company laid its first kilometre of track, the Canadian Northern had connected Winnipeg with Lake Superior. Its founders now owned 1,930 km of trackage but they didn't stop at that.

By 1905, the year Saskatchewan and Alberta entered Confederation, their lines had crossed the Prairies to Edmonton. Track was laid quickly and perhaps not too well, because Mackenzie and Mann were in a hurry to get things moving. They did, however, keep upgrading it to meet the demands of use as traffic increased.

The Canadian Northern was known as "the farmers' railway", because it served the often isolated people of the Prairies as individuals even while earning money from them. There is a story about one of its trains stopping near a cabin, and staying there so long that a passenger asked the conductor about the delay. He explained that the woman who lived in the cabin was going to a market down the line to sell two dozen eggs, but she was an egg short so the train had to wait until a hen laid one.

Employees of the Canadian Northern were proud of their company, and cared for it, and they all understood the importance of keeping costs down.

Le Canadian Northern Railway

La première compagnie à comprendre la situation est le Canadian Northern, dirigé par deux Ontariens courageux et pleins d'imagination : William Mackenzie et Donald Mann. Ils construisent d'abord la ligne Portage Laprairie-Dauphin, au Manitoba. En 1902, six ans à peine après la pose des premiers rails dans l'Ouest, le Canadian Northern inaugure la ligne qui relie Winnipeg au lac Supérieur. Ses fondateurs sont propriétaires de 1 930 km de voies ferrées, mais ils ne s'arrêtent pas là.

En 1905, année de l'entrée de la Saskatchewan et de l'Alberta dans la Confédération, leurs lignes ont franchi les Prairies jusqu'à Edmonton. Comme Mackenzie et Mann sont pressés de l'exploiter, la voie, construite très rapidement, n'est pas toujours très solide. L'accroissement du trafic les contraint d'ailleurs à reconstruire de longues sections de voie.

Le Canadian Northern est familièrement baptisé «chemin de fer des fermiers» parce que, même s'il y trouve son compte, il assure un service personnalisé à chacun des cultivateurs souvent isolés des Prairies. On raconte l'histoire du convoi arrêté si longtemps près d'une cabane qu'à un des voyageurs s'inquiétant de l'importance du retard, le chef de train répond que la fermière doit prendre le train pour aller vendre deux douzaines d'oeufs au marché, et qu'elle attend qu'une poule ponde le dernier.

Les employés du Canadian Northern sont très fiers de leur compagnie et défendent ses intérêts.

With the development of hardy strains of wheat the Prairies prospered and railways took the produce to market.

Les provinces des Prairies se sont développées grâce aux céréales qui le acheminaient vers les marchés.

On one occasion, a train struck a heifer, breaking its legs. The crew knew from experience that the farmer would make a claim against the railway for the animal without taking into account the additional value of its meat. So a brakeman who had been a butcher quickly killed and dressed it, the carcass and hide were put in the baggage car, sold that same day, and after the farmer's claim was paid in full there were four dollars left for the company.

Having reached Edmonton, Mackenzie and Mann saw the Pacific as their next goal. That, of course, meant building in the mountains, which was much more difficult than on the flat central plain. Still, although progress was slow, the Canadian Northern line to Vancouver was opened in 1915.

Une fois, un train heurte une génisse et lui casse une patte. Comme les cheminots savent que l'éleveur va réclamer au chemin de fer le prix de sa bête sans exiger la valeur de la viande, un serre-frein exboucher abat rapidement la génisse et la découpe. Il cache le corps du délit dans un fourgon à bagages, et vend le tout le jour même, permettant à la compagnie de réaliser un bénéfice de quatre dollars après indemnisation de l'éleveur.

Après Edmonton, le nouvel objectif de Mackenzie et Mann est le Pacifique. Il va leur falloir construire en montagne, ce qui est autrement plus difficile qu'en plaine. Bien qu'on progresse lentement, la ligne du Canadian Northern atteint Vancouver en 1915.

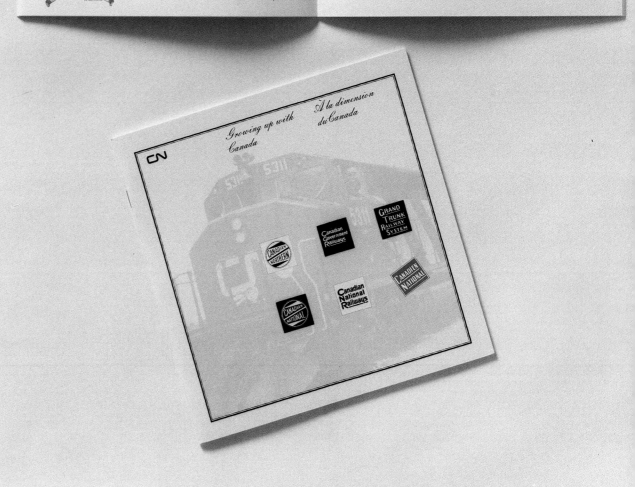

Book Title:
Night Walking
Author:
Judy Anderson
Designer:
Judy Anderson
Design Firm:
Studio Studio
Denver, CO
Illustrator:
Judy Anderson
Publisher:
X Press
Typographer:
Egan Type
Printer:
X Press
Paper:
Arches and UV Ultra
Binder:
X Press

Book Title:
Night Walking
Author:
Judy Anderson
Designer:
Judy Anderson
Design Firm:
Studio Studio
Denver, CO
Illustrator:
Judy Anderson
Publisher:
X Press
Typographer:
Egan Type
Printer:
X Press
Paper:
Arches and UV Ultra
Binder:
X Press

Book Title:
Having Tea
Authors:
Catherine Calvert and
Tricia Foley
Art Director:
Gael Towey
Designer:
Rita Marshall
Photographer:
Keith Scott Morton
Publisher:
Clarkson N. Potter/Crown
Publishers, Inc.
New York, NY
Typographer:
Dix Typesetting Co., Inc.
Printer:
Dai Nippon Printing Co.,
Ltd.
Production Manager:
Kay Riley
Paper:
Japanese Gloss coated
85#
Binder:
Dai Nippon Printing Co.,
Ltd.
Jacket Designer:
Rita Marshall
Jacket Photographer:
Keith Scott Morton

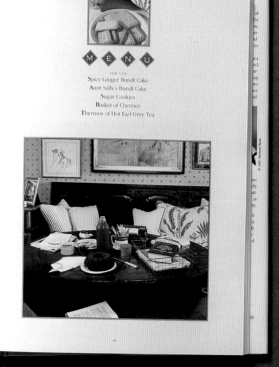

Book Title:
Clay Revisions: Plate, Cup,
Vase
Author:
Vicki Halper
Art Director:
Helen Abbott
Designer:
Anne Traver
Design Firm:
Anne Traver Graphic
Design
Seattle, WA
Photographer:
Paul Macapia
Publisher:
Seattle Art Museum
Seattle, WA
Typographer:
Thomas & Kennedy
Printer:
Dai Nippon Printing Co.,
Ltd.
Production Coordinator:
Paula Thurman
Paper:
Satin Kinfuji
Binder:
Dai Nippon Printing Co.,
Ltd.
Jacket Designer:
Anne Traver
Jacket Photographer:
Paul Macapia

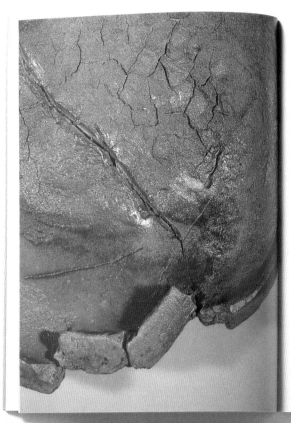

As painter alone, the artist can brush thin washes or thick impastos of color onto the finished clay form. As sketcher, using stick rather than pen, the artist can engrave the most responsive of lines. As sculptor the artist can build up or subtract from the clay surface, layering and attaching or gouging and carving with the simplest of tools or with the hand alone.

Fine European porcelains minimized the sense of any direct modeling by hand and emphasized a sleek glazed surface for display of the most painterly aspect of the ceramic arts. The Leach revival turned attention away from polished porcelain to the surfaces created by Japanese and folk potters—rougher, less regular, more likely to bear the marks of the earth, the hand, and the fire. It is this sensibility that Voulkos applies to his own work. His plates display tension between spontaneity and control—boldness of gesture and the restraint in making marks; between the control of the circular plate shape and its seeming geological dissolution; and between the pattern of handmade marks and the pattern of the fire. In these unglazed pieces, clay speaks for itself.

CLAY
REVISIONS
PLATE
CUP
VASE

Book Title:
Blues
Author:
John Hersey
Art Director:
Virginia Tam
Designer:
Dorothy Schmiderer
Illustrator:
James Baker
Endpaper Map:
David Lindroth
Publisher:
Alfred A. Knopf, Inc.
New York, NY
Typographer:
Maryland Linotype
Composition Co.
Printer:
Halliday Lithographers
Production Manager:
Andrew W. Hughes
Paper:
SDW 60#
Binder:
Halliday Lithographers
Jacket Designer:
Wendell Minor
Jacket Illustrator:
Wendell Minor

Book Title:
Defending the Constitution
Authors:
John Jay, Alexander
Hamilton, James Madison,
Thomas Jefferson, and
Noah Webster
Art Director/Designer:
Jerry Kelly
Illustrations:
18th- and 19th-century
paintings
Publisher:
A. Colish, Inc.
Mt. Vernon, NY
Typographer:
A. Colish, Inc.
Printer:
A. Colish, Inc.
Production Managers:
Jerry Kelly and Karen
Lasser
Special Paper:
Curtis Ragston Laid
Binder:
Publishers Book Bindery

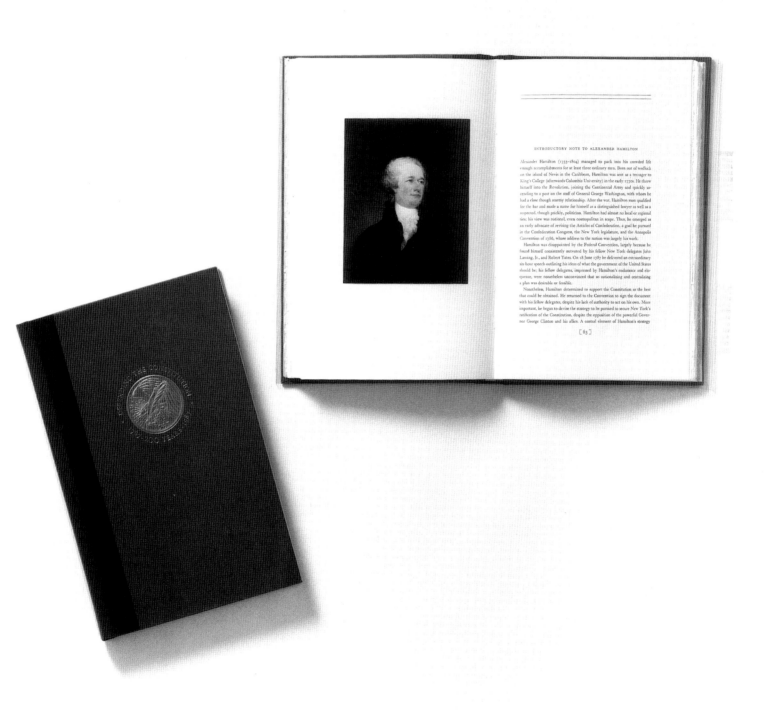

Book Title:
Robert Finigan's
Essentials of Wine
Author:
Robert Finigan
Art Director:
Virginia Tam
Designer:
Iris Weinstein
Cartographer:
Jean Paul Tremblay
Publisher:
Alfred A. Knopf, Inc.
New York, NY
Typographer:
Dix Type, Inc.
Printer:
Halliday Lithographers
Production Manager:
Tracy K. Cabanis
Paper:
Sebago 50#
Binder:
Halliday Lithographers
Jacket Designer:
Sue Keston
Jacket Illustrator:
Anthony Russo

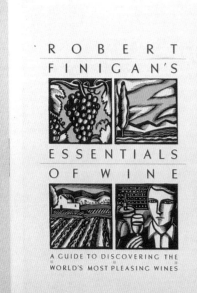

Book Title:
Japanese Tales
Author:
Royall Tyler
Art Director/Designer:
Susan Mitchell
Publisher:
Pantheon Books
New York, NY
Typographer:
PennSet Inc.
Printer:
R.R. Donnelley & Sons Co.
Production Manager:
Marlene Zack
Paper:
Sebago Antique 50#
Binder:
R.R. Donnelley & Sons Co.
Jacket Designer:
Louise Fili
Jacket Illustrator:
Anthony Russo

Book Title:
The Devils Who Learned To
Be Good
Author:
Michael McCurdy
Art Director:
Trisha Hanlon
Designer:
Jeanne Abboud
Illustrator:
Michael McCurdy
Publisher:
Little, Brown & Co. and Joy
Street Books
Boston, MA
Typographer:
American-Stratford Graphic
Services, Inc.
Printer:
Eastern Press, Inc.
Production Manager:
Linda Jackson
Paper:
Matte coated 80#
Binder:
Horowitz/Rae Book
Manufacturers, Inc.
Jacket Designer:
Jeanne Abboud
Jacket Illustrator:
Michael McCurdy
Jacket Printer:
John P. Pow Co., Inc.

Book Title:
Madam I'm Adam
Author:
William Irvine
Art Director:
Ruth Colbert
Designer:
Peter Davis
Illustrator:
Steven Guarnaccia
Publisher:
Charles Scribner's Sons
Publishers
New York, NY
Typographer:
Talbot Typographics, Inc.
Printer:
R.R. Donnelley & Sons Co.
Production Manager:
Olga Leonardo
Paper:
Warren Sebago 50#
Binder:
R.R. Donnelley & Sons Co.
Jacket Designer:
Susan Hochbaum
Jacket Illustrator:
Steven Guarnaccia

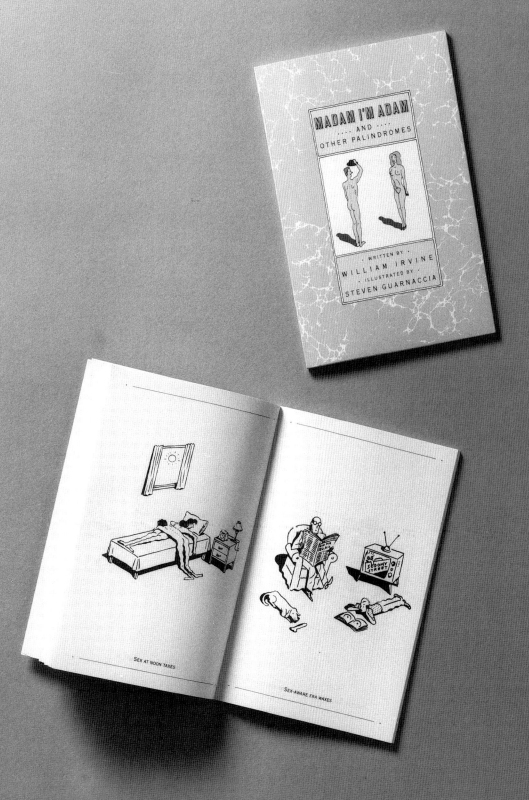

Book Title:
Mary Emmerling's American
Country Cooking
Author:
Mary Emmerling
Art Director:
Gael Towey
Designers:
Stephen Doyle and Rose
Marie Sohmer
Design Firm:
Drenttel Doyle Partners
Photographer:
Michael Skott
Publisher:
Clarkson N. Potter/Crown
Publishers, Inc.
New York, NY
Typographer:
Dix Typesetting, Inc.
Printer:
Toppan Printing Co., Inc.
Production Manager:
Joan Denman
Papers:
Gloss coated 86# and
white u/c, w/f 105#
Binder:
Toppan Printing Co., Inc.
Jacket Designer:
Drenttel Doyle Partners
Jacket Photographer:
Michael Skott

Book Title:
The Natural Cuisine of
Georges Blanc
Author:
Georges Blanc
Designer:
Rita Marshall
Photographer:
Christopher Baker
Publisher:
Stewart Tabori & Chang
New York, NY
Typographer:
Trufont Typographers, Inc.
Printer:
Dai Nippon Printing Co.,
Ltd
Production Manager:
Kathy Rosenbloom
Paper:
Gloss coated 106#
Binder:
Dai Nippon Printing Co.,
Ltd
Jacket Designer:
Rita Marshall
Jacket Photographer:
Christopher Baker
Jacket Typographer:
Affolter & Gschwend AG

Book Title:
Certain Places:
Photographs by William Clift
Author:
William Clift
Art Director/Designer:
Catherine Waters
New Haven, CT
Photographer:
William Clift
Publisher:
William Clift Editions
Typographer:
Display: Meriden-Stinehour
Press
Text: Michael and Winifred
Bixler
Printer:
Meriden-Stinehour Press
Tritone negatives by Robert
J. Hennessey
Production Managers:
Catherine Waters and
Susan Medlicott
Paper:
Mohawk Superfine text
smooth white 100#
Binder:
Publishers Book Bindery
Jacket Designer:
Catherine Waters

Book Title:
Jan Groover
Author:
Susan Kismaric
Art Director:
Jim McDonough
Designers:
Homans/Salsgiver
Photographer:
Robert J. Hennessey
Publisher:
The Museum of Modern Art
New York, NY
Typographer:
Trufont Typographers, Inc.
Printer:
Stamperia Valdonega
Production Manager:
Jim McDonough
Papers:
Text: Patty Matte 150 gsm
Cover: Sottrici Primat 250
gsm
Binder:
Stamperia Valdonega

Book Title:
Alden Mason: A Selected
Survey
Editor:
Joseph Newland
Art Director/Designer:
Douglas Wadden
Seattle, WA
Publisher:
Henry Art Gallery
Seattle, WA
Typographer:
Thomas & Kennedy
Printer:
Nissha Printing Co., Ltd.
Paper:
Espel Dull
Binder:
Nissha Printing Co., Ltd.

Book Title:
Grrrhhhh: A Study of Social
Patterns
Authors:
Warren Lehrer, Sandra
Brownlee Ramsdale, and
Dennis Bernstein
Art Director/Designer:
Warren Lehrer
Photographers:
Phil Zimmerman and Jack
Ramsdale
Letterers:
Jan Baker and Warren
Lehrer
Publisher:
ear/say
Purchase, NY
Typographer:
Warren Lehrer
Printer:
Center for Editions and Lori
Spencer
Production Manager:
Warren Lehrer
Paper:
Mohawk Superfine text 70#
Binder:
Publishers Book Bindery
Jacket Designer:
Warren Lehrer

Book Title:
The Culture of Fragments
Authors:
Gianmarco Vergani, Peter
Shinoda, and David Kesler
Art Director/Designer:
Willi Kunz
Design Firm:
Willi Kunz
New York, NY
Photographers:
Various
Publisher:
Columbia University,
Graduate School of
Architecture
New York, NY
Typographer:
Brill & Waldstein
Printer:
Lucas Printing
Production Manager:
Thomas Cox
Paper:
LOE dull text 80#
Binder:
Lucas Printing

Book Title:
Mario Bellini, Designer
Author:
Cara McCarty
Art Director:
Tim McDonough
Designer:
Steven Schoenfelder
Publisher:
The Museum of Modern Art
New York, NY
Typographer:
Concept Typographic
Services, Inc.
Printer:
Eastern Press, Inc.
Production Manager:
Tim McDonough
Papers:
Text: LOE Dull 80#
Cover: Curtis Tweedweave
Black 80#
Binder:
Mueller Trade Bindery Corp.

Book Title:
Harmony by Hand: Art of
the Southwest Indians
Authors:
Patrick Houlihan, Jerold L.
Collings, Sarah Nestor, and
Jonathan Batkin
Art Directors:
Don McQuiston and Debra
McQuiston Smith
Designer:
Debra McQuiston Smith
Photographers:
Various
Publisher:
Chronicle Books
San Francisco, CA
Typographer:
Thompson Type
Printer:
Dai Nippon Printing Co.,
Ltd. and Interprint
Production Managers:
McQuiston & Daughter, Ken
Coburn
Paper:
Satin Kinfuji Dull, 150 gsm
Binder:
Dai Nippon Printing Co.,
Ltd.
Jacket Designer:
McQuiston & Daughter
Jacket Illustrator:
Debra McQuiston Smith
Jacket Photographers:
Kathleen Norris Cook, San
Diego Museum of Man, and
Southwest Museum

Book Title:
New Mexican Furniture
1600-1940
Authors:
Lonn Taylor and Dessa
Bokides
Designer:
Jim Miho
Project Supervisor:
Jim Mafchir
Photographers:
Mary Peck and Jim Bones
Publisher:
Museum of New Mexico
Press
Santa Fe, NM
Typographer:
Business Graphics, Inc.
Printer:
Dai Nippon Printing Co.,
Ltd.
Production Manager:
Jim Mafchir
Papers:
Text: Art Glossy 86#
Colored Wood Free 86#
Jacket: Art Glossy 106#
Binder:
Dai Nippon Printing Co.,
Ltd.
Jacket Designer:
Jim Miho
Jacket Illustrator:
Jim Miho

Book Title:
Measuring Medical
Practice: Statistics for the
Physician
Author:
American Medical
Association
Art Director:
Mark Oldach, American
Medical Association
Designer:
Kym Abrams
Design Firm:
Kym Abrams Design
Illustrator:
David Povilaitis
Publisher:
American Medical
Association
Chicago, IL
Typographer:
Master Typographers
Printer:
First Impression
Production Manager:
Gail Patejunas, Kym
Abrams Design
Papers:
Starwhite Vicksburg Text,
Smooth 100#
Lustro Gloss Cover 100#
Binder:
Adhesive Binding

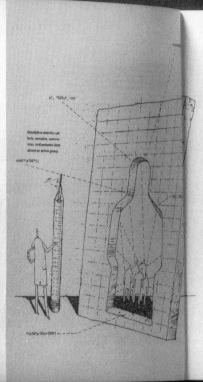

Book Title:
The Berlin Diary
Author:
William L. Shirer
Editor:
Marian Waxman
Art Director:
Joe Marc Freedman
The Sarabande Press
New York, NY
Designer:
Gregory Gillbergh
Mapmaker:
David Lindroth
Photo Research:
Joan Kerr
Publisher:
Book-of-the-Month Club
New York, NY
Typographers:
The Plimpton Press and The
Sarabande Press
Printer:
The Maple Press
Production Manager:
Sally Long
Jacket Designers:
Gregory Gillbergh and Joe
Marc Freedman
Jacket Photographer:
Heinrich Hoffman

PARIS, JUNE 30, 1934

Berlin was cut off for several h...
this afternoon telephone comm...
established. And what a story! ...
a post in Berlin. It's a story I...

WITH AN INTRODUCTION BY
DAVID HALBERSTAM

ILLUSTRATIONS FOR
THIS EDITION SELECTED BY
JOAN PATERSON KERR

BERLIN DIARY

THE JOURNAL
OF A FOREIGN
CORRESPONDENT
1934 · 1941

WILLIAM L. SHIRER

THE AMERICAN PAST
BOOK·OF·THE·MONTH CLUB, INC.
NEW YORK

Book Title:
American Photography 3
Editor:
Edward Booth-Clibborn
Art Director:
Fred Woodward
Designers:
Fred Woodward and Jolene
Cuyler
Photographers:
Various
Publisher:
Harry N. Abrams, Inc.
New York, NY
Typographers:
Phil's Photo, Inc. and
Type Foundry
Printer:
Dai Nippon Printing Co.,
Ltd.
Project Director:
Donna Vinciguerra
Paper:
Coated 157 gsm
Binder:
Dai Nippon Printing Co.,
Ltd.
Jacket Designer:
Fred Woodward
Jacket Photographer:
Annie Leibovitz

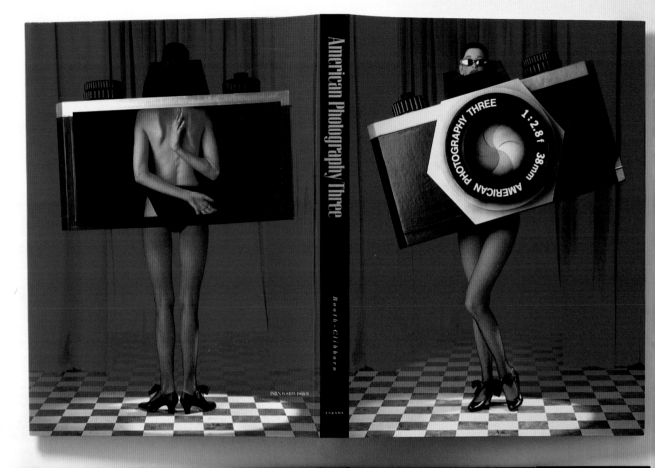

Book Title:
American Illustration 6
Editor:
Edward Booth-Clibborn
Art Director:
Walter Bernard
Designers:
Walter Bernard and Colleen
McCudden
**Illustrators and
Photographers:**
Various
Publisher:
Booth-Clibborn Editions
New York, NY
Typographer:
Seven Graphic Arts
Project Manager:
Donna Vinciguerra
Jacket Designer:
Walter Bernard
Jacket Illustrators:
Barbara Nessim and James
McMullan

Book Title:
The Dissolution of Freddie
Author:
Juliet Wittman
Designer:
Judy Anderson
Design Firm:
Studio Studio
Denver, CO
Illustrator:
Judy Anderson
Publisher:
X Press
Typographer:
Egan Type
Printer:
X Press
Paper:
Strathmore and UV Ultra
Binder:
X Press

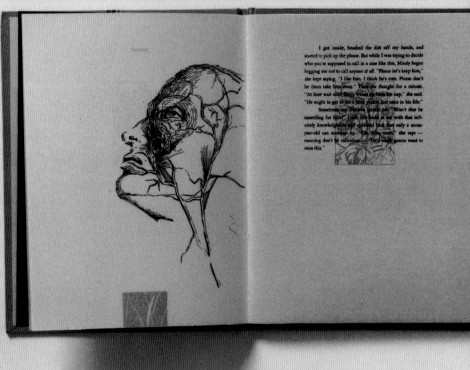

Book Title:
1988 Leap Year of Fate
Art Director:
Esther K. Smith
Publisher:
Purgatory Pie Press
New York, NY
Typographer:
Dikko Faust
Printer:
Dikko Faust
Production Manager:
Georgia Luna Smith Faust
Paper:
Shutan & Kasugami
Binder:
Esther K. Smith
Jacket Designer:
Esther K. Smith

Book Title:
Alberto Giacometti
Author:
Mercedes Matter
Photographer:
Herbert Matter
Art Director:
Sam Antupit
Designer:
Herbert Matter
Design Assistant:
Doris Leath
Artist:
Alberto Giacometti
Publisher:
Harry N. Abrams, Inc.
New York, NY
Typographer:
Concept Typographic
Services
Printer:
Nissha Printing Co., Ltd.
Production Manager:
Shunichi Yamamoto
Paper:
157 GSM Matte Coated
Binder:
Nissha Printing Co., Ltd.
Jacket Designer:
Herbert Matter
**Jacket Photographer and
Letterer:**
Herbert Matter

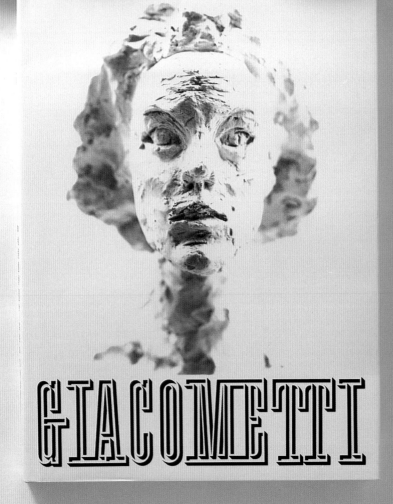

Shoe Show Invitation, Fall 1986

Another season's shoe announcement was produced out of the corrugated plastic used for shoe boxes. This same material was used in display at the Shoe Show. The silkscreened printing for this project was unique. Because of the translucent character of the material, the ink was applied in layers to achieve a two-dimensional image when looking through the material to the back side. The fun fur popular that season inspired the printed texture. This plastic card was then inserted into a translucent glassine envelope. Altogether an ingenious invitation, making the most of the material's translucent quality and silkscreen printing.

ok Title:
rit's Graphic Work
84-1986
thor:
Rae Roth
Director:
notsu Yagi
signers:
notsu Yagi and
berto Carra
otographer:
berto Carra
blisher:
rit De Corp
Francisco, CA
pographer:
play Lettering and Copy
nter:
sha Printing Co., Ltd.
per:
ell 100 kg
der:
sha Printing Co., Ltd.
cket Designer:
notsu Yagi

ESPRIT'S GRAPHIC WORK 1984-1986

Book Title:
Posters of the WPA
1935-1943
Author:
Christopher DeNoon
Art Director/Designer:
Henry Vizcarra
Design Firm:
90 Degrees
Los Angeles, CA
Publisher:
The Wheatley Press
Typographer:
Scarlet Letters
Printer:
Dai Nippon Printing Co.,
Ltd.
Production Manager:
Freda Wheatley Vizcarra
Paper:
U-Light 128 gsm

375
Vera Bock
New York, NY
71 x 56 cm
28 x 22 in.

Portfolio Introduction

From among the many artists who created posters for the FAP-WAP nationwide, a small number have been selected for special recognition in this portfolio. Several factors have been considered in selecting the artists featured here, including that:
- Posters could be identified as the work of a particular artist.
- There was a sufficient number of identified posters available to allow a representative display of an artist's work.
- The work represents the qualities of good poster art by conveying a message through effective design and color.
- Information was available documenting that artist's career.

Identifying the designers responsible for the creation of individual posters was the first task to be undertaken, since many works are unsigned and entered institutional collections without attribution. Some identifications have been confirmed by referring to FAP exhibition catalogues. The author has made certain attributions, basing his judgement on stylistic similarities and other clues. Others have been made with the assistance of WPA poster artists, who reviewed their work and the work of their colleagues. Many posters, however, remain uncredited. The authors and publishers hope that, with this publication, additional identifications will be forthcoming.

Each of the featured artists has produced exemplary designs, which add substantially to the body of work that comprises the history of poster design in America. Many other artists, represented with extraordinary work in this book, are excluded from this portfolio only due to lack of biographical information. These include Albert Bender, Harry Herzog, Stanley Clough, and Jack Rivolta.

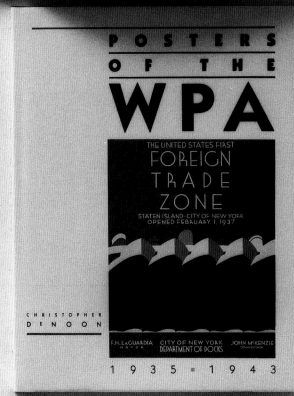

Book Title:
Manual of Instructions for
Étant Donnés
Author:
Marcel Duchamp
Art Director:
George H. Marcus
Designer:
Phillip Unetic
Artist:
Marcel Duchamp
Photographer:
Will Brown
Publisher:
Philadelphia Museum of Art
Philadelphia, PA
Printer:
Balding & Mansell
Production Manager:
Charles Field
Paper:
Parilux Matte

Book Titles:
25 Cats Name Sam and
One Blue Pussy; Holy Cats
by Andy Warhol's Mother
Author:
Andy Warhol
Art Director:
Robert Scudellari
Illustrator:
Andy Warhol and Julia
Warhol
Publisher:
Panache Press at Random
House
New York, NY
Printer:
25 Cats: Thorner-Sidney
Press, Inc.
Holy Cats: F. N. Burt Co.,
Inc.
Production Manager:
Dennis E. Dwyer
Paper:
25 Cats: Crestline soft white
vellum 70#, Allan & Gray
Holy Cats: 11 special stocks
manufactured by Hazen
Paper Co. for Alan & Gray
Slipcase Designer:
Yolanda Cuomo
Slipcase Manufacturer:
DeRidder Inc.

Book Title:
Halloween ABC
Author:
Eve Merriam
Art Director:
Cecilia Yung
Designers:
Cecilia Yung and Lynne
Arany
Illustrator:
Lane Smith
Publisher:
Macmillan Publishing Co.
New York, NY
Typographer:
Vulcan Typography Co.
Printer:
South China Printing Co.
Production Manager:
Lottie L. Gooding
Paper:
Matte Art 86#
Binder:
South China Printing Co.
Jacket Designer:
Lynne Arany
Jacket Illustrator:
Lane Smith

Book Title:
Jazz: Photographs by
William Claxton
Authors:
Terry Southern, Leonard
Feather, and William
Claxton
Designer:
Jack Woody
Photographer:
William Claxton
Publisher:
Twelvetrees Press
Pasadena, CA
Typographer:
Patrick Reagh
Printer:
Toppan Printing Co., Ltd.
Production Manager:
Jack Woody
Binder:
Toppan Printing Co., Ltd.
Jacket Designer:
Jack Woody
Jacket Photographer:
William Claxton

Book Title:
Lost Hollywood
Author:
Jack Woody
Designer:
Jack Woody
Photographers:
Various
Publisher:
Twin Palms Publishers
Altadena, CA
Typographer:
Patrick Reagh
Printer:
Toppan Printing Co., Ltd.
Production Manager:
Jack Woody
Binder:
Toppan Printing Co., Ltd.
Jacket Designer:
Jack Woody
Jacket Photographer:
Ruth Harriett Louise

Book Title:
I Want a Dog
Author:
Dayal Kaur Khalsa
Art Director:
Gael Towey
Designer:
Karen Katz
Illustrator:
Dayal Kaur Khalsa
Publisher:
Clarkson N. Potter/Crown
Publishers, Inc.
New York, NY
Typographer:
Images
Printer:
Toppan Printing Co., Inc.
Production Manager:
Milton Wackerow
Paper:
Matte coated 86#
Binder:
Toppan Printing Co., Inc.
Jacket Designer:
Karen Katz
Jacket Illustrator:
Dayal Kaur Khalsa

Book Title:
Animal Numbers
Author:
Bert Kitchen
Art Director:
Atha Tehon
Designers:
Bert Kitchen and Atha
Tehon
Illustrator:
Bert Kitchen
Publisher:
Dial Books
New York, NY
Printer:
Van Den Bossche
Production Manager:
Shari Lichtner
Paper:
Smooth white matte coated
cartridge 135 gsm
Jacket Designer:
Atha Tehon
Jacket Illustrator:
Bert Kitchen

Book Title:
Read Yourself Raw
Authors:
Art Spiegelman and
Françoise Mouly
Art Director:
Louise Fili
Designers:
Art Spiegelman and
Françoise Mouly
Illustrator:
Various
Publisher:
Pantheon Books
New York, NY
Typographer:
Maxwell
Typographers
Printer:
MJR Graphics
**Production
Managers:**
Marlene Zack and
Kathleen Grasso
Paper:
Landmark 70#
Binder:
MJR Graphics
Jacket Designer:
Art Spiegelman
Jacket Illustrator:
Art Spiegelman

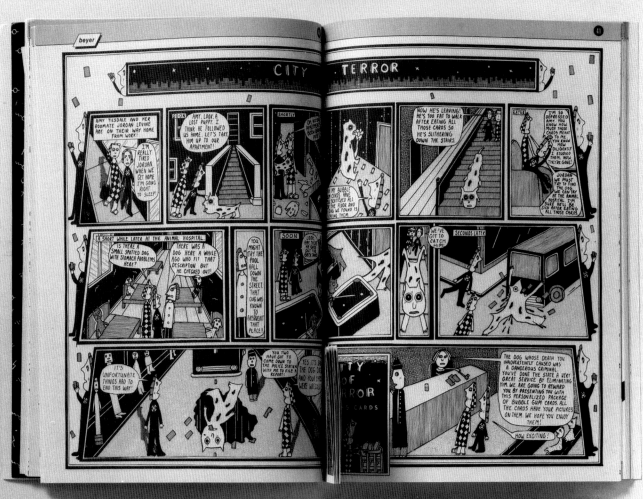

Book Title:
Agony
Author:
Mark Beyer
Art Director:
Louise Fili
Designers:
Art Spiegelman and
Françoise Mouly
Illustrator:
Mark Beyer
Publisher:
Pantheon Books
New York, NY
Typographer:
Images
Printer:
Kingsport Press
Production Managers:
Diane Ward and Kathleen
Grasso
Paper:
Alpine Opaque 70#
Binder:
Kingsport Press
Jacket Designer:
Art Spiegelman
Jacket Illustrator:
Mark Beyer
Jacket Letterer:
Tony Di Spigna

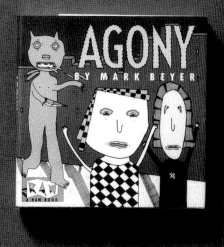

Book Title:
Agony
Author:
Mark Beyer
Art Director:
Louise Fili
Designers:
Art Spiegelman and
Françoise Mouly
Illustrator:
Mark Beyer
Publisher:
Pantheon Books
New York, NY
Typographer:
Images
Printer:
Kingsport Press
Production Managers:
Diane Ward and Kathleen

Book Title:
The Birthday Party Book
Author:
Jeremy Sage
Art Director/Designer:
Gael Towey
Illustrator:
Steven Guarnaccia
Letterer:
Steven Guarnaccia
Publisher:
Clarkson N. Potter/Crown
Publishers, Inc.
New York, NY
Typographer:
TGA Communications
Printer:
The Murray Printing Co.
Production Manager:
Kay Riley
Paper:
P & S Offset 70#
Binder:
The Murray Printing Co.
Jacket Designer:
Gael Towey
Jacket Illustrator:
Steven Guarnaccia

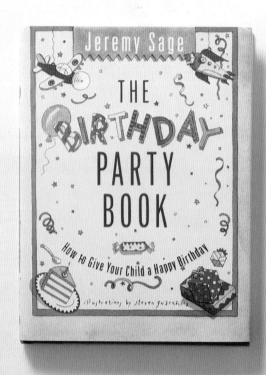

Book Title:
Sam's Bar: An American
Landscape
Author:
Donald Barthelme
Art Director/Designer:
Seymour Chwast
Illustrator:
Seymour Chwast
Publisher:
Dolphin Doubleday
New York, NY
Typographer:
Granite Graphics
Jacket Designer:
Seymour Chwast
Jacket Illustrator:
Seymour Chwast

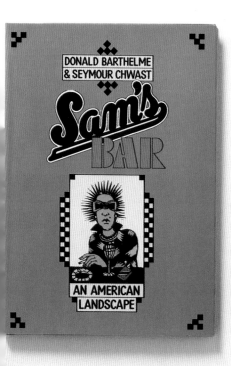

Book Title:
Stay Up Late
Author:
David Byrne
Art Director:
Tibor Kalman
Designers:
Maira Kalman, Tim Horn,
and Tibor Kalman
Illustrator:
Maira Kalman
Publisher:
Viking Penguin, Inc.
New York, NY
Typographer:
Trufont Typographers
Printer:
Dai Nippon Printing Co.,
Ltd.
Production Managers:
Liz Walker and Lisa Lenovitz
Jacket Designers:
Maira Kalman and Tibor
Kalman
Letterer:
Maira Kalman
Jacket Letterer:
Maira Kalman

Book Title:
The Book of Adam to Moses

Author:
Lore Segal

Art Director/Designer:
Denise Cronin

Illustrator:
Leonard Baskin

Publisher:
Alfred A. Knopf Books for Young Readers
New York, NY

Typographer:
Maryland Linotype Composition Co.

Printer:
Arcata Graphics Co./Kingsport Press

Production Manager:
Norann Systma

Paper:
Mohawk Vellum warm white 70#

Binder:
Arcata Graphics Co./Kingsport Press

Jacket Designer:
Denise Cronin

Jacket Illustrator:
Leonard Baskin

Book Title:
The Mountains of Quilt
Author:
Nancy Willard
Art Director:
Joy Chu
Designer:
Dalie Hartman
Illustrator:
Tomie dePaola
Publisher:
Harcourt Brace Jovanovich,
Publishers
San Diego, CA
Typographer:
Central Graphics
Printer:
Tien Wah Press (Pte.) Ltd.
Production Managers:
Eileen McGlone and
Rebecca Miller
Paper:
Matte Art 115 gsm
Binder:
Tien Wah Press (Pte.) Ltd.
Jacket Designer:
Dalia Hartman
Jacket Illustrator:
Tomie dePaola

Book Title:
Little Nino's Pizzeria
Author:
Karen Barbour
Art Director/Designer:
Joy Chu
Illustrator:
Karen Barbour
Publisher:
Harcourt Brace Jovanovich,
Publishers
San Diego, CA
Typographer:
Thompson Type
Printer:
Horowitz/Rae Book
Manufacturers, Inc.
Production Managers:
Warren Wallerstein and
Eileen McGlone
Paper:
White Karma text 80#
Binder:
Horowitz/Rae Book
Manufacturers, Inc.
Jacket Designer:
Joy Chu
Jacket Illustrator:
Karen Barbour

My dad, Nino, still makes the best pizza in the world.

But he changed the name of our restaurant.

CALL FOR ENTRIES · AIGA BOOK SHOW 1987 & BOOK JACKET & PAPERBACK COVERS SHOW 1984-87

Jacket Title:
Fantomas
Art Director:
Cheryl Asherman
Designer:
Fred Marcellino
Illustrator:
Fred Marcellino
New York, NY
Typographer:
The Type Shop
Publisher:
William Morrow
New York, NY

Jacket Title:
The Young Petrella
Art Director:
Joseph Montebello
Designer:
James Steinberg
Illustrator:
James Steinberg
Typographer:
Don Dewshap Typographic
Services, Inc.
Publisher:
Harper & Row
New York, NY

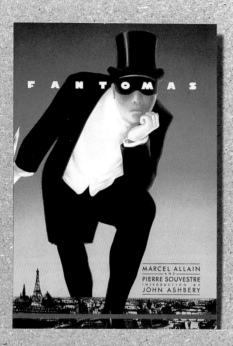

Jacket Title:
The Man Who Stole the
Mona Lisa
Art Director/Designer:
Louise Fili
Illustrator:
Dave Calver
Typographer:
Photo-Lettering
Publisher:
Pantheon Books
New York, NY
Printer:
The Longacre Press, Inc.

Jacket Title:
The Artful Egg
Art Director/Designer:
Louise Fili
Illustrator:
Robert Goldstrom
Typographers:
Louise Fili and Haber
Typographers
Publisher:
Pantheon Books
New York, NY
Printer:
The Longacre Press, Inc.

Jacket Title:
The Bonfire of the Vanities
Art Director:
Dorris Janowitz
Designer:
Fred Marcellino
Illustrator:
Fred Marcellino
New York, NY
Typographer:
The Type Shop
Publisher:
Farrar Straus Giroux
New York, NY

Jacket Title:
Big Foot Dreams
Art Director:
Louise Fili
Designer:
Fred Marcellino
Illustrator:
Fred Marcellino
New York, NY
Typographer:
The Type Shop
Publisher:
Pantheon Books
New York, NY

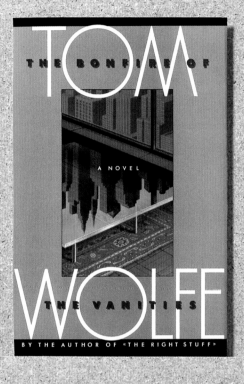

Jacket Title:
The Handmaid's Tale
Art Director:
Louise Noble
Designer:
Fred Marcellino
Illustrator:
Fred Marcellino
Typographer:
Letraset
Publisher:
Houghton Mifflin
Boston, MA
Printer:
Phoenix Color Corp.

Jacket Title:
Perfect Gallows
Art Director/Designer:
Louise Fili
Illustrator:
Robert Goldstrom
Typographer:
The Type Shop
Publisher:
Pantheon Books
New York, NY
Printer:
The Longacre Press, Inc.

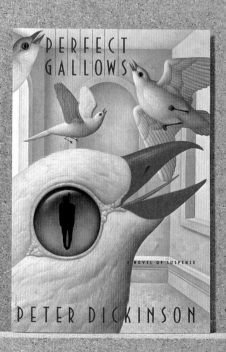

Jacket Title:
Sartre: A Biography
Art Director:
Frank Metz
Designer:
Carin Goldberg
Design Firm:
Carin Goldberg Design
New York, NY
Photographer:
Henri Cartier-Bresson
Typographer:
The Type Shop
Publisher:
Simon & Schuster
New York, NY
Printer:
The Longacre Press, Inc.

Jacket Title:
Sartre, A Life
Art Director/Designer:
Louise Fili
Photographer:
Brassaï
Typographer:
Photo-Lettering
Publisher:
Pantheon Books
New York, NY
Printer:
The Longacre Press, Inc.

Jacket Title:
Chroma
Art Director:
Frank Metz
Designer:
Louise Fili
Letterer:
Craig DeCamps
Typographer:
Louise Fili
Publisher:
Simon & Schuster
New York, NY
Printer:
The Longacre Press, Inc.

Cover Title:
Taking Care
Art Director:
Judith Loeser
Designer:
Lorraine Louie
New York, NY
Illustrator:
Rick Lovell
Typographer:
Boro Typographers
Publisher:
Vintage Contemporaries
New York, NY
Printer:
The Longacre Press, Inc.

Jacket Title:
Uncommon Wisdom
Art Director:
Frank Metz
Designer:
Paula Scher
Design Firm:
Koppel & Scher
New York, NY
Typographer:
The Type Shop
Publisher:
Simon & Schuster
New York, NY

Jacket Title:
By the Bomb's Early Light
Art Director/Designer:
Louise Fili
Photographer:
Fritz Goro
Typographer:
The Type Shop
Publisher:
Pantheon Books
New York, NY
Printer:
The Longacre Press, Inc.

Cover Title:
Where Water Comes
Together With Other Water
Art Director:
Judith Loeser
Designer:
Carin Goldberg
Illustrator:
Gene Greif
Typographer:
The Type Shop
Publisher:
Vintage Books
New York, NY
Printer:
Phoenix Color Corp.

Jacket Title:
The Lover
Art Director/Designer:
Louise Fili
Letterer:
Craig DeCamps
Typographer:
Louise Fili
Publisher:
Pantheon Books
New York, NY
Printer:
The Longacre Press, Inc.

Cover Title:
[illegible]

Art Director:
Joseph Montebello

Designers:
Paul Davis and
Jeanine Esposito

Illustrator:
Paul Davis

Design Firm:
Paul Davis Studio
New York, NY

Letterer:
Paul Davis

Publisher:
Harper & Row
New York, NY

Printer:
Murray Printing Co

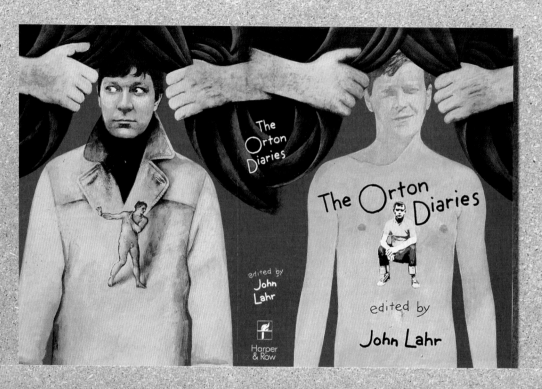

Cover Title:
Futurist Performance

Art Director:
Steven Hoffman
New York, NY

Designer:
Steven Hoffman

Publisher:
PAJ Publications

Cover Title:
Ship to Shore

Art Director:
J.C. Suares

Designer:
Rita Marshall
Lakeville, CT

Illustrator:
Étienne Delessert

Typographer:
Dix Type

Publisher:
Prentice-Hall Press

Printer:
Phoenix Color Corp.

Cover Title:
Graphic Artists Guild
Pricing and Ethical
Guidelines Handbook, 6th
Edition
Art Director:
Simms Taback
New York, NY
Designer:
Michael Doret
Letterer:
Michael Doret
Publisher:
Graphic Artists Guild
New York, NY
Printer:
Zarett Graphics, Inc.

Cover Title:
The Food Lover's Guide to
Paris
Art Director:
Paul Hanson
Designer:
Susan Aronson Stirling
Photographer:
Robert Freson
Publisher:
Workman Publishing Co.
New York, NY
Printer:
Lehigh Press Lithographers

Jacket Title:
Japanese Tales
Art Director/Designer:
Louise Fili
Illustrator:
Melanie Marder Parks
Typographer:
Photo-Lettering
Publisher:
Pantheon Books
New York, NY
Printer:
The Longacre Press, Inc.

Cover Title:
Japanese Vegetarian
Cooking
Art Director/Designer:
Louise Fili
Illustrator:
Philippe Weisbecker
New York, NY
Typographer:
Photo-Lettering
Publisher:
Pantheon Books
New York, NY
Printer:
The Longacre Press, Inc.

Cover Title:
Chanson DaDa
Art Director/Designer:
Gordon Robertson
Typographer:
The Coach House Press
Publisher:
The Coach House Press
Toronto, CAN
Printer:
The Coach House Press

Jacket Title:
An Adultery
Art Director:
Frank Metz
Designer:
Paula Scher
Design Firm:
Koppel & Scher
New York, NY
Typographer:
Collection of Paula Scher
Publisher:
Simon & Schuster
New York, NY

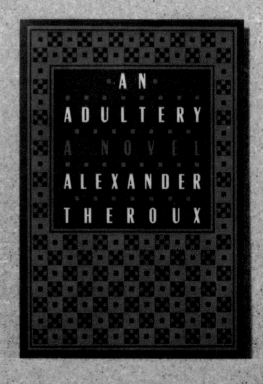

Cover Title:
Cooper's Creek
Art Director/Designer:
Robbin Schiff
Illustrator:
Ludwig Becker
Publisher:
Atlantic Monthly Press
New York, NY
Printer:
The Longacre Press, Inc.

Jacket Title:
Piazza Carignano
Art Director:
Char Lappan
Designer:
Louise Fili
Letterer:
Louise Fili
Publisher:
Atlantic Monthly Press
Printer:
The Longacre Press, Inc.

Jacket Title:
The Education of a Yankee
Art Director:
Joseph Montebello
Designer:
Julie Metz
Hand-Tinting Illustrator:
Dion Ogust
Typographer:
The Type Shop
Publisher:
Harper & Row Publishers
New York, NY
Printer:
The Longacre Press, Inc.

Jacket Title:
The Sergeant's Cat
Art Director:
Louise Fili
Designer:
Bascove
Illustrator:
Bascove
Letterer:
Bascove
Publisher:
Pantheon Books
New York, NY
Printer:
The Longacre Press, Inc.

Jacket Title:
Inner Tube
Art Director:
Sara Eisenman
Designer:
Marc Cohen
Illustrator:
Marc Cohen
Letterer:
Marc Cohen
Publisher:
Alfred A. Knopf, Inc.
New York, NY

Cover Title:
Women of the Left Bank
Art Director:
George Lenox
Designer:
Carolyn Baker
Illustrator:
Carolyn Baker

Typographer:
G & S Typesetters, Inc.
Publisher:
University of Texas Press
Austin, TX
Printer:
University of Texas Printing
Division

Jacket Title:
Fit for America
Art Director:
Louise Fili
Designer:
John Craig
Illustrator:
John Craig
Letterer:
John Craig
Publisher:
Pantheon Books
New York, NY
Printer:
The Longacre Press, Inc.

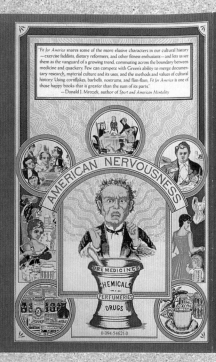
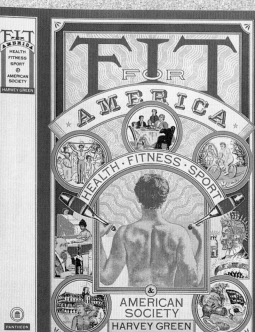

(continued from front flap)
whose symptoms included insomnia, sweaty hands, headaches, and hopelessness. Soldiers in the war on debility included not just athletes and doctors but real-estate developers, dress designers, ad men, and religious reformers. They sought to remedy the maladies of contemporary life by running magnetic currents through the body; redesigning bedrooms, bathtubs, and corsets; and alternately prescribing and proscribing fresh air, red meat, coal burners, spicy foods, indoor plumbing, and professional sports.

Harvey Green has searched out tales of America's first bodybuilders and bicycle racers, anecdotes in the annals of vegetarianism and diet reform, and even accounts of nineteenth-century corporate fitness programs—all of which add up to an astonishing picture of a population nervously tuned in to the competitive tasks, physical and mental, of the twentieth century. Heeding the sermons of the precursors to Jane Fonda, Jane Brody, and Jack La Lanne, an anxious America reshaped its body, its habits, and its attitudes with a careful eye to maintaining its tradition of superiority, individual and national—and went on to breed the generation that pounds the floors of aerobic studios today.

Harvey Green is deputy director for interpretation at the Strong Museum, in Rochester, New York. He has a B.A. from the University of Rochester, an M.A. and a Ph.D. from Rutgers University. He is the author of *The Light of the Home* ("This examination of nineteenth-century women is as interesting as the humor and persistence with which he links his Victorian subjects with the women of our day."—*Washington Post Book World*). He lives with his wife, Susan Williams, and their two dogs, Sparky and Zoe, in Palmyra, New York.

Jacket illustration and design by John Craig
Pantheon Books, New York

4/86 Printed in the U.S.A. © 1986 Random House, Inc.

Fit for America snares some of the more elusive characters in our cultural history—exercise faddists, dietary reformers, and other fitness enthusiasts—and lets us see them as the vanguard of a growing trend, commuting across the boundary between medicine and quackery. Few can compete with Green's ability to merge documentary research, material culture and its uses, and the methods and values of cultural history. Using cornflakes, barbells, nostrums, and flim-flam, *Fit for America* is one of those happy books that is greater than the sum of its parts.
—Donald J. Mrozek, author of *Sport and American Mentality*

FIT AMERICA
HEALTH FITNESS SPORT & AMERICAN SOCIETY
HARVEY GREEN

FIT FOR AMERICA
HEALTH · FITNESS · SPORT
& AMERICAN SOCIETY
HARVEY GREEN

PANTHEON

FPT $24.95

"An entertaining work of originality and synthesis, *Fit for America* highlights middle-class America's ongoing search for physical health and its connection to the tension between the pursuit of individual self-interest and the preservation of the Republic. Whether describing the 'Moses of Mastication' or 'American Nervousness,' Green tells the story well."
—Peter Levine,
Professor of History,
Michigan State University

Today's obsession with health and fitness is nothing new, as we see in this wry investigation of the way Americans have regarded, altered, healed, and preserved their bodies for over a century. Aerobics, weight-lifting, "health food" and holistic healing, and other familiar strategies to perfect the human machinery have been around for over a hundred years—marketed through ingenious ploys by men like fitness czars Charles Atlas and Sylvester Graham (of cracker fame), cereal barons C. W. Post and the Kellogg brothers, and the indefatigable Horace Fletcher, America's high priest of chewing. Harvey Green's intriguing account of the attempts by these and other visionaries, reformers, and entrepreneurs to get America in shape for the twentieth century also explores how consumerism and marketing techniques developed, how our notions about gender, race, sex, and beauty evolved, and why we remain so obsessed by the pursuit of the perfect body today.

Fit for America opens as the United States is on the brink of the modern age and (in the mind of reformers, at least) in peril of its very mortal body and soul. A once-pure nation was now choking on city air, in thrall to labor-saving technology, and genocidally plagued by the new and pernicious diseases of the "brain-worker,"

(continued on back flap)

Jacket Title:
No Pain, No Gain
Art Director:
Steven Guarnaccia
Designers:
Steven Guarnaccia and
Michael Klein
New York, NY
Illustrator:
Michael Klein
Publisher:
The Rosen Publishing
Group, Inc.
New York, NY
Printer:
Oceanic Graphic Printing
Productions

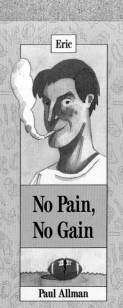

Eric

No Pain,
No Gain

Paul Allman

ROSEN
No Pain, No Gain

Jacket Title:
Savory Suppers and
Fashionable Feasts
Art Director:
Louise Fili
Designer:
John Craig
Illustrator:
John Craig
Typographer:
Solo Type
Publisher:
Pantheon Books
New York, NY
Printer:
The Longacre Press, Inc.

Jacket Title:
Elementary Education
Art Director:
Sara Eisenman
Designers:
Susan Hochbaum and
Steven Guarnaccia
New York, NY
Illustrator:
Steven Guarnaccia
Typographer:
Paragon Typographics
Publisher:
Alfred A. Knopf, Inc.
New York, NY
Printer:
The Longacre Press, Inc.

Jacket Title:
The Character Factory
Art Director:
Louise Fili
Designer:
Phil Huling
Illustrator:
Phil Huling
Letterer:
Phil Huling
Publisher:
Pantheon Books
New York, NY
Printer:
The Longacre Press, Inc.

Jacket Title:
A Scrap of Time
Art Director/Designer:
Louise Fili
Illustrator:
Anthony Russo
Typographer:
Photo-Lettering
Publisher:
Pantheon Books
New York, NY
Printer:
The Longacre Press, Inc.

Cover Title:
Groucho Letters
Art Director:
Stacey Holston
Designer:
Jackie Seow
New York, NY
Photographer:
Bettmann Archives
Typographer:
Images Typographers
Publisher:
Fireside Books
New York, NY
Printer:
The Longacre Press, Inc.

Jacket Title:
Behind the Front Page
Art Director:
Frank Metz
Designer:
Robert Anthony
Photographer:
Irv Bahrt
Typographer:
MKP
Publisher:
Simon & Schuster
New York, NY
Printer:
New England Book Co.

Jacket Title:
Julia Paradise
Art Director:
Frank Metz
Designer:
Louise Fili
New York, NY
Photographer:
Bettmann Archive
Letterer:
Louise Fili
Publisher:
Simon & Schuster
New York, NY
Printer:
The Longacre Press, Inc.

Cover Title:
Madam I'm Adam
Art Director:
Ruth Colbert
Designer:
Susan Hochbaum
Illustrator:
Steven Guarnaccia
New York, NY
Typographer:
Typogram and Paragon
Typographics
Publisher:
Charles Scribner's Sons
Publishers
New York, NY
Printer:
R.R. Donnelley & Sons Co.

Jacket Title:
Journey to the East
Art Director:
Diane Jaroch
Designer:
Julie Simms
Illustrator:
Le Corbusier
Typographer:
DEKR Corp.
Publisher:
The MIT Press
Cambridge, MA
Printer:
Henry Sawyer & Co.

Cover Title:
Aventura Series: Maira, The
Four Wise Men, We Love
Glenda So Much,
Correction

Art Directors:
Keith Sheridan and Judy
Loeser

Designer:
Keith Sheridan

Illustrators:
Melanie Marder Parks, Anita
Kunz, Bascove, and
Marshall Arisman

Design Firm:
Keith Sheridan Assoc., Inc.
New York, NY

Letterer:
Craig Warner

Typographer:
Haber Typographers, Inc.

Publisher:
Random House, Inc.

Printer:
The Longacre Press, Inc.

Cover Title:
Vintage Master Musicians:
Wagner, Bach, Dufay

Art Director:
Judith Loeser

Designer:
Carin Goldberg

Illustrators:
Various

Typographer:
The Type Shop

Publisher:
Vintage Books
New York, NY

Printer:
Coral Graphics, Inc.

DARCY RIBEIRO

MAÍRA

'One of the most delicious novels to have appeared
in Brazil in modern times....its lyrical passages read like
Song of Songs'—Jornal do Brasil

A

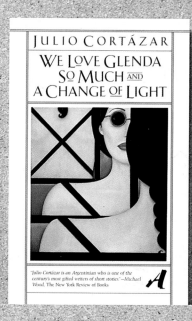

JULIO CORTÁZAR

WE LOVE GLENDA SO MUCH AND A CHANGE OF LIGHT

'Julio Cortázar is an Argentinian who is one of the
century's most gifted writers of short stories'—Michael
Wood, The New York Review of Books

A

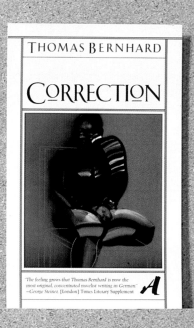

THOMAS BERNHARD

CORRECTION

'The feeling grows that Thomas Bernhard is now the
most original, concentrated novelist writing in German'
—George Steiner, [London] Times Literary Supplement

A

WAGNER

"An account of the
composer's life and
career which is as
close to the truth as
we are currently
able to get."
—Classical Music

VINTAGE
MASTER
MUSICIANS

BARRY MILLINGTON

BACH

"An excellent guide
for the amateur
Bach lover, the
professional
musician and the
musicological
researcher."
—British
Book News

VINTAGE
MASTER
MUSICIANS

MALCOLM BOYD

Jacket Title:
Taormina/Wilhelm Von
Gloeden
Designer:
Jack Woody
Photographer:
Wilhelm Von Gloeden
Publisher:
Twelvetrees Press
Altadena, CA
Typographer:
Typeworks
Printer:
Typecraft

W I L H E L M   V O N   G L O E D E N

T A O R M I N A

W I L H E L M   V O N   G L O E D E N

Jacket Title:
Robert Mapplethorpe:
Certain People
Designers:
Jack Woody and Dimitri
Levas
Photographer:
Robert Mapplethorpe
Publisher:
Twelvetrees Press
Altadena, CA
Typographer:
Typeworks
Printer:
Toppan Printing Co., Ltd.

Jacket Title:
Agony
Art Director:
Louise Fili
Designer:
Art Spiegelman
Illustrator:
Mark Beyer
Letterer:
Tony DiSpigna
Typographer:
The Type Shop
Publisher:
Pantheon Books
New York, NY
Printer:
Coral Graphics, Inc.

Jacket Title:
De Stijl
Art Director:
Diana Jaroch
Designer:
Julie Simms
Typographer:
DEKR Corp
Publisher:
The MIT Press
Cambridge, MA
Printer:
Mark Burton Printers

Doesburg became the leading figure and opened
up the magazine to a more international circle of
contributors).

Each of the nine chapters discusses an
individual artist—four are painters (van
Doesburg, Vilmos Huszár, Bart van der Leck,
Mondrian), four are architects (Robert van 't
Hoff, Oud, Gerrit Rietveld, and Jan Wils), and
one is a sculptor (Georges Vantongerloo). The
authors consider what each artist, on the basis of
his prior training and development, contributed
to De Stijl, and also what distinguished each of
them from the others. And they take up a
number of other important themes, including
the relation between the abstract work of art
and the visible reality, the use of color and form
(why and indeed whether the De Stijl artists
were committed to using primary colors and
rectilinear forms, for example), and the influence
of Frank Lloyd Wright (who received his first
critical accolades in the Netherlands).

Carel Blotkamp, who wrote the introduction
and the chapter on van Doesburg, is Professor of
Art History at the Free University of
Amsterdam.

jacket photograph:
Georges Vantongerloo, *Triptiek* (1921).

Of related interest

The MIT Press
Massachusetts Institute of Technology
Cambridge, Massachusetts 02142

The De Stijl Environment
by Nancy J. Troy

"A splendid volume of De Stijl literature."
Suzanne Frank, *Progressive Architecture*

"Nancy Troy offers a brilliant analysis of De Stijl theory and practice that will add immeasurably to our
understanding of one of the most significant movements in twentieth-century art. She provides new information about the impact of De Stijl on architecture and interior design and tackles with gusto the critical issues
artistic collaboration among the members of this seminal Dutch group. Her book will be eagerly read by
everyone interested in the genesis of modern ideas about space and formal abstraction."
Helen Searing, Smith College

The Amsterdam School
Dutch Expressionist Architecture, 1915–1930
edited by Wim de Wit

Led by the talented Michel de Klerk, the Amsterdam School produced some of the most original and avant-
garde movements in the halcyon days of post–World War I modernism. This book documents all the School's
major projects, from renderings of furniture and interiors to completed buildings.

BLODH 0-262-0224-

Cover Title:
Read Yourself Raw
Art Director:
Louise Fili
Designer:
Art Spiegelman
Illustrator:
Art Spiegelman
Design Firm:
Raw Books
Letterer:
Vladimir Studio
Publisher:
Pantheon Books
New York, NY

RAW is
unReasonable
unAssimilated and
unWavering

RAW is
Refined, Angry, and Wired
Radiant, Antagonistic,
and Wary
Radioactive, Alive, and Warm

RAW is
A Rhythmic Abstract
Whimper
A Ruthless Affectionate
Weapon
A Rectangular Accusatory
Window

RAW isn't
Interested in New Waves or
Old Waves
RAW is interested in
Permanent Waves

Now, *Read Yourself Raw* brings
back the best of the long-out-
of-print first three issues of
RAW, the magazine that first
published Art Spiegelman's
Maus. Here are the golden old-
ies of "New Wave" cartooning
in a stunningly reproduced new
anthology with: the full-color
covers of each issue; Art Spiegelman's *Two-Fisted Painters*
all-color comic; Mark Beyer's
City of Terror bubble–gum
cards; Gary Panter's dazed
punkabilly *Jimbo* strips;
Charles Burns's *Dogboy*; José
Muñoz's and Jacques Tardi's
hard-edged cartoon *noir* city-
scapes, and a host of other
startling and intriguing picture
stories.

For those who remember, for
those who are just discovering
how new the world of comics
can really be, *Read Yourself
Raw* is a book not to miss.

"*RAW* will rearrange your head…"

"The hippest, artiest, and most intense of the New Comix publications."

"A magazine of visual literature, occupying new terrain outside the comic book
art world."

"The best-looking satire magazine in the country today."

Pantheon Books, New York

0-394-75551-0

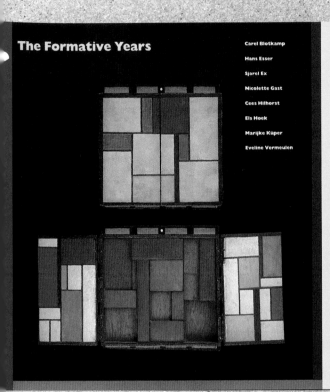

The Formative Years

Carel Blotkamp

Hans Esser

Sjarel Ex

Nicolette Gast

Cees Hilhorst

Els Hoek

Marijke Küper

Eveline Vermeulen

$45.00

De Stijl: The Formative Years
by Carel Blotkamp, Hans Esser, Sjarel Ex,
Nicolette Gast, Cees Hilhorst, Els Hoek, Marijke
Küper, and Eveline Vermeulen
translated by Charlotte I. Loeb and Arthur L. Loeb

"Based upon their extensive research in
previously inaccessible archival resources, the
authors provide a cogent and detailed analysis of
the early work and development of the De Stijl
group, whose complex personal and professional
relationships are here thoroughly examined
for the first time. The wealth of new visual and
documentary material this study presents
will insure its lasting value in the literature about
De Stijl."
Nancy J. Troy, Northwestern University

These nine essays underscore the fact that De
Stijl was first and foremost a periodical, not a
group. Marshaling new evidence drawn from
previously untapped Dutch sources, the authors
suggest—and, to a large extent, prove—that
only in the minds of critics did De Stijl ever
constitute a movement. What emerges is a more
biographically vivid and pluralist view of De Stijl
in the important early period of its development
than any of De Stijl's previous historians have
provided.

The Dutch magazine *De Stijl*, published from
1917 to 1928 with a final commemorative
number issued in 1932, was the focus of a
remarkable group of artists and architects who
sought to integrate painting with architecture,
sculpture, and graphic design, and who had a
significant influence on contemporary
architecture and design.

Whereas most books emphasize De Stijl as a
collaborative movement, these writings—
augmented by over 260 illustrations—
concentrate on the specific works and the
temperaments, practices, and visions of the
various artists and architects. They reveal
fundamental differences in the aesthetic bearings
of the artists who formed the magazine's
identity, and they establish that a major
discontinuity appeared around 1922 (the end of
the period in which De Stijl was dominated by
Piet Mondrian, Theo van Doesburg, and J. J. P.
Oud and the start of the period in which van

READ YOURSELF

RAW

PAGES FROM
THE RARE
FIRST 3 ISSUES
OF THE COMICS
MAGAZINE FOR
DAMNED
INTELLECTUALS!

CITY
OF
TERROR

EDITED BY ART SPIEGELMAN AND FRANÇOISE MOULY

Cover Title:
Vintage Contemporary
Artists Originals Series:
Clemente, Fischl, Salle
Art Director:
Elizabeth Avedon
Designer:
Elizabeth Avedon
Photographer:
Richard Avedon

Typographer:
Typographic Images, Inc.
Publisher:
Vintage Books
New York, NY
Printer:
Coral Graphics, Inc.

Jacket Title:
Pantheon Modern Writers:
The Woman Destroyed:
Simone de Beauvoir; The
War Diaries: Jean-Paul
Sartre; The Assault: Harry
Mulisch
Art Director/Designer:
Louise Fili
Photographers:
Various

Hand-Tinting Illustrator:
Christine Rodin
Typographer:
Haber Typographers
Publisher:
Pantheon Books
New York, NY
Printer:
The Longacre Press, Inc.

SCHL

CLEMENTE

CLEMENTE

CLEMENTE

CLEMENTE | GORE | WASH

ANSORY / VINTAGE

ISBN 0-394-74787-9

JEAN-PAUL SARTRE

THE WAR DIARIES
NOVEMBER 1939 – MARCH 1940

"An extraordinary book.
His mental agility here.....is dazzling."
Alfred Kazin

Pantheon Modern Writers

Fiction $7.95

These three long stories draw us into the lives of
three women, all past their first youth, all facing
unexpected crises. In the title story, the heroine's
serenity is shattered when she learns that her
husband is having an affair. In "The Age of
Discretion," a successful, happily married professor finds herself increasingly distressed by her
son's absorption in his young wife and her
worldly values. In "The Monologue," a rich,
spoiled woman, home alone on New Year's Eve,
pours out a lifetime's rage and frustration in a
harrowing diatribe. Enthralling as fiction, suf-
fused with de Beauvoir's remarkable insights
into women, *The Woman Destroyed* gives us a
legendary writer at her best.

. . . .

"Witty, immensely adroit....These three women
are believable individuals presented with a wry
mixture of sympathy and exasperation."
—The Atlantic

"A remarkable feat of empathy."
—Times Literary Supplement

"Brilliant craftsmanship."   —Harper's

. . . .

Born in Paris in 1909, Simone de Beauvoir is
celebrated as novelist, feminist, and lifelong
companion to Jean-Paul Sartre. The author of
The Second Sex, *The Mandarins*, and many
other books, she died in 1986.

Cover photograph by Christine Rodin
Cover design by Louise Fili

Pantheon Books, New York

1187 Printed in the U.S.A. ©1987 Random House, Inc.

0-394-71103-3

DE BEAUVOIR : THE WOMAN DESTROYED : PANTHEON

SIMONE DE BEAUVOIR

THE WOMAN DESTROYED

"Immensely intelligent stories about
the decay of passion."
London Sunday Times

Pantheon Modern Writers

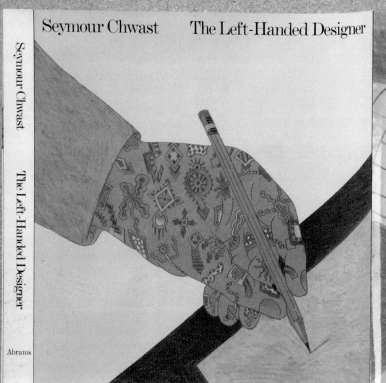

Jacket Title:
The Left-Handed Designer
Art Director/Designer:
Seymour Chwast
New York, NY
Illustrator:
Seymour Chwast
Typographer:
Concept Typography
Service, Inc.
Publisher:
Harry N. Abrams, Inc.
New York, NY

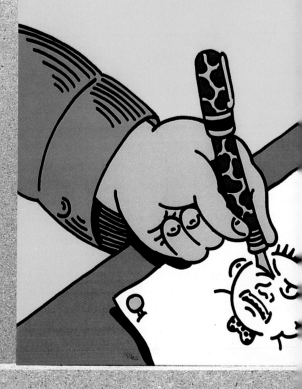

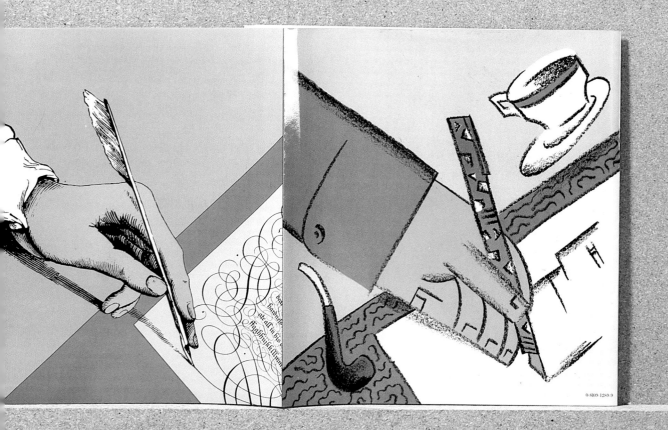

Jacket Title:
Psychology: Perspectives
on Behavior
Art Director/Designer:
Karin Gerdes Kincheloe
Illustrator:
Roy Wiemann
Typographer:
Exper-Type
Publisher:
John Wiley & Sons
New York, NY
Printer:
Phoenix Color Corp.

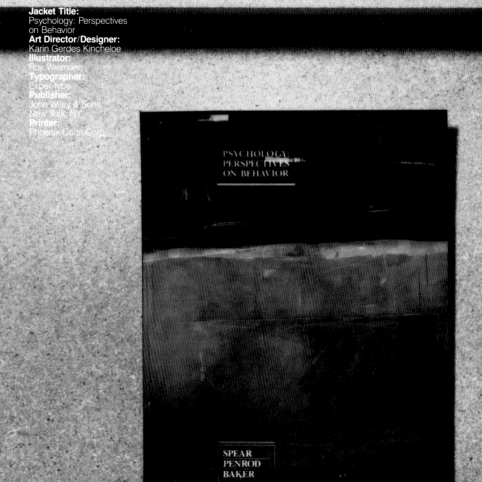

Jacket Title:
Houses of Glass
Art Director:
Diane Jaroch
Designer:
Rebecca Daw
Hand-Tinting Illustrator:
Rebecca Daw
Typographer:
DEKR Corp.
Publisher:
The MIT Press
Cambridge, MA
Printer:
Henry Sawyer & Co.

Jacket Title:
Dear Diego
Art Director/Designer:
Louise Fili
Typographer:
Louise Fili
Publisher:
Pantheon Books
New York, NY
Printer:
The Longacre Press, Inc.

Jacket Title:
He Got Hungry and Forgot
His Manners
Art Director:
Louise Noble
Designer:
Seymour Chwast
Illustrator:
Seymour Chwast
Design Firm:
The Pushpin Group
New York, NY
Letterer:
Seymour Chwast
Publisher:
Ticknor & Fields
New York, NY
Printer:
John P. Pow Co.

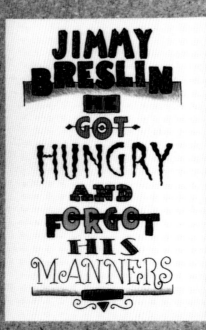

Jacket Title:
Once in Europa
Art Director:
Louise Fili
Designer:
Dugald Stermer
Illustrator:
Dugald Stermer
Letterer:
Dugald Stermer
Publisher:
Pantheon Books
New York, NY
Printer:
The Longacre Press, Inc.

Jacket Title:
The Seven Ages
Art Director:
Louise Fili
Designer:
Dugald Stermer
Illustrator:
Dugald Stermer
Letterer:
Dugald Stermer
Publisher:
Pantheon Books
New York, NY
Printer:
The Longacre Press, Inc.

Mikhail Anikst
Publisher:
Robert E. Abrams
Abbeville Press
New York, NY

Paul Browning and
Scott Taylor
Designer:
Diti Katona
Design Firm:
Taylor & Browning Design
Toronto, Canada
Illustrator:
Wendy Wortsman
Typographer:
XY Typesetting Services
Publisher:
Indecs Publishing Inc.
Canada
Printer:
Dai Nippon Printing Co.,
Ltd.

(Continued from front flap)

   This volume is not only compiled but also
designed by the distinguished Russian graphic artist
Mikhail Anikst. His aim is to recreate the period in all
its richness and variety by including both State and
private-sector commissions, in both new and more
traditional styles, from the provinces as well as from
Moscow: posters, book jackets, candy wrappers,
emblems, cigarette and matchboxes, and much
more. Very few of these items have ever been seen
before in published form.
   These advertisements, always powerful and
often humorous, evoke with great immediacy the
realities of the young Soviet State; they have also
stood the test of time as works of art in their own
right. The artistic energy of those years has
continued to influence generations of graphic
designers around the world.
   Soviet Commercial Design of the Twenties
should be read by anyone with a love of the truly
innovative in art and design.

With 323 illustrations, 211 in full color.

About the Authors

Mikhail Anikst was born in Moscow in 1938. After
training at the Moscow Architectural Institute, he
worked for a time as an architect before beginning
to design books and stage sets. One of the most
noted graphic designers in the Soviet Union, he has
worked on a wide variety of art books as well as
posters, logos and other graphics; he has also been
responsible for the design of several productions in
leading Moscow theaters. His many international and
Soviet awards include the honor of Best Book in the
World at the Leipzig Book Fair. He is a member of the
Soviet Union of Artists, and since 1976 he has been
the chief art director of the publishing house Soviet
Artist.

Elena Chernevich was born in Moscow in 1938.
Since 1964 she has specialized in the theory and
history of graphic design and is currently a lecturer
at the Faculty of the Artistic Design of Printed
Products of the Moscow Polygraphic Institute. Her
courses cover photographics, graphic design and the
development of the contemporary poster. She is a
member of the Soviet Union of Artists and
contributes frequently to anthologies and journals.

Write for a free catalog of books.

Abbeville Press
488 Madison Avenue
New York, N.Y. 10022

Jacket design by Mikhail Anikst

Printed in Singapore

ISBN 0-8965

**ПРОЧТИ
ЭТУ
КНИГУ**

A PUBLICATION OF
INDECS PUBLISHING INC.

ISBN 0-9697019-2-3
ISSN 0929-5298
PRINTED IN JAPAN

ISBN 0-9697019-2-3

272   Jackets and Covers

Soviet Commercial Design of the Twenties

Edited and designed by Mikhail Anikst
Introduction and texts by Elena Chernevich

The art of the Soviet avant-garde from the nineteen-twenties on is at last becoming known and its significance appreciated. This book, published with the unprecedented co-operation of the Soviet government, opens up one of the most visually compelling aspects of artistic culture soon after the Russian Revolution: advertising design.

Vladimir Mayakovsky's poster slogan — 'From the old world all that remains is Ira cigarettes' — was barely an exaggeration: after 1917, everything was different. This selection of vivid illustrations tellingly reflects the changes. It also reveals a lesser-known aspect of the young Soviet State — the allowance, under its New Economic Policy, of commercial competition in those momentous early years.

At that time, artists dedicated themselves to commercial graphic design with the same boldness they brought to all tasks of the new Soviet art, their advertisements for State products vying for attention with those of the private sector. The hundreds of striking designs reproduced here represent the work of figures who are long forgotten as well as legendary names such as Mayakovsky, Rodchenko and the leading Constructivists – Lissitzky, Gan, Stepanova and the Stenbergs.

(Continued on back flap)

Jacket Title:
Sondheim and Co.
Art Director:
Joseph Montebello
Designer:
Carin Goldberg
Illustrator:
Jean Tuttle
Design Firm:
Carin Goldberg Design
New York, NY

Typographer:
The Type Shop
Publisher:
Harper & Row
New York, NY.
Printer:
New England Book
Components

Jacket Title:
People Will Talk
Art Director:
Sara Eisenman
Designer:
Daniel Pelavin
New York, NY
Illustrator:
Daniel Pelavin
Letterer:
Daniel Pelavin
Typographer:
Boro Typographers
Publisher:
Alfred A. Knopf, Inc.
New York, NY

Jacket Title:
The Society of Mind
Art Director:
Frank Metz and Carin
Goldberg
Designer:
Carin Goldberg

Illustrator:
Eugene Mihaesco
Design Firm:
Carin Goldberg Design
New York, NY
Typographer:
The Type Shop

Publisher:
Simon & Schuster
New York, NY
Printer:
The Longacre Press, Inc.

Jacket Title:
The Day Room
Art Director:
Carol Devine Carson
Designer:
Chip Kidd
Photo Treatment:
Chip Kidd
Photographer:
Richard Feldman
Letterer:
Chip Kidd
Typographer:
Photo-Lettering
Publisher:
Alfred A. Knopf, Inc.
New York, NY
Printer:
Coral Graphics, Inc.

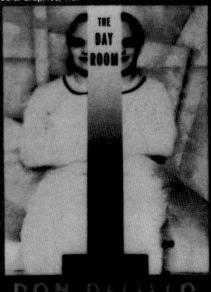

Cover Title:
Diana Cooper
Art Director:
Joseph Montebello
Designer:
Carin Goldberg
Typographer:
The Type Shop
Publisher:
Perennial Library/
Harper & Row Publishers
New York, NY
Printer:
The Longacre Press, Inc.

Jacket Title:
Debutante
Art Director:
Sara Eisenman
Designer:
Lorraine Louie
New York, NY
Photographer:
Horst
Letterer:
Daniel Pelavin

Publisher:
Alfred A. Knopf, Inc.
New York, NY
Printer:
Coral Graphics, Inc.

Cover Title:
The Hungarian Cookbook
Art Director:
Joseph Montebello
Designer:
Diana Cook
Illustrator:
Karen Baumann
Typographer:
All-American
Publisher:
Harper & Row Publishers
New York, NY
Printer:
Phoenix Color Corp.

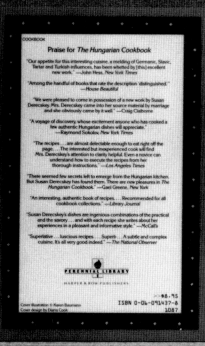

Design for the Public Good

When calling for entries for the "Design for the Public Good" competition, we intentionally cast a broad net in order to draw from as wide a cross-section of related design endeavors as possible. Works which pertained to advocacy of public causes or to non-profit or public-spirited events were obvious. However, we also felt that graphic work done for funding and promoting nonprofit or public institutions or for the benefit and enlightenment of the general public in its day-to-day activities was also within the parameters and spirit of the exhibition.

From the outset of the jury process, it was apparent that entries were unevenly dispersed among the possible categories. Work done for charitable organizations and events, or promoting colleges and universities and other nonprofit public institutions was abundant, while entries in areas such as advocacy or educational and informational graphics were sparse.

If we accept the mix of entries for the exhibition as an accurate indication of the design being done in these areas, it is amazing and alarming to find that in a time when there are many issues which threaten us and our planet, none has galvanized the design community as, for example, the Vietnam War did twenty years ago. This came as quite a surprise to the jury.

By any measure, the 95 pieces finally selected for the exhibition were rich, diverse, and consistently excellent. Unfortunately, their excellence is undercut somewhat by a narrower scope to the exhibit than had been anticipated and by the speculation as to the reasons why.

Lanny Sommese
Chairperson
Pennsylvania State University

DESIGN FOR THE PUBLIC GOOD
CALL FOR ENTRIES

Call for Entry:
Design for the Public Good
Design:
Kristin Breslin
Typographer:
Snavely Vidmar & Associates
Lithographer:
Nittany Valley Offset
Paper:
Butler Paper Co. and
Plainwell Paper Co.

Jury
Ralph Caplan
Freelance Writer and
Design Consultant

John Morning
President
John Morning Design

Leo Mullen
President
Invisions, Ltd.

Lanny Sommese
Professor and Head
of Graphic Design
Pennsylvania State University

Deborah Sussman
President
Sussman/Prejza & Co., Inc.

Alina R. Wheeler
Partner
Katz Wheeler Design

Artists:
Woody Pirtle and Jeff
Weithman
Design Firm/Agency:
Pirtle Design
Dallas, TX
Client:
Dallas Society of Visual
Communication
Typographer:
Southwestern Typographics
Printer:
Heritage Press

Could You?

It was a smashing year, all
right, but the challenge
isn't over. If PCA is to fully
realize its goal of becoming
the finest art college
anywhere, we still have a
job to do. Not just in terms
of the Bread and Pine
restoration but studios,
equipment, facilities and
faculty, making them
second to none.

But quality costs more.
Our 1982-83 Alumni Fund
goal is $75,000 by June 30.
A pretty tall order but we
think that PCA students,
and their importance to
the future, are worth it.

Take on the challenge with
us again. With your help
we can continue to build on
the artistic excellence that
is the hallmark of the
Philadelphia College of Art.

Thank You!

Client:
AIGA/Texas
Typographer:
Characters, Inc.
Printer:
Grover Printing Co.

Poster:
ArtXArchitecture
Art Director:
Michael Vanderbyl
Artist:
Michael Vanderbyl
Design Firm:
Vanderbyl Design
San Francisco, CA
Clients:
AIA, San Francisco and San
Francisco Museum of
Modern Art
Printer:
Seriphics

FROM SELF TO SHELF

How to develop your idea into a marketable product.

Bringing a product to market. If you've ever had a great idea, but didn't know how to get it off the ground, or even if you've just wanted more insight into the role design plays in the overall conception and marketing of a product, you'll benefit from AIGA/Texas' upcoming seminar, "From Self to Shelf". ◆ The day-long seminar will be on Saturday, February 28 at Innova Design Center in Houston. Three internationally recognized speakers will share their ideas about what makes an idea strong and how to make it marketable. ◆

ARTXARCHITECTURE

Heartbreak House

by George Bernard Shaw

directed by Alvin Epstein
September 16 – October 11, 1986

Yale Repertory Theatre

Lloyd Richards, Artistic Director
Corner of Chapel & York
New Haven, Connecticut
203/432-1234

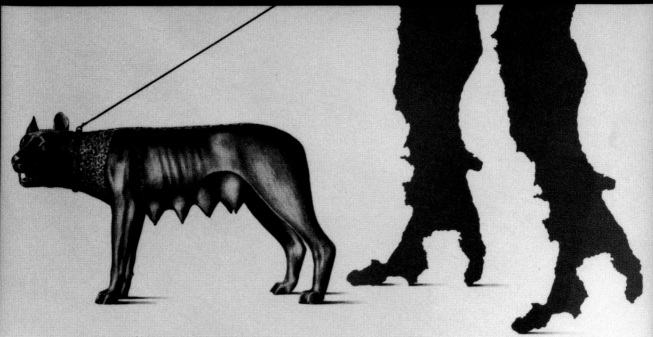

SUMMER ART IN ROME

Temple University
Tyler School of Art

Lynn Schulte and Joe Duffy
Design Firm:
The Duffy Design Group
Minneapolis, MN
Client:
First Tennessee Bank
Typographer:
Great Faces
Printer:
Litho Specialties

Poster:
Hoover Dam: Fiftieth
Anniversary
Art Directors:
Anderson/Mattos
Designers:
Mattos/Anderson
Artists:
Mattos/Anderson
Design Firm:
John Mattos Illustration
San Francisco, CA
Client:
Bechtel
Typographer:
Lance Anderson
Printer:
Redwood Litho

1935 1985
HOOVER DAM FIFTIETH ANNIVERSARY

Poster:
Prenez-Place
Art Director:
Gerard Bochud
Designers:
Jean-Marie Benoit, Martin
Beauvaise, and Jacques
Cournoyer
Design Firm:
Bretelle, UQAM
Montreal, CAN
Client:
Module de Sign Graphique
Typographer:
TAO, UQAM
Printer:
BCR Litho

Poster:
The Chair Fair
Art Director/Designer:
Milton Glaser
Artist:
Milton Glaser
Design Firm:
Milton Glaser, Inc.
New York, NY
Client:
The Architectural League of
New York

The Chair Fair

AN OPEN EXHIBITION OF CHAIRS DESIGNED DURING THE PAST TEN YEARS

Chairs are at once practical and metaphoric, everyday objects and expressions of individuality. The challenge of this program (inescapable size and a universal form) has attracted designers, architects, and others: how to combine performance and personality? Everyone wants to design a truly new chair, the "better mousetrap" of the design profession. *Call for Entries:* Chairs submitted by architects, designers, artists, manufacturers, craftspeople and others are welcome; maximum of three chairs per entrant. Chairs must be designed within the last ten years, and fit within a 3' x 3' footprint. A jury of distinguished designers and artists will choose winners in several categories.

Registration via the official entry form is mandatory by 1 October 1986. Please read the form carefully for complete rules and conditions of entry. If no forms are available, write or call.

The Architectural League of New York
457 Madison Avenue, New York, NY 10022
212/753-1722

Sponsored by The Architectural League of New York at the International Design Center, New York (IDCNY)
30-20 Thomson Avenue, Long Island City, New York

Exhibition open 10 November–6 December 1986

MADE POSSIBLE BY:

IDCNY
Osmose Corporation
Furniture Consultants, Inc.
Knoll International
Herman Miller, Inc.
Steelcase Inc.
Atelier International
The Gunlocke Company
Sunar Hauserman

JURORS:

Richard Artschwager, artist
Mario Bellini, architect and designer
Milton Glaser, designer
T. Merrill Prentice, Jr., sculptor and architect
Lella Vignelli, designer

Art Directors:
Clement Mok and Stephen
Sieler
Designer:
Stephen Sieler
Artist:
Brad Holland
Design Firm:
Apple Creative Services
Cupertino, CA
Client:
Apple Computer, Inc.

To an earthquake, nothing is sacred.

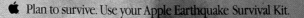

 Plan to survive. Use your Apple Earthquake Survival Kit.

Poster:
Endangered Cuban
Crocodile
Art Director:
Judy Kensley McKie
Artist:
Judy Kensley McKie
Design Firm:
The Graphic Workshop
Boston, MA
Publisher:
Judy Kensley McKie
Printer:
Orange Line Press

Poster:
An Evening with Bobby
Short
Art Director/Designer:
Malcolm Grear Designers
Artist:
Richard Merkin
Design Firm:
Malcolm Grear Designers
Providence, RI
Client:
Trinity Repertory Theater
Typographer:
Typesetting Service
Printer:
Bizzaro Screen Printers

eNDaNGered CubaN cr

Murkin

AN EVENING WITH
BOBBY SHORT
TRINITY REPERTORY
COMPANY
APRIL 22, 1985

Client:
The Museum of
Contemporary Art, Los
Angeles
Typographer:
Vernon Simpson
Printer:
Alan Lithograph Co.

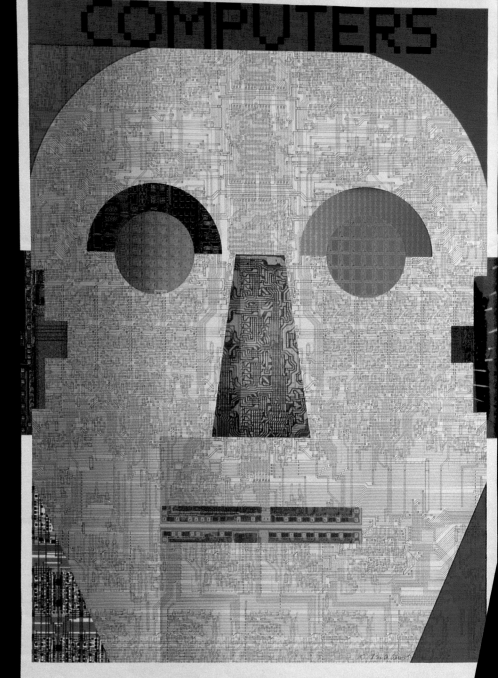

COME TOUCH TOMORROW 🖐 THE CALIFORNIA MUSEUM OF SCIENCE AND INDUST

THE MUSEUM OF CONTEMPORARY ART LOS ANGELES

Architect: Arata Isozaki

Poster:
Earth Zero
Art Director/Designer:
Malcolm Grear Designers
Design Firm:
Malcolm Grear Designers
Providence, RI
Client:
The Shoshin Society
Typographer:
Malcolm Grear Designers
Printer:
Bizzaro Screen Printers

Poster:
Peace
Art Director:
Ivan Chermayeff
Photographer:
Alan Shortall
Design Firm:
Chermayeff & Geismar
Assoc.
New York, NY
Client:
The Shoshin Society
Printer:
Virginia Lithograph Co.

Peace.

Poster:
1987 Italian Film Festival
Art Director:
Michael Osborne
Designers:
Michael Osborne and Bill
Reuter
Design Firm:
Michael Osborne Design,
Inc.
San Francisco, CA
Client:
College of Marin
Typographer:
Eurotype
Printer:
Seriphics

Poster:
Seton Cardiac Classic
April 5
Art Director:
Mike Hicks
Artist:
Michael Schwab
Design Firm:
HIXO, Inc.
Austin, TX
Client:
Seton Medical Center
Printer:
Mercury Art Editions

THE SETON CARDIAC CLASSIC. SUNDAY, APRIL 5, 1987 IN DOWNTOWN AUSTIN. THE LAST STAGE OF THE WORLD-CLASS BRANDERS JEANS TOUR OF TEXAS. BENEFITTING THE SETON CENTRAL TEXAS HEART INSTITUTE.

Poster:
Man of La Mancha
Art Director:
Ron Sullivan
Designers:
Linda Helton and Diana
McKnight
Artist:
Linda Helton
Design Firm:
Sullivan Perkins
Dallas, TX
Client:
Eastfield College Theatre
Typographer:
Robert J. Hilton
Typographers
Printer:
Williamson Printing Co.

Poster:
Unforgettable Fire/Drawings
from Hiroshima
Art Director:
Lisa DeFrancis
Design Firm:
DeFrancis Studio
Boston, MA
Client:
Massachusetts College of
Art
Typographer:
Monotype
Printer:
Meridian Printing

Poster:
Nuclear Disarmament
Art Director/Designer:
Rafal Olbinski
Artist:
Rafal Olbinski
Design Firm:
Rafal Olbinski Studio
Forest Hills, NY
Client:
American Peace
Typographer:
Rafal Olbinski
Printer:
Repro-Form

303

Poster:
War is Madness
Art Directors:
Seymour Chwast and
Charles Michael Helmken
Designer:
Seymour Chwast
Artist:
Seymour Chwast
Design Firm:
The Pushpin Group
New York, NY
Client:
The Shoshin Society

Poster:
American Museum of
Natural History
Art Director:
Ivan Chermayeff
Artist:
Ivan Chermayeff
Design Firm:
Chermayeff & Geismar
Assoc.
New York, NY
Client:
Mobil Corp.
Typographer:
Latent Lettering
Printer:
Crafton Graphic Co., Inc.

Poster:
War is Madness
Art Directors:
Seymour Chwast and
Charles Michael Helmken
Designer:
Seymour Chwast
Artist:
Seymour Chwast
Design Firm:
The Pushpin Group
New York, NY
Client:
The Shoshin Society

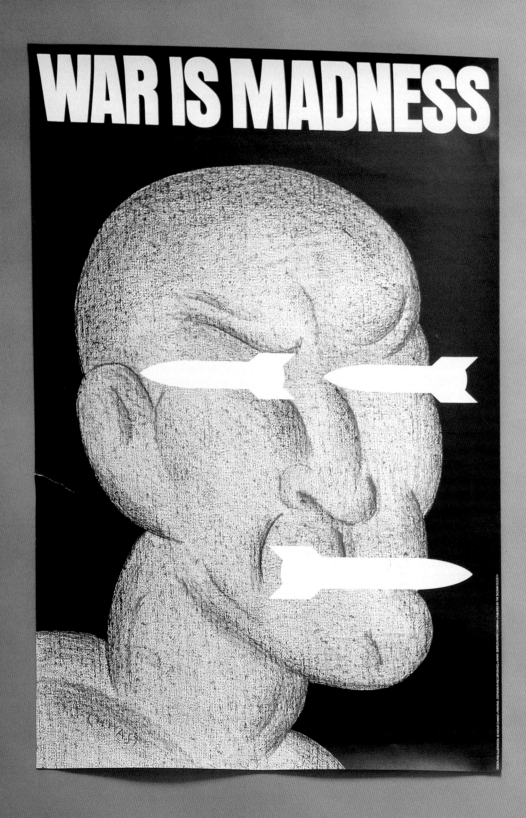

American Museum of Natural History
Central Park West at 79 Street
Open FREE Friday and Saturday evenings 5-9

Made possible by a grant from Mobil

305

U.S. Postage Stamp:
Science and Industry
Art Director:
Saul Bass
Artist:
Saul Bass
Design Firm:
Saul Bass/Herb Yager &
Assoc.
Los Angeles, CA
Client:
United States Postal Service

Poster:
Games of the Twenty-third
Olympiad/Los Angeles
1984
Art Director:
Saul Bass
Photographers:
Donald Miller and Saul
Bass
Design Firm:
Saul Bass/Herb Yager &
Assoc.
Los Angeles, CA
Client:
Los Angeles Olympic
Committee

Poster:
Rape Line
Art Director/Designer:
Lanny Sommese
Artist:
Lanny Sommese
Design Firm:
Lanny Sommese Design
State College, PA
Client:
Penn State Rape Line
Printer:
Design Practicum (Penn
State)

RAPE LINE 234-5050 !

Environmental Graphics:
DAV National Vietnam
Veterans Memorial
Project Director:
Mark Barensfeld
Designers:
Mark Barensfeld and Heinz
Schenker
Design Firm:
Schenker, Probst,
Barensfeld
Cincinnati, OH
Client:
Disabled American
Veterans

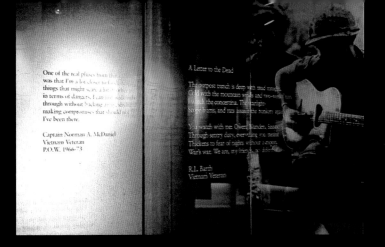

One of the real pluses from that
was that I'm a lot closer to God. In
things that might scare a lot of others
in terms of dangers, I can just walk on
through without backing away, shying
making compromises that should not
I've been there.

Captain Norman A. McDaniel
Vietnam Veteran
P.O.W. 1966–73

A Letter to the Dead

The outpost trench is deep with mud enough,
Cold with the mountain winds and too-well run.
I watch the concertina. The strange
Scope hunts, and runs against the tonkin mud,

You watch with me, Quyet, Munden, Sisson.
Through sentry duty, everything you mean,
Thickens to fear of nights without passion.
War's war. We are, my friends, are different.

R.L. Barth
Vietnam Veteran

**Patient Communication
Aid for the Impaired:**
Communicard
Art Director:
Rudolph de Harak
Designers:
Linda Kondo and Frank
Benedict
Design Firm:
de Harak & Poulin
Associates, Inc.
New York, NY
Client:
Mount Sinai Patient
Representative Dept.
Typographer:
Wizard Graphics
Printer:
Rapoport Printing Corp.

Communi-Card

This card has been prepared to assist you in communicating with your family, friends and hospital staff.

Estos dibujos se han preparados para que usted se pueda comunicar con su familia, sus amistades, y los empleados del hospital.

Yes / Sí

 Afraid/Sad *Miedo/Triste*

 Angry/Upset *Enojado/Nervioso*

 Drowsy/Tired *Soñoliento/Cansado*

 Dizzy *Mareado*

 Doctor *Médico*

 Nurse *Enfermera*

Family/Friends *Familia/Amigos*

Clergy *Clérico*

No

 Pain/Ache *Dolor*

 Vomit/Full Stomach *Sensación de Plenitud*

 Difficulty Breathing *Dificultad en Respirar*

 Suction *Succión*

 Intravenous *Intravenosa*

 Lower/Raise Bed *Subir/Bajar la Cama*

 Turn Me Over *Dar Vuelta de Lado a Lado*

In/Out of Bed *Entrar a/Salir de la Cama*

Please Leave *Por Favor Destídese*

 House *Casa*

 Medicine/Laxative *Medicina/Laxativo*

 Toilet/Commode *Servicios Sanitario*

 Wash *Lavarse*

 Shave/Hair Care *Afeitarse/Cuidado de Pelo*

 Mouth Care *Higiene Oral*

 Lotion *Crema*

 Pillow/Blanket *Almohada/Frazada*

 Drink *Bebida*

 Food *Alimento*

 Time *Hora*

 Dentures *Dentadura*

 Eyeglasses *Espejuelos*

 Hearing Aid *Audífono de Oír*

 Robe/Slippers *Bata de Casa/Chancletas*

 Pajamas *Pijama*

 Telephone *Teléfono*

 Television *Televisión*

 Money *Dinero*

 Mail *Cartas*

 Reading Material *Algo para Leer*

A B C D E F G

H I J K L M N

O P Q R S T U

V W X Y Z ?

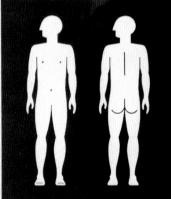

Please indicate on these figures where your problem is located.
Usando estos dibujos, por favor señale donde tiene la molestia.

Yes / Sí | **When / Cuando** | **Where / Donde** | **Why / Porque** | **How / Como** | **OK** | **No**

Patient Representatives *Representante de Pacientes*

Social Worker *Trabajador/a Social*

Physical Therapist *Terapista Física*

Dietician *Dietista*

Occupational Therapist *Terapista Ocupacional*

Speech Therapist *Terapista de Lenguaje*

The Mount Sinai Medical Center, New York, N.Y. Patient Representative Department. Principal Investigator: Ruth Ravich. Concept: Linda Micchi. Supported by: The Robert Wood Johnson Foundation. Design: Rudolph de Harak & Associates, Inc.

Environmental Graphics:
Penns Landing
Art Director:
Joel Katz
Designers:
Joel Katz and Christine
Nardello
Design Firm:
Katz Wheeler Design
Philadelphia, PA
Client:
City of Philadelphia
Fabricators:
Various

Billboard:
Actual Size
Art Director:
Tatsuya Higashi
Artist:
Gary Jacobsen
Design Firm:
Sharp Hartwig Advertising
Inc.
Seattle, WA
Client:
Pacific Science Center
Typographer:
Thomas & Kennedy

← **Great Plaza**

No alcoholic beverages permitted in
public areas.
Bikes permitted 6 to 10 a.m. only.
No swimming.
No unauthorized vendors or solicitors.
Dogs must be leashed.
No excessive noise (including radios).

ACTUAL SIZE.

DINOSAURS AT PACIFIC SCIENCE CENTER

G. Lois Grossmann, E. W.
Faircloth, and others
Design Firm:
Philadelphia Daily News
Philadelphia, PA
Publisher:
Philadelphia Daily News,
Inc.
Typographer:
Philadelphia Daily News,
Inc.

315

Journal:
PS/The Journal of The
Poster Society, Spring 1987
Art Director/Designer:
Keith Godard
Editor:
Robert K. Brown
Design Firm:
Works Design Group
New York, NY
Publisher:
The Poster Society
Typographer:
George Dembo
Printer:
RAE/Horowitz

Informational Graphics:
Around the world on one
tank of gas
Art Director:
Dale Glasgow
Artist:
Dale Glasgow
Washington, DC
Publisher:
USA TODAY
Printer:
USA TODAY

Poster:
Possibilities
Art Director:
Darby Roach
Designers:
Darby Roach and Jack
Simmen
Design Firm:
Graphic Design Practicom
(Penn State)
State College, PA
Client:
Penn State College of Arts
and Architecture
Typographer:
Grove Printing

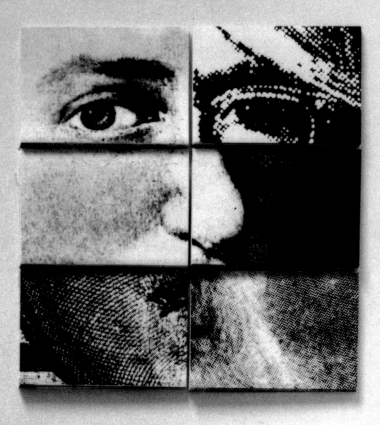

Penn State College of Arts and Architecture   Architecture Art History Landscape Architecture Music Theatre Visual Arts

POSsiBiLiTies

116 Arts Building University Park, PA 16802 814-865-·2523

Newsletter:
Art Center Review, May
1987
Art Director:
Kit Hinrichs
Designer:
Kit Hinrichs and Lenore
Bartz
Photographers:
Steven A. Heller, Henrik
Kam, John Blaustein, and
Jeffery Dunn Studios
Illustrators:
Gerard Huerta and John
Mattos
Design Firm:
Pentagram
San Francisco, CA
Client:
Art Center College of
Design
Typographer:
Eurotype
Printer:
Color Graphics

Newsletter:
Art Center Review,
September 1987
Art Director:
Kit Hinrichs
Designer:
Kit Hinrichs and Lenore
Bartz
Photographers:
Steven A. Heller, Henrik
Kam, Gary Meyer, and Joe
Henninger
Illustrators:
Walid Saba and John
Mattos
Design Firm:
Pentagram
San Francisco, CA
Client:
Art Center College of
Design
Typographer:
Eurotype
Printer:
Color Graphics

REVIEW
REVIEW
REVIEW
REVIEW

ArtCenter

ONE OF A KIND

ArtCenter

BULLETIN *16*

Art Center

ArtCenter

Center

REVIEW 2

8

10

2

MAGAZINE DESIGN (over the Top!)

DESIGN
COMPETITIONS:

THE FAME CIRCUIT

UNDER FIRE

SEATTLE
DESIGN
OCT...

ILLUSTRATION BY JOHN C. SMITH

Newsletter

March/April

1987

As Seattle's graphic design community has grown over the last decade, designers have begun to take a closer look at many things affecting their work. The changing social and economic climate, Political and aesthetic movements, present and past. As the design arena will call to... more... in some... The varied graphics shows competitio... these shows creat... so the tie... surroundings. Are the shows getting too c... ive? Is real world" business design overlooked in favor of "R&D" work? Are all the shows starting to look the same? Is the prestige attached to winning any design award fading as the sheer number of competitions continues to rise? Finally, there's the great conspiracy theory: Is there really an inner circle of national designers awarding – and receiving – all the accolades?

Sit in on any bull session at awards time and you'll hear the standard round of complaints about entry fees, screening procedures, the jury selection, etc. A good percentage will be sour grapes, but with the usual chagrin that accompanies rejection comes a certain education in practical business survival. Because... are here to stay. For all their idiosyncracies, design competitions still provide many graphic designers the peer recognition (and client recognition) they need to break out of regional markets.

This issue of the newsletter is centered around competitions – their pros and cons – with comments and recommendations for change from several Seattle designers who've ridden the awards circuit and returned to tell about it.

Our thanks to Rick Eiber, Art Chantry, Kathy Eitner, John VanDyke, Carole Jones, Sue Cummings and Sancho for their comments and their candor. ∎

Instructions   Wiggle thumb

STAR WARS

TAKING AIM AT THE STAR SYSTEM AND ITS SHOWS

By Rick Eiber

Every designer I know wants to create award-winning work.

Do you know anyone who doesn't? Yet wanting to do it and actually accomplishing it are two very different things. Similarly, the national shows set up to recognize outstanding achievement by designers aim high but frequently end up shooting themselves in the foot. What follows is a brief examination of some of the battles designers are waging in their fight for recognition.

When design shows were created (and most are still quite young), they were to satisfy several needs. First, a jury of recognized performers to evaluate the creative output of their respective specialties would help bring credibility to the work judged and serve as a critical review of the state of the art. Second, these shows would expose outstanding work to the largest possible audiences. Third, the shows would be an opportunity to recognize excellence before peer group members, and fourth, they would record development within the specialties aiming at professional status.

Every show wants to bring out the biggest stars available to judge the work submitted. Consequently, juries have become inbred with the same individuals and firms judging several major shows in a short period of time. The abilities of the judges are not the issue; their creative output defines their qualifications. Rather, their objectivity and openness to differing criteria and new work in different shows are issues. Next, with alarming speed, the judges' own work has assumed (or consumed) a major portion of the winning entries of the shows they judge. Finally, by publishing the jury members' names on the calls for entries, the character of the shows is already defined as entries are submitted in light of the judges' previous show choices and personal design styles.

So, you ask, what can put the star system back on its proper course? While there are countless answers, what follows is an explanation of just one way each of the identified problems might be solved.

Except for the *Print Regional Design Annual*, which is broad and well-judged by its own editorial staff, all of the major national graphics shows, i.e., AIGA shows, N.Y. Type Directors Club, STA 100, *CA Annual*, TIA, *Industrial Design Annual Review*, N.Y. Art Directors Club, etc., would submit a list of ranked choices and travel budgets for judges to a single source (like AIGA). This organization would then combine and monitor all requests, obtain schedules and ranked choices from the jury candidates, and notify jurors

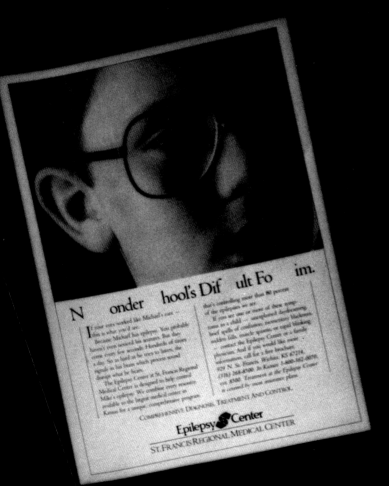

Casebooks:
Art Center College of
Design/Why Design? Why
Art Center?
Art Directors:
Neil Shakery and Kit
Hinrichs
Photographers:
Jim Blakely and Steven A.
Heller
Design Firm:
Pentagram
San Francisco, CA
Client:
Art Center College of
Design
Typographer:
Reardon & Krebs
Printer:
Dai Nippon

Brochure:
Three Women: Madeleine
Vionnet, Claire McCardell,
and Rei Kawakubo
Art Director:
Takaaki Matsumoto
Photographers:
Hoyningen-Huene, Horst,
Louise Dahl-Wolfe, Hans
Feurer, Steven Meisel, and
Peter Lindbergh
Design Firm:
M & M
New York, NY
Client:
Fashion Institute of
Technology
Typographer:
J.C.H. Graphics, Ltd.
Printer:
L.P. Thebault Co.

"Three Women: Madeleine Vionnet, Claire McCardell, and Rei Kawakubo"

is an examination of construction and style in three great designers of the twentieth century. Each designer, in a separate era of the century, provided a new concept and vision of dress. They reformulate and reform dress. All three offer clothing design as a conceptual and radical enterprise. They posit ideas as they work with material; they realize a definition of woman as they create the garment. In the instances of Vionnet, McCardell, and Kawakubo, these women make clothes that make women. These three women make clothes that foster a new intelligence and new directions in apparel. Their analytical considerations of construction, of the body, and of the social role of women were and are brave and abiding ideas about fashion.

Catalogue:
Public Art in Downtown Los
Angeles
Art Director:
Terrence Mitchell
Designer:
Yee Ping Cho
Photographers:
Chris Morland and Jay
Venezia
Design Firm:
Community Redevelopment
Agency/LA
Graphic Design Section
Los Angeles, CA
Client:
Community Redevelopment
Agency/LA
Typographer:
Composition Type
Printer:
Scott & Scott Lithography

Identity Book:
Design Process/Barcelona
Olympic Identification
Proposal
Art Director:
Miguel Soler-Roig
Artist/Photographer:
Miguel Soler-Roig
Design Firm:
Miguel Soler-Roig
Client:
Barcelona Olympic Office
Typographer:
Miguel Soler-Roig
Printer:
Newport Graphics

Guide Book:
The AIGA San Francisco
Designers Guidebook
Art Director:
Michael Vanderbyl
Artists:
Various
Design Firm:
Vanderbyl Design
San Francisco, CA
Client:
AIGA/San Francisco
Typographer:
Mercury Typography
Printer:
Mastercraft Press

**Informational Graphic
Map:**
A Walk on 53rd Street
Art Director:
Colin Forbes
Designer:
Michael Gericke
Artist:
Stephen Guarnaccia
Design Firm:
Pentagram
New York, NY
Client:
53rd Street Association

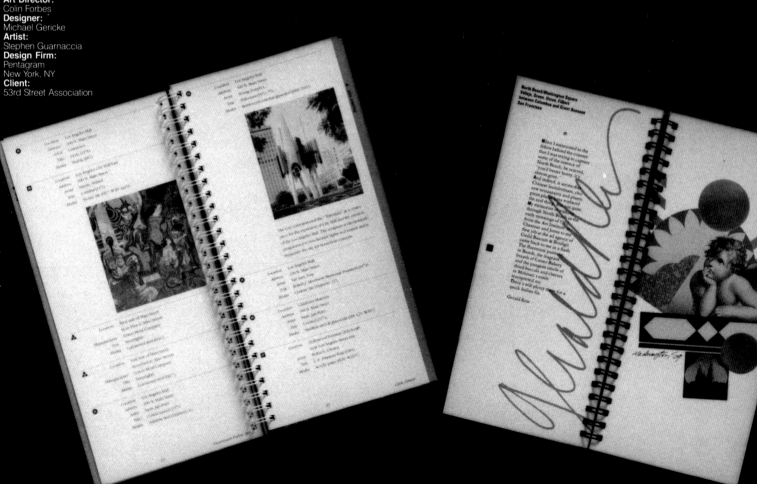

Significance

This symbol represents a series of ideas that go beyond its formal composition. The theme encompasses a strong statement about the Olympic movement; the Olympic Flame is the symbolic representation of the sacred fire that receives at Olympia.

In conjunction with the Olympic Rings, it defines the beginning of the Olympiad (period of time starting with the proclamation of the Olympic Year, and lasting for four years), linking the structure of the International Olympic Committee as a continuous organization.

Representative
Meaningful
Understandable

Announcement Folder:
10/Future Style
Art Director:
Byron Jacobs
Computer Graphics:
Roy Montibon
Design Firm:
Byron Jacobs Design
Fullerton, CA
Client:
Art Direction and Design in
Orange County
Typographer:
Orange County Typesetting
Printer:
Woods Lithographics

Brochures:
Schuylkill Expressway
Improvement Project
Art Director:
Joel Katz
Design Firm:
Katz Wheeler Design
Philadelphia, PA
Client:
Pennsylvania Dept. of
Transportation
Typographer:
Duke & Co.
Printer:
Intelligencer Printing Co.

Folder:
When two people meet, a
little something happens.
Art Director:
Susan Slover
Designer/Artist:
Susan Huyser
Design Firm:
Susan Slover Design
New York, NY
Client:
AFS International
Typographer:
Paragon Typographics
Printer:
Kenny Press

Brochures:
The Suicide and Crisis
Center
Art Director:
Ron Sullivan
Designer:
Linda Helton
Artists:
Linda Helton and Diana
McKnight
Design Firm:
Sullivan Perkins
Dallas, TX
Client:
The Suicide and Crisis
Center
Typographer:
Robert J. Hilton
Typographers
Printer:
Riverside Press

Programs:
Cincinnati Symphony
Orchestra
Art Director:
Mike Zender
Designers:
Priscilla Fisher, Dave
Steinbrenner, and Mike
Zender
Cover Photographer:
Mike Zender
Design Firm:
Zender + Assoc., Inc.
Cincinnati, OH
Client:
Cincinnati Symphony
Orchestra
Typographer:
Pagemakers
Printer:
The Merten Co.

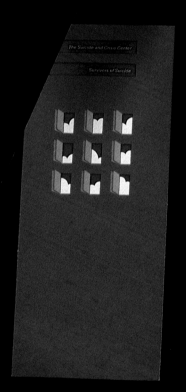
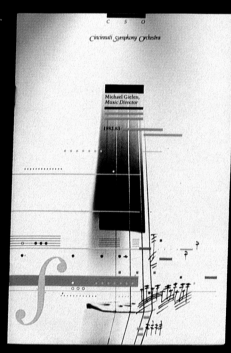

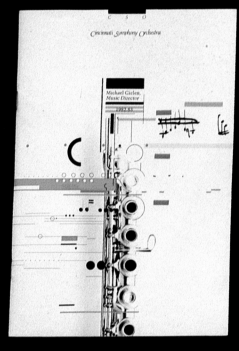

Booklet:
Washburn Child Guidance
Center/Here no Child is Left
Behind
Designer/Artist:
Charles Spencer Anderson
Design Firm:
The Duffy Design Group
Minneapolis, MN
Client:
Washburn Child Guidance
Center
Typographer:
Typeshooters
Printer:
Watt Peterson

Youth Guide Book:
Fresh Force Official Guide
Book
Designer:
Charles Spencer Anderson
Artist:
Charles Spencer Anderson
Design Firm:
The Duffy Design Group
Minneapolis, MN
Publisher:
Fresh Force Youth Volunteer
Group
Typographer:
Typeshooters
Printer:
Rainbow Sign, Inc.

Invitational Booklet:
Fort Worth Opera Ball
Art Director:
Joe Rattan
Artist:
Joe Rattan
Design Firm:
Pirtle Design
Dallas, TX
Client:
Fort Worth Opera
Association
Typographer:
Robert J. Hilton
Typographers
Printer:
Heritage Press

Booklet:
Pairs & Party
Art Directors:
Chris Hill, Jeffrey McKay
and David Lerch
Designers:
Jeffrey McKay, David Lerch
and Chris Hill
Artists:
David Lerch and Jeffrey
McKay
Design Firm:
Hill/A Marketing Design
Group
Houston, TX
Client:
The Galleria/Gerald Hines
Interest
Typographer:
Characters, Inc.
Printer:
American Photocopy &
Printing

Booklet:
A Poem by Margaret Walker
Commissioned for
Sculpture . . .
Art Director:
Hap Owen
Designer:
Lisa Stewart
Photographer:
Tom Joynt
Design Firm:
Communication Arts Co.
Jackson, MS
Client:
Linda S. Trobaugh
Typographer:
Communication Arts
Co./Aldus Pagemaker
Printer:
Graphic Reproductions

Leaflet:
Apropos of Marcel
Duchamp
Art Director:
Phillip Unetic
Design Firm:
Philadelphia Museum of Art
Philadelphia, PA
Client:
Philadelphia Museum of Art
Typographer:
John C. Myers & Son
Printer:
Franklin Town Press

Our goals for each child we serve are similar, but the way we reach those goals is often very different. We literally custom-tailor a solution to each child's specific problem. The services we offer range from preschool programs for high-risk children and early developmental screening, to perceptual motor training, tutorial classes, and pyschological and educational evaluation. We also serve as advocates for schools and courts, provide parenting education groups, and offer in-service training for educators and day-care personnel.

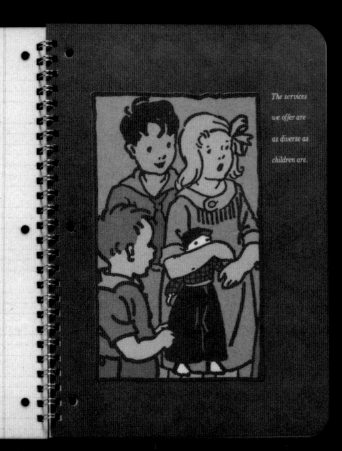

The services we offer are as diverse as children are.

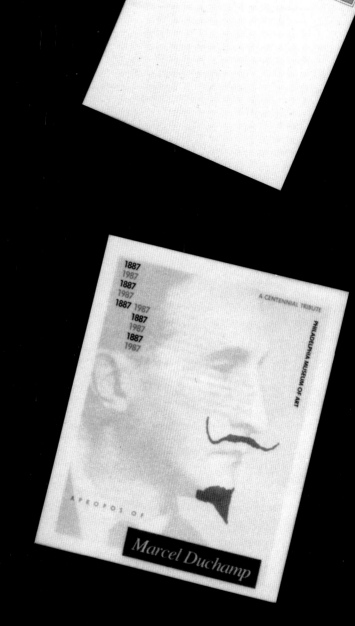

A POEM BY **MARGARET WALKER** COMMISSION ED FOR SCULPTURE IN FARISH STREET GREEN: COMMISSIONED SCUL PTURE BY **TROBAUGH**

1887
1987
1887
1987
1887 1987
1887
1987
1887
1987

A CENTENNIAL TRIBUTE

PHILADELPHIA MUSEUM OF ART

APROPOS OF

Marcel Duchamp

Brochure:
Capitol Campaign: Lucile
Salter Packard Children's
Hospital at Stanford
Art Director:
Linda Hinrichs
Illustrator:
Michael Reardon
Photographer:
John Blaustein
Design Firm:
Pentagram
San Francisco, CA
Client:
Stanford Children's Hospital
Typographer:
Spartan Typographers
Printer:
Warren's Waller Press

Annual Report:
Juvenile Diabetes
Foundation
Art Director:
Hershell George
Photographer:
Nelson Bakerman
Design Firm:
Hershell George Graphics
New York, NY
Client:
Juvenile Diabetes
Foundation International
Typographer:
CTC
Printer:
George Rice & Sons

Annual Report:
MSPCC, 1986
Art Director:
Tom Kaminsky
Copywriter:
Jennifer Blair
Photographer:
Jay Maisel
New York, NY
Design Firm:
ClarkeGowardFitts Design
Client:
Massachusetts Society for
the Prevention of Cruelty to
Children
Typographer:
Wrightson Typography
Printer:
Eussey Press

Annual Report:
The L.J. Skaggs and Mary
C. Skaggs Foundation,
1985 Annual Report
Art Director:
Michael Vanderbyl
Photographer:
Various
Design Firm/Agency:
Vanderbyl Design
San Francisco, CA
Client:
The Skaggs Foundation
Typographer:
On-Line Typography
Printer:
Mastercraft Press

Exhibition catalogue:
Manifeste, 1984/Jean-Pierre
Raynaud
Art Director:
Byron Jacobs
Designer:
Mary Thonneson
Artist:
Jean-Pierre Raynaud
Design Firm:
Byron Jacobs Design
Fullerton, CA
Client:
Newport Harbor Art
Museum
Typographer:
Orange County Typesetting
Printer:
Woods Lithographics

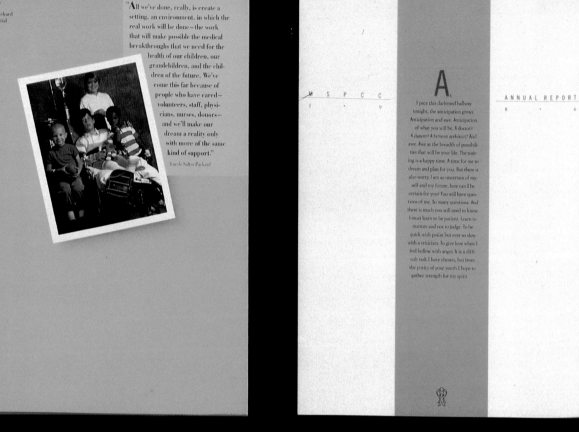

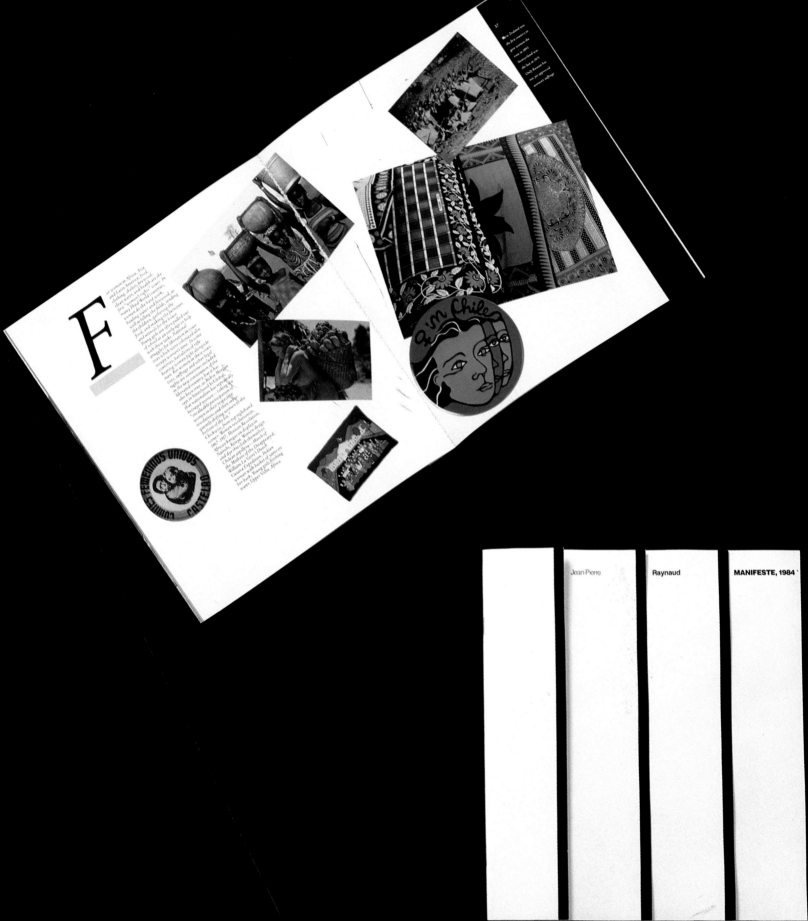

Jean-Pierre Raynaud **MANIFESTE, 1984**

Press Kit:
Artists of Books for Children
Art Director/Designer:
Lois Ehlert
Artist:
Lois Ehlert
Design Firm:
Ehlert Studio
Milwaukee, WI
Client:
Milwaukee Art Museum
Typographer:
Trend Typography
Printer:
Burton & Mayer

Brochure:
Circle Ten Council
Boy Scouts of America
Art Director:
Brian Boyd
Photographer:
Jim Sims
Photography Firm:
Sims/Boynton
Houston, TX
Design Firm:
Richards Brock Miller
Mitchell & Associates
Dallas, TX
Client:
Boy Scouts of America
Typographer:
Chiles & Chiles
Printer:
Williamson Printing Co.

Facilities Brochure:
Alternative Education in
Portland Public Schools
Art Director/Designer:
Loren Weeks
Copywriter:
Tim Leigh
Design Firm:
Bronson, Leigh, Weeks
Portland, OR
Client:
Paula Kinney
Typographer:
Paul O. Giesey
Printer:
R.G. Wilkes

Brochure:
Faith Ranch
Art Director:
Jerry Herring
Photographer:
Jim Sims
Photography Firm:
Sims/Boynton
Houston, TX
Design Firm:
Herring Design
Houston, TX
Client:
Faith Ranch
Typographer:
Characters, Inc.
Printer:
Wetmore & Co.

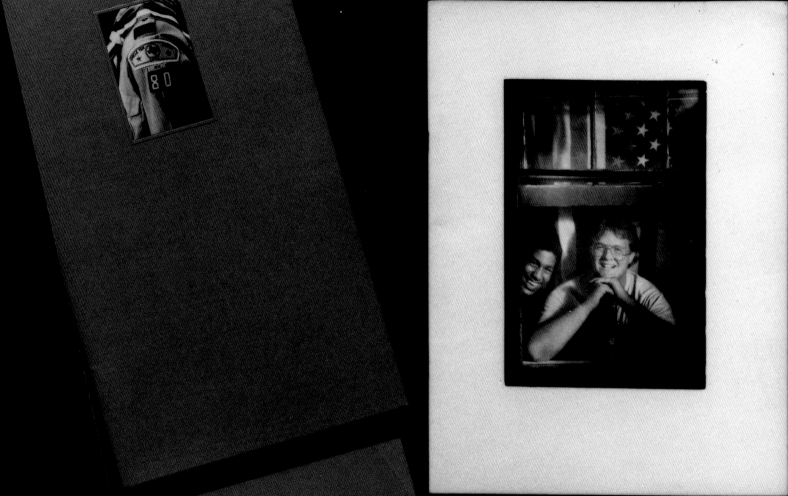

Brochure:
Seton Maternity Services
Art Director/Designer:
Mike Hicks
Photographer:
Ave Bonar
Design Firm:
HIXO, Inc.
Austin, TX
Client:
Seton Medical Center
Typographer:
Typecrafters
Printer:
Lithoprint

Catalogue:
Art + Environment
South Coast Plaza
Art Director:
John Coy
Designer:
Laurie Handler
Photographer:
Steve Klimek
Design Firm:
COY, Los Angeles
Culver City, CA
Client:
South Coast Plaza
Typographer:
Continental Typographics
Printer:
George Rice & Sons

Brochure/Folder:
Creative Learning Center
Art Directors:
Alan Taylor and Dean
Corbitt
Photographer:
Stewart Cohen
Design Firm:
Corbitt/Taylor Design
Dallas, TX
Client:
Creative Learning Center
Typographer:
Typography Plus
Printer:
Monarch Press, Inc.

Catalogue:
Viewbook
Art Director/Designer:
John Coy
Photographer:
Steven Gunther and others
Design Firm:
COY, Los Angeles
Culver City, CA
Client:
California Institute of the
Arts
Typographer:
CCI Typographers
Printer:
Nissha Printing Co.

Catalogue:
California Institute of the
Arts 1987/88, 1988/89
Art Director:
John Coy
Designers:
John Coy and Kevin
Consales
Photographer:
Steven Gunther and others
Design Firm:
COY, Los Angeles
Culver City, CA
Client:
California Institute of the
Arts
Typographer:
CCI
Printer:
Nissha Printing Co.

Invitation:
Let us pick up your cans
Art Director/Designers:
Forrest and Valerie
Richardson
Design Firm:
Richardson or Richardson
Phoenix, AZ
Client:
St. Vincent De Paul
Typographer:
DigiType
Printer:
DigiType

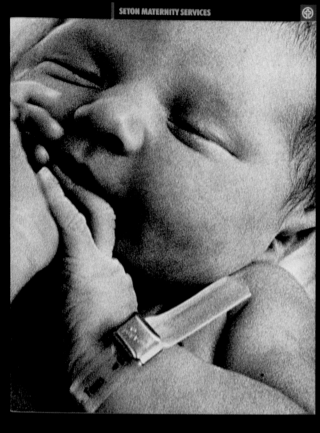

Brochure:
Adolescent Care Program
at Saint Joseph Hospital
Art Director:
Scott Eggers
Photographer:
Jim Sims
Photography Firm:
Sims/Boynton
Houston, TX
Agency:
Knape & Knape
Client:
Saint Joseph Hospital

Folder:
Channeling Children's
Anger
Art Director:
Terri Bogaards and Ellen
Shapiro
Designer:
Terri Bogaards
Artist:
Terri Bogaards
Design Firm:
Shapiro Design Associates,
Inc.
New York, NY
Client:
Institute for Mental Health
Initiatives
Typographer:
Ultra Typographic Services,
Inc.
Printer:
Metropolitan Printing
Service

Brochure/Folder:
Interchange
Art Director:
John Sayles
Design Firm:
Sayles Graphic Design, Inc.
Des Moines, IA
Client:
National Interfraternity
Conference
Typographer:
Push-Pen Studios
Printer:
Garner Printing Co.

Brochure:
How do you plan to survive
Art Directors:
Clement Mok and Stephen
Sieler
Designer:
Stephen Sieler
Artist:
Lou Beach
Design Firm:
Apple Creative Services
Cupertino, CA
Client:
Apple Computer, Inc.

Folder:
Friends of Modern Art,
87/88
Art Director:
Jacques Auger
Designer:
Babette Herschberger
Design Firm:
Jacques Auger Design
Assoc.
Coral Gables, FL
Client:
Detroit Institute of Arts
Typographer:
Supertype
Printer:
Gold Coast Graphics

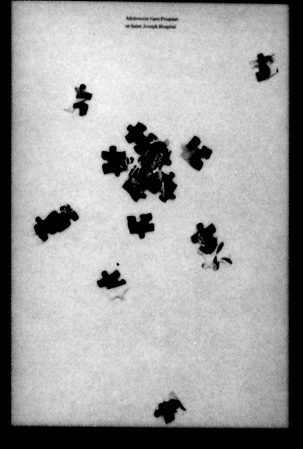

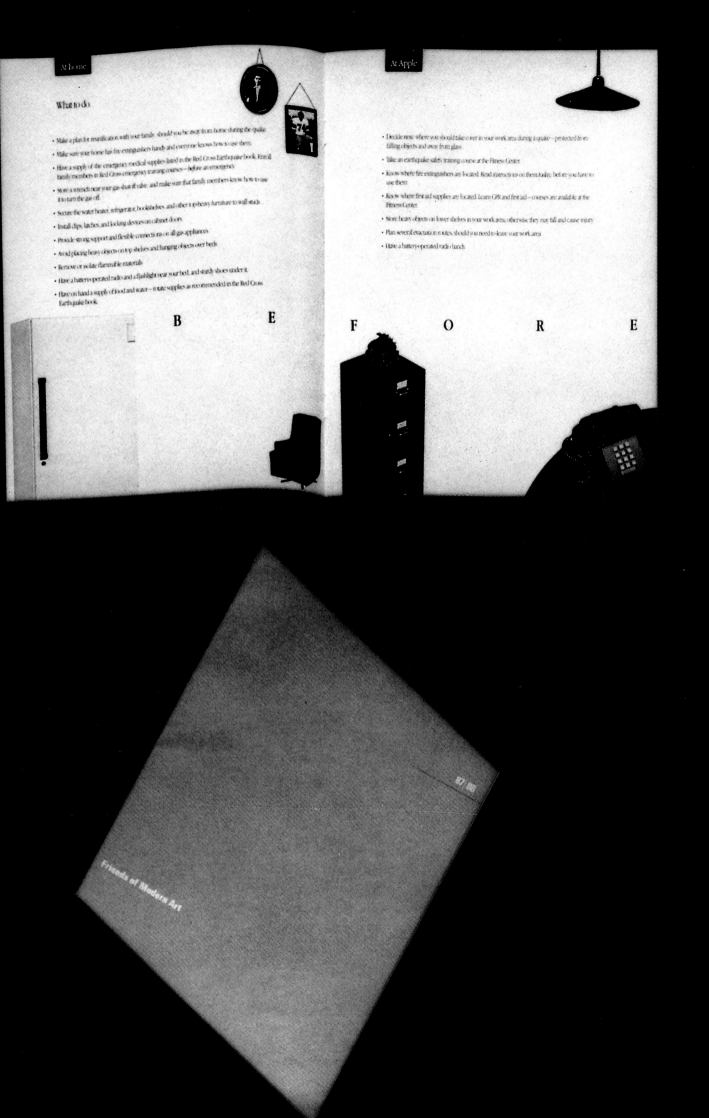

Leaflet:
UCLA Extension/Winter
Quarter begins January 4,
1988
Art Director:
Inju Sturgeon
Designer/Artist:
Ken Parkhurst
Design Firm:
Ken Parkhurst & Assoc.
Los Angeles, CA
Client:
UCLA Extension Dept.
Printer:
Forms Engineering

Folder:
Penn State's Department of
Architecture
Art Director:
Bill Kinser
University Park, PA
Publisher:
Penn State Arts &
Architecture
Typographer:
Penn State University
Printing Services
Printer:
BSC Litho. Co.

Invitation:
Un Ballo in Maschera. . . .
Art Director:
Gill Fishman
Designer:
Conde Freeman
Artist:
Conde Freeman
Design Firm:
Gill Fishman Associates
Cambridge, MA
Client:
Museum of Fine Arts
Council
Typographer:
Lithocomp
Printer:
United Litho

**Invitational
Announcement:**
The Princess and the Baker
Art Director:
Robin Ayres
Artist:
Robert Forsbach
Design Firm:
Richards Brock Miller
Mitchell & Assoc.
Dallas, TX
Client:
The March of Dimes
Typographer:
Chiles & Chiles
Printer:
Heritage Press

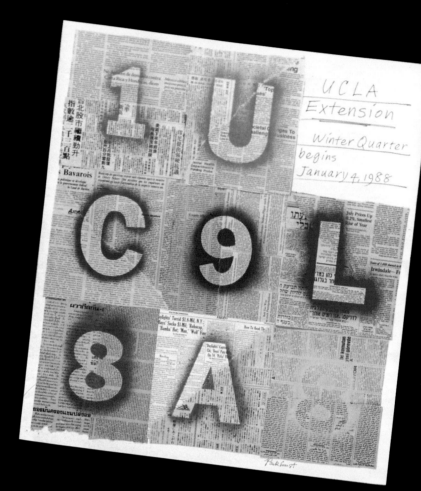

Stationery:
The Kentucky Foundation
for Women, Inc.
Art Director:
Julius Friedman and Walter
McCord
Design Firm/Agency:
Images
Louisville, KY
Client:
The Kentucky Foundation
for Women, Inc.
Typographer:
Adpro
Printer:
Hamilton Printing Co.

Logo:
Dallas Ballet
Art Director:
Scott Ray
Artist:
Don Grimes
Design Firm:
Eisenberg, Inc.
Dallas, TX
Client:
Dallas Ballet

Logo:
Twenty-Five Years of the
Arts
Art Director/Designer:
John Coy
Artist:
John Coy
Design Firm:
COY, Los Angeles
Culver City, CA
Client:
UCLA College of Fine Art
Typographer:
Skil Set Typographers

Logo:
Southfield Symphony
Orchestra
Art Director/Designer:
James V. Tocco
Design Firm:
Design Network, Inc.
Southfield, MI
Client:
City of Southfield
Typographer:
Alpha 21

Logo:
New Jersey State Council
on the Arts
Art Directors:
Roger Cook and Don
Shanosky
Design Firm:
Cook and Shanosky
Assoc., Inc.
Princeton, NJ
Client:
New Jersey State Council
on the Arts
Typographer:
Tristin, Inc.

Logo:
Minneapolis Arts
Art Director:
Ivan Chermayeff
Design Firm:
Chermayeff & Geismar
New York, NY
Client:
Minneapolis Arts

Logo:
Teen Forum/Christian
Issues Debate
Art Director/Designer:
Gary Templin
Artist:
Gary Templin
Design Firm:
Richards Brock Miller
Mitchell & Assoc.
Dallas, TX
Client:
South Center Baptist
Church

Logo:
Dallas Zoo
Art Director:
Dick Mitchell
Artist:
Dick Mitchell
Design Firm:
Richards Brock Miller
Mitchell & Assoc.
Dallas, TX
Client:
Dallas Zoo

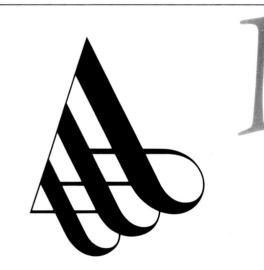

DALLAS ZOO

Index

Design Firms and Agencies

Publishers, Publications and Clients

Typographers, Letters and Calligraphers

Printers, Binders, Engravers, Fabricators and Separators